—A MAVERICK PUBLICATION—

D0555515

Sacred Cows
at the
Public Trough

Denzel and Nancy Ferguson

Drawings by Ginny Rosenberg

Maverick Publications
Drawer 5007 • Bend, Oregon 97708

*This book is dedicated to the handful of
courageous public employees who have suffered
the wrath and intimidation of the western
livestock industry for daring to put the
public's interests first.*

ACKNOWLEDGMENTS

The information in this book is derived from many disciplines, thus in a broad sense, we are indebted to a legion of contributors. But most publications dealing with livestock uses of public lands have been written by and for livestock interests and suffer a debilitating myopia. We are, therefore, especially grateful to the small cadre of individuals who view public lands as a diversified national resource rather than mere pastures for livestock. These few have steadfastly reminded the rest of us of the adverse consequences of grazing and called our attention to the shenanigans of western stockmen. Truth is not always welcomed on western rangelands, and those who speak it often risk public humiliation or worse. But critics of the industry have persevered, and to them we are indebted, for our story is theirs.

Many friends and acquaintances have encouraged and assisted us along the way. To all, we are most grateful. To Bruce Bowler, Stuart Croghan, Nancy Herman, Steven G. Herman, Carroll Littlefield, Don McKenzie, Ginny Rosenberg, Terry Steele, Mark Stern, Caryn Talbot Throop, Elaine Urban, and Karl Urban, all of whom read the manuscript and offered many useful suggestions, we owe special thanks.

Contents

PREFACE

In the early 1970's, we were employed by a consortium of 22 colleges and universities to operate a field station in southeastern Oregon near the Malheur National Wildlife Refuge. Neither of us knew much about cows and cared less. But we gradually became aware that Malheur Refuge had been converted into a gigantic cow pasture. Waterfowl production had plunged from 151,000 ducks in 1948 to only 21,300 in 1974 as cattle grazing increased from 74,385 animal units in 1948 to 125,000 animal units in 1972. The chorus of complaints from bird-watchers and other refuge visitors about the absence of wildlife could not be ignored.

We started a letter-writing campaign to get some of the cows off the refuge. Shortly afterwards, we were physically ejected from a public dance in the small ranching community of Diamond, Oregon. We were perfunctorily tossed out the door by a gang of five robust cowmen, considerably more force than was actually needed to eject one woman and a middle-aged college professor, and warned that if we did not leave the county immediately, we would be killed. For the next few weeks additional threats were made on our lives by telephone, and we received a barrage of nuisance calls.

Later, the Harney County Cattlemen's Association and eventually the Oregon Cattlemen's Association passed resolutions seeking to have us dismissed from our employment. Failing in this endeavor, the Oregon Cattlemen's Association, working through State Senator Robert Smith, a rancher and currently U.S. Congressman, began a campaign in the state legislature to deny state funds to the field station. Additional anonymous threats were made upon us by phone, including the admonition, "Sucker, you're going to die."

While it is true that removing some of the cows from Malheur Refuge would have caused a degree of economic hardship to certain local ranchers, the violent intensity of the cattlemen's reaction seemed out of proportion with a mere economic threat to a few local cowmen. There seemed to be more to it—something sinister—like skeletons in the closet that dared not be brought to light.

We began to dig. And the more we dug, the more incredible and sordid it became—perhaps awesome is a better word. No wonder the cowboys were so intent upon silencing us, for theirs is a story of special privilege, ruthless greed, plunder of public coffers, and violations of public trusts that boggles belief. That story had to be told.

In our country, the cowboy is much admired. In the eye of the public, he rivals sainthood. Library shelves strain with the weight of volumes testifying to the virtues of cowmen, magazines make a business of garnishing his image, and if that weren't enough, movies and television drive the point home. Because of all this favorable testimony, we feel no compulsion to add even a word to what has already been said in behalf of cattlemen. Furthermore, we feel not the least tinge of academic guilt in telling only one side of a story—a side intended to inject some balance into the public perception of the western livestock industry and the people who run it.

Stockmen and their apologists will accuse us of being emotional—they always do. But after learning what we have learned about the livestock industry on public lands in the West, our reply to that accusation is, "You're damn right we're emotional—we have ample reason to be." When you have read *Sacred Cows at the Public Trough*, we think you will agree.

Buck Gulch
Bates, Oregon 97817
July 13, 1983

Denzel Ferguson
Nancy Ferguson

MADISON AVENUE
ON THE RANGE

In Nevada, the cowboy reins his horse to a stop on a high knoll. He surveys the landscape—sagebrush and desert shrubs, rolling hills, and a vast sky—the arid West. Scattered over the scene are the cattle, wandering among the shrubs, seeking grasses and herbs. It's a good life. No turmoil or confusion here.

There is little need to describe the cowboy—he conforms to the stereotype—Levi's, colorful snap-buttoned shirt, boots, bandana, and his most distinguishing trademark, the 10-gallon hat. His eyes are squinted and steel gray. He is well-tanned and a bit weathered, reflecting his life out-of-doors in all kinds of weather. He sits tall, but comfortably in the saddle, revealing an inner confidence and contentment. Here is a man admired and revered by his fellow Americans. Because he is a cowboy, he is tough, courageous, and independent. He is close to the land, knows nature, and loves and communes with all he surveys.

The cowboy is an American idol, part of a western legacy and a cultural heritage of a romantic and fascinating era. He is what little boys want to become. He is, in every way, the galactic opposite of the greedy and scheming occupant of corporate executive suites. The evils and human weaknesses of Wall Street are foreign to him. When this man rides into the sunset, we know the world is right, we can rest assured, and we can grant him our full trust. And we will, for he is a cowboy.

Seldom in history have so many been so thoroughly brainwashed by so few. The truth of the matter is: No industry or human activity on earth has destroyed or altered more of nature than the livestock industry. The slow-talking cowboy and his docile cows rival the H-bomb as instruments of destruction. Cowboys and cows are the center of a monstrous myth, a part of Americana that rests on concocted imagery and fabrication—an enormous falsehood based on profound ignorance.

The American beef industry is divided geographically into two distinct operations. In states east of the Rocky Mountains, where there is little public land, cattle are kept on privately owned pastures and closely husbanded. Because soils are fertile and rainfall ample, a high density of cattle can be supported. Beef production is high. In the West, where much of the land is publicly owned and managed by federal agencies, many cattle operations depend in part or wholly on public forage. Because much of the area is arid, only a few cattle can exist on large acreages and the cattle roam extensively without close supervision. The West's beef contribution from public lands is minor—only 3 percent of the nation's total production.

Basically, the eastern states follow practices imported from northern Europe, while the West has adopted customs introduced by the Spaniards. Thus the cowboy is a western phenomenon, although his dress and certain other peculiarities have now been exported throughout the world, producing such absurdities as pointy-toed boots and cowboy hats in Tokyo and "western" bars in Brooklyn.

The legend began early. Even as the West was opened for settlement, the larger-than-life tales of the frontier livestock industry reached the eastern press and quickly spread abroad. Investors were told of fantastic profits, minimal expenses, free land, inexhaustible supplies of grass, and eager markets. "Grass is gold" was the selling pitch in those days. Easterners regarded anyone associated with the western livestock industry as a shrewd businessman destined for high success. Already, the dudes were hooked.

Much of the romance, adventure, and idealism attributed to the cowboy dates back to the times of the great cattle drives. As the cattle industry took hold, spread, and then

"ACTUALLY, HE'S A BROOKLYN CAB DRIVER!"

flourished in the frontier West, surplus cattle had to be driven to the nearest railhead for shipment to eastern markets. These were, indeed, epic times—incredible distances, extreme hardships, enormous herds of cattle, the Chisholm Trail, Abilene, gunplay, dust, cold, heat, and stampedes. Such ingredients had to produce legends. They did and rightly so. Empire building is exciting business. To many Americans, the great cattle drives *were* the West. But this narrow view denigrates the real West—pristine wilderness, great herds of bison, and free-roaming tribes of American Indians.

Today, the western cattle business has changed. There are still cowboys and cows, but they are a vestige—a partially serious charade. The cattlemen still chase their cows around, and there is dust, yelling and yipping, whiskey from the bottle, and other reminders of former times. Although legends persist and grow in books, the modern cowboy—caught up in the fantasy—merely acts out and enlarges an inherited role, provides atmosphere and authenticity for tourists, bends his image to accommodate modern conveniences, and stubbornly strives to perpetuate the myth. He has had a great deal of assistance from entrepreneurs, opportunists, and large segments of the general public.

Today, historical reality accounts for only a small portion of the esteem and admiration given cowboys by the rest of the population. Substance and legend have been grossly embellished by fantasy and fiction in movies, television, and paperback novels. For profit and entertainment, these media have completely embellished and exploited the cowboy image, turning him into a folk hero—a sort of bigger-than -life "Sagebrush Robin Hood."

Suddenly the cowboy has almost nothing to do with anything as mundane as cows, his attire has evolved from strictly utilitarian to outlandishly ornate, and he is depicted as articulate, socially aware, and incredibly athletic—a remarkable transformation from the cowpoke of the old West. With no visible means of support, this gallant force against evil dashes about the countryside performing good deeds for the downtrodden, charming the ladies, and occasionally even singing.

All this is good show business—it has made some wealthy movie stars, it has created a splendid outlet for the fantasies of real cowboys, and it has brightened many a rainy day for imaginative youngsters and urban adults. But it is imperative that the American public realizes that the intent, behavior, and aspirations of the western cattle industry are totally contradictory to the Hollywood versions.

While Americans were creating an exhalted place in society for cowboys, they were, perhaps unwittingly, bestowing upon him financial security by showing enormous national approval of his commodity—the cow. We are reminded that dining on the biggest steak in the house is a symbol of the good life and high attainment. For the less affluent, there is the hamburger, served in thousands of convenient locations, quickly, and with all the trimmings. Beef has become the national status food, and beef consumption has increased drastically in the last few decades. The environmental and public costs of this national beef-craze have been exorbitant, particularly in the West on public lands. Although beef may be a delicious food and a valid symbol of affluence, it, like the gigantic gas-guzzling automobile, seems destined to become a luxury beyond the means of an environmentally aware nation compelled to live within finite limits. Even now, the costs exceed acceptable levels of prudence.

History, fantasy, fables, and antiquated values have conspired to mold public opinions about the livestock industry in the West. The result is widespread misinformation, commonly held illusions, and quite a lot of plain naivete. Changing the public's perception of the cowboy would be a Herculean task, and an unpopular one, for the cowboy ranks right along with ice cream and motherhood as an inalienable American institution. Nevertheless, there is a clear need for putting matters in proper perspective and telling it like it is. A close examination of the beef industry on the publicly owned lands of the West reveals many surprises and explodes many favorite myths.

While western cattlemen and other spokesmen for the industry vociferously hew to a conservative viewpoint and publicly proclaim absolute independence, they are, in fact, wards of the federal government—coddled, privileged, and heavily subsidized. Few minority groups or special interests wield the political clout of cattlemen. In exchange for a minor contribution to the nation's total beef production, the public pays an enormous price to ranchers using the public lands. The environmental costs in impaired watersheds, lost soil, destruction of wildlife habitat, and other damages are incalculable. In dollars, the cost of benefits gained clearly removes the industry from the realm of private enterprise and places it squarely among other government-supported ventures. The price of a steak at the market is only the tip of the iceberg.

In the process of exposing the seamy side of the western cattle industry, one must differentiate between the people and the industry. Ranchers have a reputation for being good neighbors—friendly and generous. That reputation is richly deserved, for many of them would, as the saying goes, "give you the shirt off their backs." No doubt ranchers are represented by a range of personality types similar to that found among any other group of Americans. But the same could be said about strip miners. And there is the point. People may be friendly, generous, interesting, good companions, or anything else, but that does not mean that one must approve of their business. Good people can be involved in terribly destructive vocations.

Despite their apparent warmth and social graces, ranchers seem to have a special hardness expressed as a diminished regard for life, creatures, and the designs of nature. A willingness to resort to violence—bare knuckles, vigilante-type actions, and the use of weapons—is shallowly concealed and easily set in motion. The rodeo, with its violence, physical abuses, and man-over-beast theme, seems to be a manifestation of this attitude toward surroundings. Force has always been a way of life among cattlemen.

The origin of this hardened view of life and nature may be found in the everyday activities of ranching. The cattleman's most prized possession, his cattle, must be viewed with cold, unemotional detachment—they are destined to be slaughtered and replaced by others. Meanwhile, calves will be pulled at birth, with a chain and tractor if necessary, each animal will be branded by burning a symbol into its living skin, young males will be perfunctorily castrated, horns will be cut off, notches will be cut in the animal's ears, and wattles will be cut on the head and necks of many. The cattle will be lassoed, dragged, punched, prodded, beaten, and driven. And any predators daring to approach within shooting distance of the cattle will be promptly dispatched.

What is the impact of such violence and gore upon the impressionable children who are destined to become the next generation of ranchers? It seems a small wonder that cattlemen are unable to fathom the sentiments of environmentalists, or muster empathy for a rare and endangered species, or concern themselves with the habitat needs of bighorn sheep or native trout. Dollars are real; life and nature are transitory—to be used, recycled, and manipulated—not made into objects of affection.

In Africa, the Masais and Zulus keep large herds of cattle, not for food, but as indicators of wealth and high social position. As the Masai population increased, cooking fuels became difficult to find, and the people took to gathering grasses and shrubs to burn. Very quickly the cattle and people denuded the land, the soil washed away, and the already destitute people were reduced to a life of extreme poverty. There are important lessons here; we too have judged a man's worth by counting his cows.

Everyone knows about the sacred cows of India—large numbers of free-roaming beasts, competing with man and native animals, creating havoc, and diverting valuable resources to little useful purpose. The Indian sacred cows are zealously protected by the establishment. The West too has had its sacred cows for only a couple of centuries, but the story is the same.

Although the mistakes of the early cattlemen are usually attributed to enthusiasm and ignorance, we must remember that the prevailing motivation was greed. Even though concepts of carrying capacity and range management were yet to be developed, cattlemen must have known that land and grass really weren't inexhaustible. They were warned repeatedly by newspaper editors and others and chose to disregard sound and well-intentioned advice. Today's ranchers are better informed, yet they have retained a reckless set of ethics and practices, little changed from former times. They are content to doggedly mine dollars from sick land and resist all efforts to mend the range or husband range resources. For this they must be held accountable.

The cow has kind eyes, the calf is frisky and playful, and the vegetation is removed one bite at a time. The cowboy sits astride his mount and smiles approvingly. This pastoral scene is disarming to the critic. How could anyone object? But the story of the cattle industry in the West is not pastoral.

THE GREAT STAMPEDE

The first cattle may have been brought to North America by the Vikings in the eleventh century, but neither the Vikings nor their cattle survived.

The first meaningful cattle introductions, those that started the great stampede, are credited to the Spaniards. As early as 1521, Hernando Cortez unloaded Spanish cattle in Veracruz, then moved on to conquer Mexico City and consolidate his conquests. The Spaniards brought with them to the New World a long history of disregard for conservation. Spain was seriously overgrazed, Spanish forests had been wantonly cut and burned, and vast areas of the nation were reduced to desert and semidesert. Spanish cattle were tough, hardy, mobile, long-horned, and ideal for running wild in the wilderness of the new continent. They were well-adapted to thrive and increase in the face of whatever adversities the New World offered.

The Spanish occupation of Mexico spread northward in the form of presidios (military installations), pueblos (colonial settlements), and missions. Livestock of all types moved with the occupation, especially with the missions. Wherever the Spanish influence extended, huge grants of land were given to promote livestock production on the open range, where cattle essentially ran wild. By 1700, cattle had spread throughout Mexico. Although cattle reached New Mexico in the 16th and 17th centuries and spread into Texas, Arizona, and California, large-scale operations did not develop in the United States until about 1800 and did not peak until the 1880's.

In 1792, Captain George Vancouver, the British explorer, found cattle at a Spanish settlement on Nootka Sound on Vancouver Island in southwestern British Columbia. A few California cattle were brought to Astoria at the mouth of the Columbia River in 1814 by British fur traders.

On the eastern seaboard, cattle arrived with the first colonists. Most of these cattle were of breeds found in England and western Europe and were less formidable and of better quality than Spanish cattle. At first, communal herds were grazed on commons near settlements, often with a supervising herdsman. Although large herds and long drives occurred, these never approached the proportions that would be seen in the West. The practice of confining cattle and fattening them on grain began early. Fencing, irrigation, pasture improvement, and other husbandry techniques restrained numbers and movements of cattle. In spite of close supervision, considerable overgrazing occurred, and numerous exotic plants arrived with livestock from Europe, escaped, and often replaced native species of plants. Today, some exotic plants from Europe have been around long enough to have become naturalized and acquire New World names, such as Kentucky bluegrass. The eastern cattle industry continued to expand westward to the limits of the forests, but halted temporarily at the plains in deference to a wild and explosive growth of the open-range cattle industry on the Great Plains.

Herds of Spanish cattle, soon to be known as Texas Longhorns, multiplied rapidly in Spanish Texas and California. Because of a lack of ready markets for large quantities of beef, tens of thousands of cattle were slaughtered just for hides and tallow. Ships from Boston worked in the hide and tallow trade along the coast of California, as described in Richard Dana's classic book, *Two Years Before the Mast.* Even the hide and tallow business was profitable to Texas cattlemen.

Eventually, Texas cattle were used to supply army posts and feed Indians confined on reservations. When gold was discovered in California, cattle drives were used to deliver meat to the miners. Other cattle were driven from Texas to markets in Louisiana, but when Union forces captured New Orleans, delivery routes to the Confederacy were severed. By the end of the Civil War, incredible numbers of cattle had accumulated in Texas. Thus, Texas had about 4.5 million cattle in 1860, but from 1865 to 1885 about 5.5 million head were driven from Texas to railroad terminals and other western states for stocking new ranges.

The Civil War, Indians, bison, and a lack of ready markets delayed and impeded the spread of the open-range cattle industry in the Great Plains. But the war's end ushered in the historic era when enormous herds of cattle were driven north to shipping points along railroads being built westward. The Chisholm Trail, between San Antonio, Texas, and Abilene, Kansas, became an American legend, as did other trails, towns, and events. By about 1870, the Plains Indians were subdued and forced to live on reservations. The native bison were systematically slaughtered to clear them from railroad tracks and to keep Indians on reservations; eventually the bison were almost eliminated.

Now the livestock industry was free to expand. And expand it did. As wealthy investors from the East and Europe joined the mounting cattle boom, the expansion became a craze—a frenzied quest for easy money that spread like wildfire through the West. Huge herds of Longhorns were driven from Texas to other western states and even Canada. For example, a herd of 10,000 went to Idaho and southeastern Oregon in 1869. In the haste to get all the western ranges fully stocked, buyers began to bring large herds from the East to the West.

In the Far West, the Hudson Bay Company had brought cattle to its trading post at the mouth of the Columbia River in 1814. From there surplus cattle were transferred to other posts throughout the Oregon Territory. By 1837, the number in the Oregon Territory had reached 1,200 head, most belonging to the British. But in that year, settlers in the Willamette Valley of Oregon began purchasing large numbers of Spanish cattle and driving them north from California.

The great westward migration of settlers was merely a trickle until 1843, when 1,000 people came west in wagon trains. But thereafter, the human migration became a veritable flood. Wagon trains were usually accompanied by cattle, mostly breeds much superior to the Texas Longhorns. When gold was discovered in California in 1849, the Northwest had plenty of cattle and began driving them south to provide meat to hungry miners. In 1858, as many as 20,000 head were taken to California. As other gold and silver strikes were made, large numbers of Oregon and California cattle were driven to mines in Nevada, Idaho, Montana, Washington, and British Columbia.

Between the 1860's and the 1890's, the most fertile lands west of the Cascade and Sierra mountains were being diverted to croplands, so the open-range cattle industry moved onto the vast stretches of open rangeland of the arid intermountain region. As early as 1862, 46,000 cattle were brought to interior ranges—some from settled areas west of the Cascades and others from the East with newly arriving immigrants. By the 1870's, much of the interior was stocked, and numerous reports of overstocking began to surface.

These were times when enormous holdings were accumulated—cattle kingdoms stocked with as many as 75,000 cattle. The first transcontinental railroad was completed in 1869, and during the 1870's and 1880's, huge numbers of cattle were driven or shipped from the Far West to stock newly opened ranges in Montana, Wyoming, Colorado, Kansas, and the Dakotas. In 1880 alone, more than 170,000 head were driven east from Oregon, Idaho, and Washington. One large drive, involving 30,000 head, travelled as three great herds. Meanwhile, large numbers of cattle from the eastern states were also being moved into these newly developing states.

Adding to the growing pressures on western rangelands were the huge herds of free-roaming horses, derived from breeding stock escaped from Spanish missions or stolen by Indians. Lewis and Clark found horses to be abundant among Northwest Indians in 1804. And by 1825, more than a million domestic sheep inhabited California. Soon, the great bands of sheep began to follow the well-trodden pathways laid down by the cattle and quickly spread throughout the West. In 1850 the number of sheep in western states other than California was only about 514,000 but the numbers soared to near 20 million by 1890.

In 1870, the total number of cattle in the Arizona Territory was only 5,000. But numbers were increased recklessly, and by 1891 the population of cattle in the territory had grown to an estimated 1.5 million. Although actual numbers varied from area to area, similar increases occurred throughout the West. In 1870, the cattle population in 17 western states was estimated to be 4-5 million head; by 1890, that had grown to 26.5 million. These estimates are probably quite conservative—censusing methods were crude.

Thus, within the brief span of about 25 years, the great empty rangelands of the West, once thought to be inexhaustible, had been filled with cattle and other livestock. Tensions and serious problems had already begun to appear.

Except for portions of California, the entire West had been transformed into a gigantic, unfenced, free, and unrestricted cattle pasture. Wherever cattlemen went, they spread their enthusiasm and standard promotional lines—unending supplies of forage, plenty of vacant range, and opportunities for huge profits. But as these fantasies grew, reality began to intrude. Settlers bent on agriculture began to claim rich bottomlands, plant crops, and deny cattlemen access to some of the more productive lands. The competition from sheepmen was a growing and intolerable problem. As early as the 1850's, some ranges were devastated, but now productivity was declining on much more of the western rangeland.

Throughout the era of the cattle explosion in the West, cattle were permitted to run unsupervised on the open range, without supplementary feed or shelter in the winter. During exceptionally bad winters in the 1840's and 1850's, many cattle died. Such losses were regarded as one of the costs of being in the business. Then in the winter of 1861-62, temperatures plunged and remained far below zero for several weeks. Deep accumulations of snow and a thick crust of ice denied cattle access to buried forage. Cold rains and sleet aggravated the dangerous situation. By spring, the results were disastrous, with some losses as high as 90 percent in eastern Oregon.

Newspaper editors fretted about the rotting carcasses littering the countryside, wondered who was responsible for their disposal, and openly feared for the health of the citizenry. Editors also chided cattlemen for their stubborn and inhumane refusal to provide winter feed and shelter for the cattle. All manner of arguments were published against the foolish economics of such waste and negligence. Although cattlemen admitted that losses were greater on overgrazed ranges, their solution was merely a vow to drive their cattle to better rangelands next time. But memory and common sense were short-lived, and after a couple of mild winters, resolve and promises of change were forgotten. Experience was not an effective teacher because the cattlemen preferred to gamble—to risk making high profits with minimal expenditures and effort. Damage to the range was of no concern because it belonged to the government. Furthermore, most cattlemen had only a vague idea of how many cattle they owned and were not easily convinced of the extent of their losses.

Other bad years followed, but not often enough to force drastic changes. The winter of 1880-81 was particularly severe, both in the Far West and in the Great Plains. Even the few ranchers who had started winter feeding ran out of feed and suffered enormous losses.

Public revulsion against the inhumanity of the cattlemen continued to grow, and even the livestock journals published complaints about the barbarous cruelty on public lands and asked the government to intervene and stop the practice of allowing cattlemen to starve hundreds of thousands of cattle each year. But the winter of 1886-87 brought more cattle deaths and range devastation to the West, especially in the northern Great Plains, where one corporation, the Bay State Land and Cattle Company, lost 100,000 head.

In Montana in the spring of 1886, rainfall was scant, and many watering sites dried up in early summer. Fires swept over large areas of range. Nevertheless, cattlemen were scurrying to bring in more cattle to get the rangelands fully stocked. In the fall of the year, more than a million head of cattle roamed Montana ranges, and at the 1886 meeting of the Montana Stockgrower's Association, long-time residents complained of overstocking, but newcomers and southern cattlemen professed only optimism. Snow fell early, covered the grass, and then froze. In mid-December, a 3-day blizzard struck. Then on January 9, a record-smashing storm swept in from the north—it lasted 10 days, during which as much as 16 inches of snow fell, winds lashed the landscape, and temperatures plunged as low as 46 degrees below zero.

Herds of cattle that had just arrived in the state were still weak from the drive and perished almost immediately. Young animals and others unaccustomed to the Montana climate soon died. Resident cattle, unable to survive on sprigs of sagebrush protruding above the snow, moved into willow thickets along stream courses to find protection from the wind and to feed on limbs and bark. One rancher remembered seeing segments of wood the size of lead pencils in cow manure. Some cattle wandered into towns and ate tar paper from the walls of buildings.

When it was over, 70 percent of the cattle in eastern Montana lay frozen, stacked where they died in piles in willow thickets along various streams. Dugouts and old shacks were stuffed with carcasses of cattle that had jammed into any refuge offering protection from the bitter storm. Wolves and coyotes had a heyday. When the snow finally melted, thousands of dead cattle bobbed among the ice floes moving down the swollen streams—a procession of bodies testifying to the immensity of the tragedy. Many of the surviving cattle had wandered such distances that owners did not recover them for as long as a year after the storm. During the spring thaw, emaciated and helpless cattle, barely alive, were everywhere—stuck in mud or simply too weak to travel. One rancher lost only 66 percent of his herd and seemed to consider himself lucky. Eventually, the total loss was estimated to be $20 million. Only the small operators, who had seen fit to set aside a little hay, escaped

"I THOUGHT YOU SAID HE'D JUST EAT GRASS!!"

the wrath of the storm; by doing so, they set an example for major cattlemen to follow in the future.

In the intermountain region of the West, the late 1880's brought a series of dry summers. In 1889, a drought year, cattlemen approached the winter with inadequate feed supplies, and the cattle were in poor condition at the end of the summer. The exceptionally cruel winter of 1889-90 ended, for most cattlemen, the reckless and negligent era of running cattle year-round on open range. Many ranchers including some of the largest operators, were forced into bankruptcy. For example, a Nevada-Idaho operation branded 38,000 calves in 1885, but recovered only 68 of them in 1890!

In parts of the Southwest, cattle numbers reached a peak in 1891 when rainfall was below normal. With continuing drought in 1892, cattle began to die. In the spring of 1893, the losses grew incredibly, amounting to 50-75 percent of the total cattle population. Dead cattle were everywhere. Witnesses stated that a person could stand at one carcass and throw rocks to others nearby. In retrospect, the massive die-offs were a blessing, otherwise the entire West would have been turned into a desert.

Although some winter losses of cattle continued into the 20th century, the great stampede and era of virtual madness had clearly come to an end in the early 1890's. Decades of abuse and carelessness had left valuable range resources in ruin, and for the next 50 years, it would not be possible to build cattle herds in the West much above the numbers attained in the early 1890's. The era had scarred the land, altered the vegetation's composition, and set in motion drastic changes in the total environment of the western rangelands—changes that in some instances would require centuries to reverse, if indeed, reversal were possible. Much of the damage continues today.

Perhaps the saddest and most unfortunate result of the long and undisciplined period of "boom or bust" in the western cattle industry is that it set a pattern for the future—the industry developed outside the law. Not that certain practices and attitudes haven't changed, for they certainly have—they had to. But the ethics, free-wheeling individualism, attitudes toward government, defiance against suggestions and regulation, relationships with other users of public lands, and many of the most objectionable current ranching practices have their roots in that outrageous period. Because these roots are historical and anchored in that mythical era, they are stubbornly retained, practiced, revered, and even cherished. This inheritance from the days of the great stampede survives and forms the basis for many problems, disputes, and public costs associated with the modern cattle industry on public rangelands.

CHICANERY AND FORCE

The occupation and domination of the West by cattlemen were not fortuitous events. On the contrary, from the beginning, cattlemen systematically adopted and ruthlessly employed techniques designed to assure their control and exclusive occupancy of newly opened public lands. Unlike most businesses, the raising of cattle on open range could be done in remote areas far from centers of commerce, consequently, the cattlemen were usually first on the scene. Once a power base had been established, influence, wealth, and force were used to protect interests and enlarge holdings. Chicanery and force were part of the normal procedure in gaining control of rangelands, dealing with various competitors, and taking command of social, economic, and legislative systems. In large areas of the West, modern cattlemen and their organizations have retained much of this power and influence.

Except for fur trappers, explorers, and a few military parties, cattlemen were often the first white men to reach remote parts of the West. Often, cattle were driven to uninhabited rangelands far beyond settlements and simply abandoned to fend for themselves. After returning to civilization for the winter, the owners would go back to the open range in the spring to brand and mark cattle, collect animals to be driven to market, and perform other chores. In some instances, a shack or cabin might be constructed to house cowboys at the site. Sometimes, corrals were built in convenient locations for working and sorting the cattle. Although the land belonged to the federal government, it was used according to need, and little thought was given to acquiring deeds, even when structures were erected.

Later, home ranches established in grazing areas were strategically located to control available water supplies and rich bottomlands. By gaining command of water and nearby fertile lands, a cattleman could repel potential competitors and assure himself exclusive use of all surrounding public rangelands without actually taking ownership. At first, only the lands surrounding the home ranch were patented. In some cases squatters elected to remain without deeded property, relying upon the force of arms to protect holdings.

Through purchase, treaty, and theft, the United States acquired vast tracts of land in the West and formulated a national policy of land disposal to encourage settlement of these lands. The encouragement of settlement was hardly altruistic, but served national interests and security by putting an American presence in these frontier regions so remote from the seat of government. In any event, congress enacted a series of laws designed to transfer publicly owned land into private ownership, e.g., Pre-emption Act of 1841, Homestead Act of 1862, Timber Culture Act of 1873, Desert Land Act of 1877, Stone and Timber Act of 1878, and others.

Under the provisions of these acts, cattlemen could obtain deeded property for home ranches and a limited amount of the better surrounding lands. Various schemes were used to gain title to more land than the law permitted, including filing under names of employees and their families, filing under names of persons living in an eastern state, inventing fictitious names, and so forth. Abuses under these laws, however, were generally minor compared to certain other devices used to obtain land.

As new states joined the Union, each received extensive tracts of federal land for support of schools and local governments. In most states, much of this state land was sold to wealthy ranchers and speculators for a few cents or a few dollars an acre. Many of these land deals were openly fraudulent and amounted to outright theft. Furthermore, because the first legislatures were dominated by cattlemen, state policies for selling lands and prices were set to benefit ranchers and to exclude other interests.

Unlike other states, Texas retained ownership of all lands within the state upon coming into the Union and, therefore, had millions of acres to dispose of. This fact, together with its size, explains why Texas has always had far more than its due share of cattle kings.

Both state and federal governments gave liberal grants of land in payment for the construction of roads and railroads, often in the form of alternate sections of land for some distance on either side of the proposed route. Not infrequently, builders failed to perform the assigned task, and governments had to go to court to retrieve the granted land. Over the years many of these lands became involved in abuses and scandals, and even today, several large railroads in the West retain immense landholdings and wealth dating back to these land grants. In Texas, one railroad builder was promised 16-20 sections of land for every mile of track laid. When the job was completed, the state owed the builder 12 million acres—more than the state had. The obligation was finally settled for a mere 5 million acres!

Although some cattlemen bought large parcels of state and railroad lands, others purchased only isolated sections distributed in a manner to confer control of large tracts of interspersed public lands. By acquiring small parcels here and there and using hired gunmen, a cattleman could gain exclusive use of hundreds of square miles of public rangelands.

Throughout the latter half of the 1800's, cattle kings and corporate cattle kingdoms sprouted up throughout the West. Some of these operations were founded upon large holdings of deeded land, but depended, to a large extent, upon public lands for grazing. Others had little land of their own. Many of the larger outfits operated in several states and grew so powerful that nothing short of the full force of the federal government could budge them. Several of these cattle kingdoms controlled more than a million acres, and the XIT in Texas, the largest of all, once held dominion over 5 million acres—an area the size of New Jersey. Some, such as the

Bay State Land and Cattle Company in Nebraska and Wyoming, ran as many as 150,000 head of cattle.

Once the large operators gained control of rangelands, they adopted various devices to keep other cattlemen out of their territory. Several states and territories recognized an unwritten law of customary range. Ranchers in a given geographic region, usually an area delineated by rivers, mountain ranges, or other natural boundaries, mutually agreed that certain public rangelands belonged to the person who got there first and had used the range for several years. Obviously, this policy favored large operators and the *status quo.*

Often, ranchers in a specific area would form associations and hire gunmen to enforce agreed-upon arrangements and to insure that outsiders did not infringe on lands controlled by the association. Associations sometimes passed and enforced illegal regulations specifying that a particular area was fully stocked and closed to additional cattle. In Wyoming, one association decreed that no person could run cattle on the range without first posting a deposit of $3,000, an amount calculated to insure continued use by the wealthy current users and to exclude small ranchers and settlers. If that weren't enough, the association also refused to recognize or honor any brands except those of established cattlemen. Acting as vigilantes or through hired agents or gunmen, associations were able to attend to rustlers and competitors without resorting to legal channels.

When barbed wire became available in 1874, many cattlemen erected illegal fences to protect "their" public rangelands. Charles Goodnight, a Texas cattle baron, controlled 3 million acres of public range with illegal fences, and it took the personal intervention of President Theodore Roosevelt to get the fences taken down. In 1885, the Unlawful Exclosures Act forbade excluding other users of public-domain lands with illegal fences or intimidation.

Because all public lands were open to settlement by homesteaders, there was no legal way for cattlemen to keep settlers out. However, plenty of illegal methods were available, including cutting off water supplies, cutting fences and

letting cattle devastate crops, denying credit (banks and businesses were usually owned by cattle barons), gunplay, forced land sales in times of economic hardship, and so on.

Most eastern states adopted fencing laws based on English common law, which specified that the person owning livestock must *fence animals in*. Should livestock escape, the owner of the offending animals was liable for any damage to crops. Although California approved such a law, causing many large cattle operations to relocate in adjacent states, most western states passed open-range laws stating that cattle were free to roam, the person owning crops must *fence cattle out*, and all fences must meet legal specifications prescribed by law. Thus, if a rancher's cow sustained injury while attempting to squeeze through an unlawful type of fence to raid a farmer's crops, the farmer was liable for the damage to the cow! Ironically, farmers were forced to fence deeded lands against the incursions of cattle using public lands—lands not belonging to the owner of the offending cattle. But even railroads were liable for killing cows that wandered onto tracks. And in most parts of the West, if a motorist collides with a cow on a highway, even though the highway is fenced on both sides, the driver or next of kin is liable for the cost of the cow—which usually turns out to be the rancher's "most valuable" brood cow!

When sheep began to spread throughout the West and compete with cattle for the use of public ranges, cattlemen were incensed. The major complaints were that sheep grazed the vegetation too close to the ground, and cattle would not feed where sheep had been. Various steps were taken to discourage the sheepmen.

In some areas, associations declared large tracts of rangeland to be for cattle only, patrolled the range, and enforced the edict. Other cattlemen resorted to illegal fencing of public lands, or simply retreated to ranges not used by sheep. Sheep were poisoned, clubbed, and denied access to watering holes, sheepherders were beaten or murdered, and groups of men were hired to shoot sheep. In Oregon, the Crook County Sheep Shooters brazenly published their annual tallies in newspapers.

In Idaho, a cattleman-dominated legislature enacted laws forbidding sheep to graze within two miles of a dwelling or on lands normally grazed by cattle. Even though the laws were applied to publicly owned, federal lands, the Idaho laws were upheld in court tests.

Despite obstacles, sheep continued to come in ever-increasing numbers. When it became apparent that sheep raising was highly profitable, many cattlemen joined the opposition and went into the sheep business. The value of the sheep industry eventually surpassed that of the cattle industry in many portions of the West. With the coming of federal regulations governing the grazing of public lands, cattlemen and sheepmen buried their differences, and in recent times, have often acted in concert to oppose federal grazing policies, wilderness and other environmental issues, big game protection, and sensible methods of predator control.

Cattlemen saved their most dastardly bag of tricks for the Indians. Early cattlemen tolerated Indians as long as they didn't get in the way, but the accepted belief was that "the only good Indian is a dead Indian." When Indians were forced onto reservations, they were usually given generous allotments of land by the federal government. But as the public rangelands became crowded, cattlemen began to covet the unused forage on reservations—forage that was being wasted on savages. Soon ranchers were demanding that western congressmen reduce the size of reservations to make more land available for cattle grazing. In 1880, four reservations in Oregon contained 3,567,360 acres, but by 1890, these reservations were reduced to only 1,788,800 acres; similar reductions in the size of reservations took place in other western states.

But stealing a portion of the Indian land failed to satisfy greedy cattlemen—they wanted more. As encroachment by sheep and homesteaders crowded them, the cowboys began to run cattle on reservations. Indian agents reported swarms of cattle and counted as many as 10,000 trespassing cattle on a single reservation, but they were helpless to stop it. On some reservations, trespassing thrived for 20 years, after which, Indian agents reported that the native bunchgrasses had been eaten out and destroyed. Even when agents reported names of offending ranchers and numbers of trespassing cattle to their superiors, little was done. Eventually, some of the bolder cattlemen actually built homes on reservations, mowed hay, and refused to leave when ordered to do so—telling the government to fence the reservation if they wanted them off. Trespassing cattlemen contended that the only solution was to move the Indians and sell the land to the trespassers.

Because of the prevailing belief that all the good Indians were underground, law officers, courts, and juries refused to punish trespassers. Meanwhile, not only did cattlemen encroach upon Indian reservations, but they had the audacity to use force to keep homesteaders from doing the same.

On a few occasions, the military was summoned to clear cattlemen from reservations. But whenever it became apparent that the government meant business, the ranchers usually resorted to more subtle ploys. For example, they would drive herds across a reservation, on the pretense of moving them to another range, but drive the cattle so slowly that they would get fat along the way. Others took Indian wives in an attempt to gain a legal foothold on reservation grazing lands. Still others consigned cattle to a willing Indian already living on the reservation. Besides, cattlemen could always claim that they didn't know where the boundaries were, for congress steadfastly refused to appropriate funds needed to survey the reservations. In the few cases where surveys were actually done, trespassers pulled up and destroyed the boundary markers.

Initially it was illegal to lease Indian grazing lands, although many tried. In Oregon, a large cattle corporation offered to rent 500 square miles of the Malheur Reservation for 15 years at the rate of $200 per year! Eventually, leases were authorized by congress, and the leasing of Indian land became one of the most despicable chapters in American history—filled with graft, corruption, and cheating of every description—always at the Indians' expense. Many cattle kings got a start by leasing reservation land. Only within recent times, with the use of sealed bids and the arrival of a generation of educated Indians who hire good lawyers, have the abuses begun to subside.

Open range invited a certain amount of rustling, and although most cattlemen didn't know how many cattle they owned, they were positively paranoid about having any stolen. Although laws dealt severely with rustlers, the charge being grand theft and the penalty 1-15 years in prison (reduced in later years), the law was seldom around when needed. Cattlemen preferred to handle rustling through associations or vigilante actions. Remedies differed from place to place and time to time.

In 1875, a dozen rustlers were caught and their bodies dumped in the town square of Brownsville, Texas, for relatives to claim and identify. Many others were strung up to the nearest tree. In other cases, the suspected rustlers were taken to the nearest town, given a speedy trial, and then hanged. Occasionally, suspected rustlers were given a few hours to leave the territory—then hanged if they weren't gone in the specified time.

The task of determining guilt or innocence seemed not to weigh heavily upon the rustling proceedings. The primary objective was to hang someone—anyone to set an example for all others who might be tempted to try a hand at rustling. The irate farmer who shot cattle trespassing in his fields could expect much the same treatment.

Some large corporations, such as the Swan Land and Cattle Company, Limited—a British-owned firm that operated in Wyoming and Nebraska—illegally ran cattle on Indian land, fenced public lands, and controlled with force nearly every aspect of business and government in the area. President Cleveland threatened to send in the cavalry when the Swan Company and other big operators, acting through the Wyoming Stockgrower's Association, openly flaunted the law. When the corruption continued, President Theodore Roosevelt hauled many of the major offenders into court, where they were given light fines or acquitted. But when government surveyors continued to be murdered and other atrocities were undiminished, an exasperated President

Roosevelt sent in the Secret Service, fired a U.S. Marshall, and shook up the local judiciary. Eventually, a brother of the Governor of Wyoming was sent to prison. It was one of the few times the cowboys lost, and the effect was to end an era of open lawlessness. Unfortunately, not every generation has had a Teddy Roosevelt.

Cattlemen have always exerted legislative clout and political power far beyond their numbers. By being on the scene early, they played a dominant role in the establishment of territorial governments and many state governments. Wealth and power, gained from dominating the land, were easily transferred to politics in sparsely populated regions. Cattlemen liked politics and sought office at all levels of government. Their influence is particularly evident in state legislation in the West, which favors and perpetuates the cattle industry. In contrast, federal laws, showing the influence of eastern legislators, are more likely to protect public lands and to regulate grazing abuses.

Wealthy cattlemen used their economic power to gain influence in settlements and towns where they invested in banks, property, and stocks in enterprises such as railroads. Many managed to become power brokers at a national level and were accustomed to dealing with important and influential people.

Men in the cattle business were often picturesque and resourceful. Political and economic power gave them great self-confidence, spirit, and command. Being held in high regard by others caused many ranchers to become assertive, even arrogant. Early on, all this heady power began to be expressed as a distinct class consciousness. Cattlemen considered themselves superior to farmers, settlers, public employees, and other persons who labored for a regular salary. The attitude was almost medieval, with the cattleman seeing himself in the role of a baron or aristocrat overseeing his fiefdom. Even today, this aristocratic aura attracts many people—the wealthy, the cultured, the professionals—people who buy cattle ranches because they relish the role of being a baron.

Although much has changed in the West, a great deal has remained the same. Cattlemen have largely retained their unchallenged domination of the public rangelands. While chicanery and force have become a bit more subtle, the industry is as ruthless as ever in gaining its objectives and protecting its interests. Associations continue to exert disproportionate influence in regional and local matters. In the more rural western states, legislatures have large contingents of cattlemen, and many are still dominated by stockmen.

In hundreds of small western towns, one can easily recognize the wealthy rancher swaggering down the street, and from two blocks away, his demeanor telegraphs his firm conviction that he is indeed a baron. And if you were to ask him whether or not he has grazing *privileges* on public lands, chances are, he would reply, "Privilege, my ass—I have a *right* to those lands."

AT THE PUBLIC TROUGH

When the great stampede ended, 700 million acres of grass west of the Mississippi River had been depleted or destroyed in only 50 years. Much of the western rangeland had suffered damages that would carry over into the 20th century and beyond. Because range management did not yet exist, the damages would not be scientifically documented until the 1930's, when all the public rangelands were finally surveyed. But the greed and ignorance of the last third of the 1800's, especially the period from 1880 to 1895, had laid waste to public rangeland resources and signalled a clear need for ending the unfettered raising of cattle on open range. Not only were changes needed—they were inevitable—the land was simply incapable of tolerating more of the same.

Flagrant overstocking of ranges, deterioration of vegetation and soils, and the shocking extravagance of massive winter starvation demanded reform. But other factors dictated change as well. For one, grass-fed beef began to lose its command of the market as more cattle were fattened on grain before slaughter. Furthermore, Texas Longhorns were gradually replaced by superior breeds, such as Herefords, Shorthorns, and Angus, which required closer supervision and winter feeding. Finally, barbed wire, invented in 1874, spread to cattle ranges and increasingly interfered with long drives and wide-ranging operations that permitted cattle to roam at will.

As the number of homesteaders increased and the civilizing effects of law and order began to take charge, the scandalous social customs evolved during the great stampede became increasingly unacceptable. Unbridled force, the concept that bigger is better, the strong taking whatever they want—all were questioned and challenged. Ordinary citizens began to expect legal equality with wealthy and powerful ranchers. Also, western society came to respect more commonplace virtues relating to family, the home, and the true worth of an individual to the community. Eventually, with the support and approval of law-abiding citizens, lawmen and legal authorities were able to suppress the vigilante shenanigans of cattlemen and their associations. Even the federal government, which discovered that cattlemen had illegally fenced 7.25 million acres of public land in 14 states, ran out of patience. But because cattlemen had enjoyed so much freedom and become accustomed to it, change would come at a painfully slow pace.

By the end of the Civil War, a few perceptive observers began to warn about the long-term consequences of the nation's reckless and destructive exploitation of natural resources. These concerns grew, spread, and eventually gave rise to a system of ethics for dealing with lands and resources that has persisted into modern times. Grazing abuses were not the focus of these first warnings—that would come later. Instead, exploitation of forests and destruction of water supplies were the initial causes of public reaction—these being more visible and immediately urgent. Grazing, however, was so intimately entwined in these other resource problems that it would prove impossible to deal with one without the others. In time, the call for action in the national interest became a force that could no longer be denied.

In 1891, a law providing for the setting aside of federal forest reserves was passed. Reserved lands did not have to have commercial timber and were closed to homesteading. Using the provisions of the law, President Benjamin Harrison set aside more than 13 million acres of public land as forest reserves. Because the law failed to provide for the administration and ultimate use of the forest reserves, it erected perpetual barriers to would-be exploiters. Lumbermen, miners, railroaders, stockmen, and others were incensed, especially when President Grover Cleveland proclaimed 13 additional forest reserves—21 million acres.

After much debate and political maneuvering, congress revised the controversial law in 1897 to limit future forest reserves to lands having forest and water resources. Also, the Secretary of Interior, whose agency administered the reserves, was instructed to devise rules to regulate and provide for the occupancy and use of the forest reserves. In 1905, during the presidency of Theodore Roosevelt, the forest reserves were transferred to the Department of Agriculture, designated as national forests, and placed under the jurisdiction of the newly created Forest Service, whose first administrator was Gifford Pinchot. Cattlemen and others, who had freely exploited these forest lands in the past, didn't like the course of events.

It should be noted, however, that stockmen and their livestock were already using the lands that became national forests. In setting out to manage the lands to insure the permanency of the resources and for the benefit of the greatest number for the longest time, the Forest Service set high goals and challenged the customs and rights of current users. But the ranchers were already out there, operating just as they pleased. Thus, the new agency faced the difficult task of taking charge—deciding who would continue to graze the lands, how many livestock would be permitted, and the length of the grazing season. It was a task fraught with controversy.

But the sharpest blow to livestock owners came when a charge was levied for forage on Forest Service lands and put into effect for the 1906 grazing season. The fee was ridiculously modest—5 cents a month for a cow and her calf and 1 cent a month for a ewe and her lamb or lambs. Nevertheless, stockmen, accustomed to free forage, were irate and brought strong pressures upon Pinchot and President Roosevelt (a western rancher) through associations, congressmen, and other allies. When Roosevelt and Pinchot refused to yield, congress retaliated by withdrawing presidential authority to create additional national forests in several western states. Roosevelt, however, hastily proclaimed 16 million acres of new national forests in those states—*then* signed the bill into law. The livestock industry and other special interests challenged the action in court and heaped further abuse upon the Forest Service, but to no avail. Immense credit belongs to Pinchot and Roosevelt for standing firm when lesser men would have crumpled.

Despite strong opposition from stockmen and unrelenting political interference, the Forest Service formulated a rational grazing program and began the difficult task of healing the damages caused by decades of grazing abuse. Then came World War I. Under the guise of patriotism (i.e., producing red meat for the boys in uniform), the livestock industry managed to nullify all Forest Service gains. Once again the forests swarmed with livestock, and all the old abuses were resurrected. In 1918 and 1919, the number of cattle on Forest Service lands reached an all-time record, and then for the next 14 years, the western states suffered the longest and most serious drought since records have been kept. At the end of the war, forests were ravaged and denuded of forage—the Forest Service faced the prospect of beginning anew.

Today, little has changed. Stockmen and their political allies continue stubborn opposition to what they consider to be unwarranted interference with grazing "rights." The conflict has grown more subtle and somewhat more civil, but the old attitudes prevail and dominate the thinking of a large percentage of the permittees grazing livestock on Forest Service allotments.

While public concern was leading to the establishment and protection of national forest lands, no similar sentiments were being voiced in behalf of the public-domain lands. After homesteaders, states, federal agencies, and other recipients of public land had taken what they wanted, more than half a billion acres remained, mainly in arid and mountainous parts of the West. Lacking forests or other readily apparent values, public-domain lands were generally considered to be worthless except for grazing. These vast tracts, which no one cared about, had been the centerpiece of the great stampede and the era of unrestricted open range. And for several decades after some semblance of grazing control had come to forest lands, the public domain would continue to be grazed unmercifully—without fee, restriction, or accountability by users. This period of legalized looting of the public domain is a particularly disgraceful blemish on the nation's record of land stewardship. Although congress fretted, conducted hearings, and talked, there was little resolve and no action.

Finally in 1934, during the presidency of Franklin D. Roosevelt, the Taylor Grazing Act was passed. In its preamble, the Taylor Act proclaimed noble intentions. It would stop injury to the public grazing lands by preventing overgrazing and soil deterioration, provide for orderly use, improvement, and development, and stabilize the livestock industry dependent upon public-domain lands, and much more. The act boasted that it would promote the highest use of the public domain pending its "final disposal."

The Taylor Act created the Division of Grazing (later to become the Grazing Service) in the Department of Interior, transferred 80 million acres (eventually 157 million acres) into grazing districts, set guidelines for selecting grazing permittees entitled to use the lands, called for charging a *reasonable* grazing fee, and authorized committees of local stockmen to manage the grazing districts jointly with the Department of Interior. A fee of 5 cents per AUM (=Animal Unit Month—the amount of forage required to feed a cow and her calf, a horse, or five sheep or goats for a month) was put into effect in 1936 and not increased until 1946. Only $150,000 was appropriated to administer the grazing districts and the new program. The Taylor Act placed all other public-domain lands (i.e., those not in grazing districts) under the jurisdiction of the General Land Office, an agency whose principal function had been to dispose of the public-domain lands. A minimal grazing fee was authorized for the use of these lands, but stockmen were not restricted as to numbers of livestock or length of grazing season.

Although many stockmen opposed all forms of federal intervention, others actually welcomed passage of the Taylor

Act. To begin with, stockmen had used these lands for decades without restriction and had every reason to believe that their tenure was not seriously threatened. Furthermore, the public-domain lands were in such pitiful and unproductive condition that prospects of an infusion of federal funds seemed attractive. Finally, the act was expressed in loose language and contained ample concessions and guarantees to stockmen, while rendering the Division of Grazing virtually powerless. The first director was a rancher, and division policies originated with or were approved by stockmen.

Given such constraints, the Taylor Act amounted to little more than an expectation of federal largesse and a legal forum for the bickerings and complaints of stockmen. Grazing abuses were largely undiminished. Grazing permittees were selected, permits were issued, but no one had the slightest idea of the amount of forage available. Influential western politicians, such as Patrick McCarran, a U.S. Senator from Nevada, constantly badgered the new agency and made certain that the interests of stockmen remained foremost.

After muddling along for a decade, the Grazing Service and its equally toothless sister agency, the General Land Office, were abolished and combined to form the Bureau of Land Management (BLM). Again, the livestock industry supervised the birth of the BLM, attempted to render it harmless, and sought to intimidate the new agency's staff. A favorite ploy of stockmen has been to initiate campaigns to transfer public lands to the states or to sell them to private interests, thus threatening the job security of agency personnel. These tactics are still being employed in the 1980's (see Chapter 15).

The Forest Service, being older, born under fewer compromises, and charged with the administration of more valuable lands, has been much more effective in managing its grazing lands than has the BLM. From the beginning, both agencies have developed cozy relationships with grazing permittees. Stockmen had political clout and could help friendly agencies obtain fat budgets. Also, because grazing was a major land use (the dominant use on BLM lands), an active and expanding grazing program fueled agency growth and led to rapid advancement of agency personnel. Staff living in the same communities with stockmen learned quickly that it was easier to wear cowboy boots, attend barbecues, and maintain civil relationships with cattlemen than to get threatening phone calls, have children beaten up at school, or to be socially shunned and ostracized. Given these circumstances, the public's interests have not always fared well.

With the publication of Rachel Carson's *Silent Spring* in 1962, a tide of environmental awareness swept the nation. As the environmental movement grew, it became immensely influential, before subsiding with the election of Ronald Reagan in 1980. During the 1970's, many citizens and conservation organizations became interested in public land management and grazing programs. As a consequence of widespread public participation and the support of conservation organizations, the Forest Service and BLM found courage to stand up to livestock interests as never before.

Even congress got in the act and passed a series of laws designed to loosen the grip of commodity interests upon public lands. Although much of this legislation was tempered by the ever-present livestock lobby, it nevertheless had substantial impacts upon range policies.

The Classification and Multiple Use Act (1964-1970) officially recognized, contrary to language in the Taylor Grazing Act, that the 174 million acres of western land administered by the BLM have constituencies other than stockmen and values other than livestock grazing. Although the act's title sounded impressive, in practice, the law was minimally successful in diminishing dominant uses of public lands. Wildlife, recreation, and other less commercial uses continued to get what was left after loggers and cowboys took what they wanted. Despite its shortcomings, the act forced agencies to acknowledge other uses and provided a justification for curbing the appetites of dominant users.

The National Environmental Policy Act (1969), among other things, requires federal agencies to consider the environmental implications of their policies and actions. Furthermore, the act requires public review of proposed environmental impacts. NEPA and court decisions relating to it, for the first time brought grazing policies and problems into full public view. Disclosure has sometimes revealed shocking examples of mismanagement and costly environmental damage. Nevertheless, NEPA has without question had more beneficial effects upon rangeland management than any other legislation in the history of the American livestock industry. As bureaucrats and permittees learn to circumvent the act's intentions, as they are, NEPA's values will wane.

The Federal Land Policy and Management Act (1976) reiterates the principles of multiple use and sustained yield and requires comprehensive planning and full public participation in public land management. Perhaps more importantly, FLPMA finally settled the long-standing questions of final disposal of public lands (dating back to the Taylor Grazing Act) by specifying that the lands were to be retained in federal ownership, unless planning revealed the disposal of a given tract was in the national interest. As the Reagan Administration proceeds with plans to sell public lands to "help pay the national debt," the matter of federal ownership threatens to become a major issue in the 1980's.

The Public Rangelands Improvement Act (1978), while having an impressive name, amounts to little more than an admission that the public rangelands continue to be in an unsatisfactory condition and that vast sums of public money must be spent to keep the western livestock industry in business on public lands. In passing the act, congress authorized the spending of $365 million over the next 20 years for a program of intensified range management, principally gimmicks, such as seeding exotic grasses, constructing water holes, and building fences—none of which can help restore overall natural productivity of rangelands. Although a child knows that the way to stop overgrazing is to reduce the number of livestock on the land, congress prefers to combat overgrazing by throwing currency at it. PRIA is a grandiose and expensive scheme to force nature to accept more cows than she can accommodate.

Other legislation, such as the Endangered Species Act and numerous others dealing with water, air, watersheds, etc., relates to rangelands and influences range policies.

After starting in 1906 at 5 cents per AUM, the Forest Service's grazing fee dropped as low as 3 cents and rose as high as 14 cents during the next three decades. From the beginning, the BLM set fees to cover administrative costs and allocated more forage than was available. In 1936, when a fee of 5 cents per AUM was levied on lands governed by the Taylor Grazing Act, the Forest Service was charging 13 cents. For both agencies, the general trend for fees has been upward, with numerous temporary reversals, but neither reached a dollar until 1974, when the Forest Service charged $1.11 and the BLM $1.00. Yet an AUM of forage provides a cow a total weight gain of 28 to 90 pounds. In 1978 the two agencies began charging a uniform rate, which climbed to a maximum of $2.36 per AUM in 1980. By 1982, the fee dropped to $1.86 as grazing fees began to be set by a formula specified in the Public Rangelands Improvement Act. Because the formula takes into account beef prices and production costs, stockmen grazing public lands received substantial reductions in cost of forage during a period of high inflation when other consumer prices were rising swiftly. For example, in 1981, while the cost of grazing public land was dropping 45 cents to $1.86 per AUM, the cost of leasing private grazing lands was increasing 12 percent to an average cost of $8.83 per AUM. Finally, in 1983 the entire matter became ludicrous as grazing fees were cut to only $1.40 per AUM—a further drop of 46 cents. At this rate, the public may soon be *paying* an AUM charge to have stockmen graze public lands!

Fortunately, the section of the Public Rangeland Improvement Act setting the current formula for calculating grazing fees is due to expire in 1986. Congress has directed the Forest Service and BLM to conduct still another study of federal grazing fees and to submit the findings by the end of 1985. Presumably after 1986, congress could arrive at a sensible system of grazing fees, but if the past is to serve as an indicator, the likelihood of such an improvement seems remote indeed.

Because of fee reductions, the $13.2 million collected by the Forest Service for grazing in 1981 was expected to drop to about $12 million in 1982. A similar decline in income was expected to decrease BLM receipts from $26.5 million to about $21.3 million. Because agency costs for operating grazing programs increase with inflation and far exceed income from grazing receipts, taxpayers, in 1982, paid a subsidy of nearly $14 per animal grazed on public lands—an average of more than $2,100 per permittee. Obviously, as grazing fees decline, the amount of the public subsidy increases.

Of the grazing fees collected by the BLM, 50 percent is used to finance range improvements in the grazing district where the funds are collected, 37.5 percent goes to the U.S. Treasury, and the remainder is given to county government in lieu of taxes. Forest Service grazing receipts are distributed similarly, with range improvement funds being returned to the national forest where the funds were collected.

In recent years, the Forest Service has issued about 16,000 grazing permits for about 6.4 million AUM's (1.3 million cattle, 1.2 million sheep and goats, and 14,000 horses and burros) in 16 western states. The BLM issues about 21,000 permits for about 11.5 million AUM's (approximately 9 million cattle, sheep, goats, horses, and burros) in 11 western states. Some livestock operators hold grazing permits with both agencies.

Various types of public grazing permits exist, but those issued to ranchers are typically for a period of 10 years and and are nontransferrable, except to new owners when base property (the home ranch) is sold. Minimal requirements include citizenship and ownership of livestock and base property, the latter being a restriction designed to exclude nomadic sheepmen who were once a common phenomenon on public rangelands. Additionally, permittees must demonstrate an ability to sustain livestock during portions of the year when grazing is not permitted on public grazing allotments. Existing permits are renewed with minimal fuss, and because all available rangelands are in use, new permits are virtually nonexistent. If agencies acquire new land through purchase or from other federal agencies, the additional range is usually divided among existing permittees. During their effective lifetime, permits may be adjusted with regard to numbers of livestock or length of authorized grazing period—though they seldom are. Beyond basic regulations and directives of the parent agency, local administrators, usually forest supervisors and BLM district managers, have wide discretion in setting and varying specific terms in individual permits.

The length of the permitted grazing season ranges from year-round grazing in many parts of the Southwest, where the growing season is long, to a few weeks at high elevations, where the snow-free season is brief. The grazing season tends to be longer on open rangelands than in forested areas, but again, regional and local differences in climate and agency policy make generalization difficult. A six-month season is common.

In addition to the lands administered by the Forest Service and BLM, large holdings are controlled by other federal agencies. Many of these lands are grazed, but policies and conditions vary a great deal among and within agencies.

Most national wildlife refuges, which are administered by the Fish and Wildlife Service in the Department of Interior, have severe grazing problems, especially those in the West. In many instances these problems stem from grandfather clauses or concessions for continued use made to local ranchers who were grazing the lands at the time of refuge designation or purchase of the land by the federal government. Most grazing permits are granted at the discretion of local refuge managers and fees tend to be modest, similar to those charged by the Forest Service and BLM. Under the direction of the Secretary of Interior, James Watt, refuges have been told to increase their involvement in various commercial ventures, including grazing.

Many Department of Defense properties, such as proving grounds and similar installations, are grazed by private stockmen. In most instances, grazing permits are offered through competitive bids and sell for $7-$11 per AUM—three to four times the going rate charged by the Forest Service and BLM. Some Indian reservations, administered by the Bureau of Indian Affairs in the Department of Interior, also use competitive bids and receive a fair market value for forage. Other reservations are saddled with disastrous grazing problems. For example, when efforts began to control grazing on the Navajo Reservation in 1937, the reservation had a total of 1.3 million sheep, despite the fact that the carrying capacity was estimated to be only 600,000. In 1980, the reservation had 2,170,300 sheep and observers warned that the land was in danger of "blowing or washing away."

Even the National Park System, which is generally free of grazing by domestic livestock, is not completely immune. For example, when congress enlarged Capitol Reef National Monument in Utah in 1971 and changed its status to Capitol Reef National Park, existing grazing on the incorporated lands was continued, but scheduled to be phased out by 1992. But in 1982, when a couple of ranchers were due to be phased out, Utah congressmen introduced legislation to extend the deadline almost indefinitely. Throughout their existence, national parks have been an irritating temptation to covetous stockmen.

There are other kinds of federal lands and other administrative agencies. Without examining each of these in detail, one can safely conclude that in the West, lands not paved or permanently under water are either grazed or threatened with grazing.

When a general land survey was made in the 1930's, it documented for the first time the extent of livestock damages to public rangelands. The survey found the carrying capacity of publicly owned grazing lands to have been reduced by 50 percent—from 22.5 million AUM's to 10.8 million. Despite this fact, at the time of the survey, grazing pressure on public rangelands amounted to 17.3

million AUM's—6.5 million more than should have been authorized based on the available forage resources.

Today, after the Forest Service has existed for more than 75 years and the BLM and its predecessor, the Grazing Service, for almost 50 years, one might justifiably expect significant improvements in the condition of the nation's rangelands. Yet in a 1975 report to the Senate Committee on Appropriations, the BLM admitted that only 17 percent (27.6 million acres) of its rangeland was in good or excellent condition—50 percent (81.5 million acres) was in fair condition, 28 percent (45.6 million acres) in poor condition, and 5 percent (8.2 million acres) in bad condition. More importantly, only 19 percent (31 million acres) was improving, while 65 percent (105.9 million acres) was static, and 16 percent (25.7 million acres) was getting worse. Furthermore, soil erosion was severe, critical, or moderate on 68 million acres and slight on another 80 million acres. The report concluded that, "Public rangelands will continue to deteriorate; projections indicate that in 25 years productive capacity could decrease by as much as 25 percent. . ." After the report was issued, both the BLM and the U.S. General Accounting Office criticized the data for *understating* the poor and deteriorating state of the public rangeland. And despite such discouraging facts, both the BLM and Forest Service have announced goals of doubling forage production!

In retrospect, it is difficult today to find elements of logic in the federal government's handling of the private livestock industry on public lands. In the beginning, the industry consisted of free-wheeling entrepreneurs operating as squatters. In an effort to gain control of an intolerable situation, the federal government (i.e., the American taxpayers) accepted complete responsibility for the economic costs of past and current grazing abuses and the economic burden of perpetuating the western livestock industry.

How could such a thing have happened? To begin with, every step involved concessions to stockmen. Politicians are elected, and when the industry wasn't electing its own, it was wielding sufficient dollars and influence to accomplish desired ends. Another factor, and a most perplexing one,

"RALPH, HOW MANY CATTLE CAN
YOU FIT ON YOUR HALF
OF THE ISLAND?"

has been a general reluctance to take actions detrimental to the cow! This reluctance goes well beyond economics. Perhaps western literature and nostalgia are to blame. For whatever reasons, the cow has occupied a favored place in western affairs. Men have been hanged for stealing them. Perhaps it's the guilt of knowing what is to be the final disposition of the cow. In any event, the cow has acquired a mystical sacredness that has exerted a profound influence upon public policy in the American West.

Finally, current grazing policies on public lands could not have evolved without a total lack of interest by the eastern half of the nation. By custom, eastern legislators have deferred to the wishes of westerners in deciding issues relating to public lands in the West. With rare exception, the eastern press has ignored events on rangelands, while continuing to spread the ridiculous myth of the pulp-magazine cowboy. Ordinary citizens from eastern states know virtually nothing about livestock on public lands, and in fact, are usually shocked, when they come West to find that there *are* cows on public lands. According to one report, when people on the streets in eastern cities were asked to identify "BLM"—most thought it was a brand of underwear! The cowboy's well-known contempt for eastern city slickers is richly deserved. Nevertheless, had the East known and cared, things would have turned out much differently.

But now it's done—sacred cows are firmly ensconced at the public trough. Many history books state that the open-range cattle industry died in the 1880's. That assertion is a monstrous error of fact, for it is alive and well on the public lands of the West, where many of the old ways flourish unabated or at best diminished only in degree. Overgrazing, livestock trespass, resistance to federal authority, and all the rest survive and prosper. Guess who's paying the bill?

HOME ON THE RANGE

The *Wall Street Journal* (22 January 1982), in describing the routine operations of a large cattle ranch in Nevada, used the following lead: "Bleeding at four points on its body, a big bull calf bucks to its feet and plunges headlong into a nervous wall of cattle at the far end of a corral. What (the rancher's name) had just done to that bull is enough to make any man cringe."

The article goes on to point out that the ranch has about 7,000 deeded acres, grazes cattle on 700,000 acres (a block measuring 30 by 82 miles) of public range, and doesn't need to buy or grow hay because the cattle are able to graze all winter on desert shrubs such as white sage, shadscale, and salt bush. The ranch owner is quoted as saying, "We do things the old style"—in other words, the same way things have been done in Nevada valleys for the past hundred years.

And the results are very much in evidence, for Nevada, which has more than 25 percent of all BLM land in the West, provides an outstanding example of the low state of productivity of public rangelands. The BLM administers 49.1 million acres in that state—69 percent of the total land area—and when properly stocked, these lands have a carrying capacity of 1,836,912 AUM's. Nevada's beef production in 1979 ranked 37th in the nation—on a par with that of Vermont. In other words, an average of 26.7 acres of BLM land in Nevada is required to feed one cow for a month! The national average, which includes all public lands, is about 5 acres (95 percent of all BLM land gets less than 15 inches of rainfall a year). In contrast, an Alabama cattleman can graze one cow for an entire year on 3.5 acres—that's slightly less than 0.3 acre per AUM, 91 times the productivity of BLM land in Nevada. (Note—Alabama pastures are also taxed for support of schools and local government). Exceptionally productive ranges, as in Puerto Rico, can support a cow year-round on only 2 acres.

In sticking to the old ways, the Nevada rancher is not unique. Most western ranchers continue to use traditional practices dating back to the original Spanish cattlemen. Of course some changes have occurred—winter feeding is standard in many areas, more of the public range is fenced into smaller grazing units, and the livestock industry is highly mechanized, with pickup trucks, tractors, helicopters, eighteen-wheel cattle trucks, fancy horse trailers, and fixed-wing aircraft taking on much of the original burden borne by the horse and cowboy. Other innovations involve breeding lines and veterinary practices. But the annual cycle of events, range practices, and operating philosophy of ranchers using the public lands have changed very little.

In parts of the West, where public grazing is limited to a portion of the year, typically April through October, the date of spring turn-out on the public rangelands varies depending upon locality and agency. Ideally, the date of spring turn-out should be sufficiently late in the season to insure melting of the winter snowpack, dry soils (to minimize effects of trampling), and a good head start in the growth of range vegetation. Grazing too early in the season can devastate good range.

Where distance permits, cattle are usually driven from home ranches to allotments on public land, at which time roads and highways, including major interstate routes, are temporarily clogged with milling herds of cattle. For motorists, large cattle drives can be exasperating and frightening—a moving sea of tightly bunched cattle, towering above the average compact car and obliterating everything but patches of sky. Although some cowboys will make an effort to clear a path through the bawling brutes, many delight in standing aside and regaling in the plight of helpless motorists.

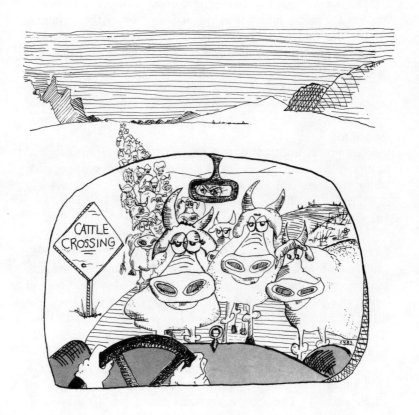

In Baker, Oregon (population about 9,400), herds of several hundred cattle are driven down main street, which is also U.S. Highway 30, forcing pedestrians to flee for cover and bringing traffic to a standstill. Bellowing cattle preempt sidewalks, block entrances to stores, fill the streets, and splatter the route with excrement. Similar scenes are repeated in towns and cities throughout the West.

Because many home ranches are far from public grazing allotments, cattle are trucked to and fro. Large cattle trucks, loaded or not, can be a nuisance as they roar along highways spewing urine and feces to the wind.

In the past, typical allotments for public grazing, especially those on BLM land, involved enormous acreages of unfenced, remote rangeland. On such allotments, herds belonging to several different owners shared the range, intermingled, and wandered great distances from original points of release. Because the cattle were unsupervised, large numbers concentrated in favorable sites and severely overgrazed the forage, while more remote or less favorable sites were lightly grazed or untouched.

On these large units, it was nearly impossible for agency personnel to detect permit violations. Knowing this, ranchers often extended the length of the authorized grazing season or put extra cattle on the allotment with little fear of being caught. Furthermore, stockmen who weren't even entitled to graze an allotment were able to trespass with relative impunity. Although some of these large units continue to exist, agencies have recently built thousands of miles of fences in a concerted effort to create smaller, more manageable units that can be assigned to individual ranchers or small groups. The extent of such fence building is well-illustrated in Oregon's Malheur National Forest, where a 28-mile segment of road crosses 22 fences at 13 single and 9 double-wide cattle guards, which cost $1,500 to $25,000 each, depending upon size and type. In recent years, smaller grazing units have gained added favor as the Forest Service and BLM have adopted various rotational grazing schemes involving periodic rest or deferred grazing allotments.

Management agencies are empowered to impound trespassing livestock and to assess charges against the owners for costs of capturing and caring for the offending animals and may even sell stock unclaimed by the owner in a specified time. But the legal procedures for dealing with cases of trespass are arduous, slow, and bound up in paper work. Consequently, the option of legal prosecution is often circumvented in favor of settlements based on gentlemen's agreement. Although conflict is avoided, violators usually get off scot-free. Ranchers choosing to trespass on public lands are fully aware that the risks and costs are minor compared to the potential gains for undetected violations. Grazing permits may be cancelled after repeated violations, but such drastic action is rare. In fact, because of widespread feelings of open resentment of federal agencies in the rural West, successful violators are often admired in the community—sort of grass-stealing Robin Hoods. Many stockmen who trespass on public lands are among the most successful citizens and may attain high office, as in the case of Robert Burford, Director of the BLM in the Reagan Administration.

In 1977, eighty ranchers in Nevada were cited for 20,500 head of trespassing cattle, sheep, and horses on BLM lands, but were fined only $26,400—considerably less than the cost of grazing the same animals legally for a month. Furthermore, BLM officials in Nevada believe that prosecuted cases are only the tip of the iceberg. Most trespassing goes undetected with as few as two or three BLM employees overseeing as much as 4 million acres of rangeland. Nevada has more cases of trespass than any other state and accounts for about a fourth of all reported cases on BLM rangelands.

John J. Casey, a multimillionaire rancher and hotel owner who is known as the king of trespassers, has made a regular business of trespassing cattle and holds a 20-year record of illegal grazing in Nevada, California, and Montana. In just one area, near Susanville, California, in an 11-year period he was cited for 89 cases of trespassing in 140 incidents on BLM land. And largely to no avail, the federal government has spent more than $1 million prosecuting Casey for numerous trespass violations. When a judge asked him if he felt he had a trespass problem, Casey replied, "I feel I have been and am being picked on." Like Casey, many ranchers are aware of the impotency of the federal government in prosecuting cases of livestock trespass and are perfectly willing to risk the consequences, if any.

At spring turn-out, cattle are put on the allotment and left to fend for themselves—the rancher goes home. In mountainous terrain, the cattle are released at low elevations and follow melting snowlines and the new growth of vegetation up the mountain, often reaching subalpine or alpine meadows and range in late summer or early fall. With the arrival of fall storms at high elevations or with the drying and depletion of forage supplies on desert ranges, cattle often head toward the home ranch of their own volition. In any event, when the authorized grazing period ends, ranchers round up their cattle and drive or haul them to the home ranch. In some areas, other federal lands may be available for winter use. In southeastern Oregon, for example, many ranchers remove cattle from Forest Service or BLM allotments and move them to Malheur National Wildlife Refuge for the winter. Because modern ranches employ few hired hands, except for summer haying, neighboring ranchers often assist each other with the fall roundup and brandings—such events being highlights of the social season, with ample food and drink.

From time to time, especially in the spring before turn-out and in the fall after roundup, new calves are branded. Using hot irons, cowboys burn the appropriate symbol into the living skin, usually on the upper thigh. The healed scar remains for the lifetime of the animal as proof of ownership. In addition to the brand, other symbols of identification are used. These include notches cut in one or both ears and the dewlap wattle, which is formed by cutting a six-inch flap of skin loose on the neck so that the bloody flap dangles free from the top of the incision as a pendant. Similar flaps of skin may be cut on the lower cheek. Some ranches use all of these disfigurements to mark their cattle. In addition, bull calves suffer the additional ordeal of castration at the time of branding and marking. Much of this gore is accomplished with a pocketknife, while the restrained animal bellows and writhes in pain. Sometimes, dehorning is added to the list of misfortunes. The entire procedure, which originated with Spanish cattlemen, has deviated but little in centuries. While this bloody mayhem remains standard throughout western rangelands, organizations devoted to the humane treatment of animals struggle to stop such atrocities as jumping frog contests, porcupine races, and greased pig contests!

Where cattle belonging to different owners intermingle, ranchers continually fuss and complain about the theft of unbranded calves. Such accusations, however, are usually delivered to a third party rather than to a neighbor who is believed to be the thief.

Today, most ranchers using public lands have cow-calf operations, in which the basic resource is a herd of brood cows. The principal income is derived from sale of yearling heifers and steers (feeder cattle) to feedlots for fattening before slaughter. In the past, steers were often kept on the range for several years before being sent to market.

In assessing grazing fees, agencies do not charge for calves less than 6 months old. Because calving time can be set, depending upon when bulls are put with the cows, it is possible to have a fall calving season, however, most calves have traditionally been born in the spring. Spring calves are not charged for grazing. They spend their first summer loafing, following the cow, taking milk, and eating little forage. In contrast, fall calves eat forage the first summer on the range and make rapid weight gains, but of course require extra care the first winter after birth and count in assessments of grazing fees.

For winter feed, hay is cut from wild hay meadows or alfalfa fields, normally located on deeded property, although some agencies, such as certain national wildlife refuges, sell hay on a permit system. Cattle are usually fed on home ranches in feedlots likely to remain accessible and convenient throughout the winter. Most often, the hay is simply thrown on the ground for the cattle to gather. Although large crews

"Haven't these guys heard about soybeans?!"

were formerly required to harvest hay, the task has become highly mechanized, and today a single worker can harvest huge quantities of hay. The principal environmental impacts of winter feeding are conversions of valuable wildlife habitats to hay lands, intensive use of surface and ground waters for irrigation, wildlife losses associated with the use of haying machinery, such as mowers, and water pollution derived from feedlots.

In areas where year-round grazing is permitted on public lands, which includes about 21 percent of all Forest Service and BLM holdings, ranges tend to suffer extreme overgrazing. Because of severe overgrazing, cattle competition with wildlife becomes especially acute when forage is depleted in drought years or during unfavorable seasons. Also, because cattle are on the range when soils are wet, much damage results to the sparse plant life and fragile soils. In some areas, as much as 100 acres (or even more) are required to provide a month's forage for a cow—obviously, such lands should not be grazed at all.

In order to appreciate the cow as an instrument of range destruction, we need to examine its basic features and behavior in greater detail.

Range cattle are out there—24 hours a day, 7 days a week, and for months or even years at a time. A standing cow exerts about 24 pounds per square inch upon the soil, and of course the pressure increases through the remaining feet if one is lifted or if the cow is in motion. Modern range cattle weigh 1,000 pounds or more, compared with the Texas Longhorn's average weight of 650 pounds. To obtain the amount of forage desired, a cow is willing to graze about 8 hours a day. When not actually gathering food, an equivalent amount of time is devoted to ruminating—regurgitating material from the first "stomach" and chewing it—or "chewing the cud," as the saying goes. About 25 pounds of native grass must be eaten to produce a pound of beef. When an 800 pound steer is butchered and the head, feet, hide, guts, etc. removed, the dressed weight is about 500 pounds. However, with removal of fat and trimmings, the finished cuts, which include a considerable weight in bone, weigh only 340 pounds (42.5 percent of the original weight). In 1982, Americans consumed an average of about 77 pounds (retail weight) of beef per person.

Cattle are usually described as being grazers, meaning that they feed primarily on grasses and other herbage near ground level, as contrasted with browsers, such as deer, which feed principally upon shrubs. If given a choice in the matter, cattle prefer to graze, usually taking the tender tops and exhibiting little selectivity. As the forage supply is depleted, grazing becomes more selective, and coarser material, such as grasses and stems, are rejected. But as the available forage continues to diminish, stems are taken and the animals begin to use larger quantities of browse. Finally, when given no choice in the matter, cattle will feed almost exclusively on shrubs and other coarse material and gain weight in the process, as was the case for over-wintering cattle on the ranch described in the *Wall Street Journal* article. So in the final analysis, the cow is a living vacuum cleaner, willing and able to move over the rangeland sucking up every bit of vegetable matter—right down to the bare soil if need be. This plasticity of the diet of cattle has made it possible for ranchers to "mine" overgrazed rangeland, while stubbornly insisting that the range is in good condition. No wonder cattlemen would rather have critics look at the cow instead of the range.

In humid climates, cattle consume about 50 pounds of forage a day, but in arid regions, such as much of the West, daily consumption is probably closer to half this amount (700-800 pounds a month). When slaughtered, a 1,000 pound feedlot steer will have consumed 12,000 pounds of forage and 2,850 pounds of grain and soy concentrates. When cattle can eat their fill every day, 70 percent of the digestible nutrients in the forage is required to maintain normal body functions, and only 30 percent goes to growth and reproduction (net gain). On the average, a range cow drinks between 35 and 70 pounds (5 to 9 gallons) of water a day. Producing a pound of beef, including the water required to grow the forage and the amount drunk by the animal, takes 25 times more water than producing a pound of bread. A hamburger for lunch and an eight-ounce steak for dinner require an investment of 3,910 gallons of water. The daily production of excrement by a cow is 52 pounds of manure and 20 pounds of urine, yet grazing does not significantly enrich range soils because large amounts of plant nutrients stored in cattle carcasses are eventually removed from the land and consumed elsewhere. According to one authority, the contribution of livestock to the nation's water pollution is 10 times that of humans and 3 times that of industry.

The carrying capacity of grazing allotments is set by agencies according to the amount of available forage. This procedure assumes that cattle will make uniform use of an allotment, regardless of terrain, slope, distance from water, and other variables. In practice, such is not the case. Cattle are basically lazy, and when they find ample food, water, and shade, they stay right there until forced to move to another site. Consequently, lush bottomlands and riparian zones (the rich streamside habitat) are severely overgrazed, while forage on steep slopes, uplands, and remote parts of an allotment may go completely unused. Cattle prefer to graze 0-10 percent slopes, and use decreases markedly on slopes of 30 percent or more. Good range management practices dicate that cattle be moved from an allotment when half the current year's production of forage has been consumed in the riparian zone—even if not a blade of grass has been removed from steep slopes and other sites avoided by cows. Because agency permits entitle ranchers to a pre-determined number of AUM's and length of grazing season, this precaution is universally ignored and accounts for a major portion of the grazing abuse on public rangelands. Given current practices, the only solution seems to be the use of riders to force cattle to disperse out from streamside and other points of concentration.

When moving about an allotment, cattle do not use random pathways, but follow well-established trails, which eventually become entrenched deep into the soil and promote erosion. Throughout the West, a conspicuous pattern of cattle trails can be seen on overgrazed hillsides as an intricate network of interlaced terraces—the "sidehill cowger" trails of western folklore. (The sidehill cowger is an animal with shorter legs on the uphill side and, thus, is unable to turn around on a slope. The poor beast is destined to spend its entire life going around the hill in concentric circles.)

On arid rangelands, particularly during the summer, cattle congregate at water holes where they lounge about during the hot part of the day and move out to feed, primarily during cooler periods in the morning and afternoon. Because the immediate vicinity of these water holes is severely trampled, littered with excrement, and devoid of forage, such places are virtually destroyed and are commonly called "sacrifice areas." Forage use decreases with distance from water, and on relatively level terrain, use drops offs sharply beyond a mile from water. The low mobility of modern cattle has intensified overgrazing—in contrast, Texas Longhorns were able to graze a radius of 100 miles from water and thrive.

In an effort to gain more uniform use of the forage on allotments, agencies and ranchers have used the spacing of water holes and salt blocks to entice cattle to graze more widely. Although such tactics work, they have severe environmental impacts. By drawing cattle into areas that were formerly ungrazed, these methods spread overgrazing and introduce cattle into areas where they did not formerly compete with wildlife. Furthermore, the immediate vicinity around salt blocks and water holes eventually become new "sacrifice areas."

The cow is a biological eating machine, and as such, is unbelievably destructive when turned loose to fend for itself on the fragile lands that make up the semiarid ranges of the West. A friend tells a story that best illustrates the fundamental nature of the cow. Her family decided to raise a beef, bought a calf, and put it in a pasture. The calf soon became a family pet, and when it came time to butcher the animal, no one was willing to kill it. Finally, a neighbor agreed to do the deed. To get the animal positioned, it was given a bucket of grain, while the neighbor stood ready with a gun. When he shot the steer between the eyes, blood issued from the wound and trickled into the pail of grain. For what seemed like minutes, the poor beast continued eating blood-soaked grain from the pail, then finally keeled over without ever lifting its head from the food. Even when "legally dead," apparently, a cow's last impulse is to get one more mouthful.

HOOVES, MOUTHS, AND SOIL

A nation with abundant and rich soil resources is blessed, just as those without adequate soil resources are damned—destined to suffer starvation, lack of vigor, and all the deprivations of national poverty. Some nations once blessed with bountiful soils have managed to squander them, and throughout the world where this has happened, overgrazing has been a principal culprit. Among human activities, only agriculture, which *intentionally* destroys native vegetation, tills soil, and exposes it to erosional agents, outranks grazing as a cause of soil loss and damage. Although public lands administered by the Forest Service and BLM are not cultivated, livestock grazing has seriously eroded vast portions of these lands (at least 40 percent of the BLM lands by the agency's own estimate, which is likely to be ultraconservative).

Because of their enormous weight and cloven hooves, cattle are exceedingly destructive to soils. When soils are wet or damp, as in the spring, hooves sink into the soil, oftentimes a foot or more. If enough cattle walk through an area, they mechanically churn the soil, compounding the destructive effects of grazing. On drier soils, just the pressure exerted through the hooves is sufficient to compact the soil. Furthermore, the litter layer, if any, is disrupted and scattered, reducing or destroying its effectiveness as a sponge for water uptake, exposing bare and unstable mineral soils to the elements, freeing the litter to be blown or washed away, and reducing soil fertility.

Churning and compacting set in motion a sequence of harmful events which often lead to the complete loss and destruction of valuable topsoils and much more—such damage being permanent as measured by ordinary human expectations. To begin with, trampling and compaction alter soil texture and reduce aeration by diminishing air spaces between soil particles. On a watershed in North Carolina, after 9 years of heavy grazing by cattle, soil-pore space in the top 2 inches of soil was reduced 44 percent and in the next 2 inches by 60 percent. On western ranges, after 100 years of overgrazing, such impacts could be critical. Once the texture and structure of soil have been altered, the infiltration of precipitation and water from melting snow is diminished, and the soil is unable to retain and hold stored water. For example, on the southern Great Plains, infiltration rates on ungrazed range were nearly four times those of grazed ranges of similar character. Obviously, when water cannot be absorbed by the soil, it runs off and is lost. As the amount of runoff increases, so does erosion. For example, in western Colorado, ungrazed watersheds produced 71 to 76 percent less sediment than did grazed watersheds. Furthermore, as soil is compacted and as water-holding capacity declines, less surface water reaches ground-water supplies and less is available for use by plants.

Organisms, such as bacteria, fungi, algae, protozoa, nematodes, numerous insects and mites, earthworms, and many others, occur by the billions in every cubic yard of soil. About 95 percent of these organisms live in the litter and top 2 inches of soil. These organisms, whose total weight may exceed several tons in an acre of soil, play indispensable roles in soil building, maintaining soil fertility, and performing the myriad complicated processes essential to healthy soils. This enormously complex biological community of soil organisms and the soil medium in which it lives are drastically disrupted by the trampling of cattle.

Besides all these direct damages to soils, there is a similar list of indirect soil damages brought about by the trampling of plant life. On undisturbed land, a cushion of mosses and lichens forms a "living skin" over the soil surface. This layer gives the soil stability, reduces water loss, and contributes to soil fertility, but is highly vulnerable to trampling

"SO THIS IS WHAT THEY MEAN
WHEN THEY TALK ABOUT
GRAZING PRESSURE!"

and disappears rapidly. In desert shrubland having a long history of cattle grazing, the moss-lichen carpet can only be found hidden under the crowns of shrubs, where cattle are unable to trod. When grazing is discontinued, the moss-lichen layer ventures out from these protected refuges and begins to spread over exposed and compacted soils between shrubs, and in a matter of a few years, if conditions aren't too drastically altered, may again form a continuous and healthy protective mat.

Many types of small plants and seedlings are easily destroyed by trampling. Furthermore, compaction of soil, physical disruptions caused by hooves sinking into soil or mud, and alteration of soil structure injure the root systems of larger plants, especially some of the esteemed perennial grasses, which are extremely sensitive to such damage. Once the root system is injured, the above-ground portion of the plant is unable to obtain sufficient nutrients and water to maintain growth and eventually dies or persists in a weakened condition.

Vigorous plant cover is essential to soil protection and development. Plant materials fall to the soil surface and form the litter layer, which is ultimately decomposed and converted into the organic components of soils. This process is vital to soil enrichment and builds water-holding capacity. Furthermore, the root systems of living and dead plants penetrate the soil and form pathways for water to enter the soil. Finally, the above-ground portion of plants shields the soil and protects if from wind and water erosion, while moderating temperature of the soil surface and reducing evaporative water losses. Raindrops landing on bare ground stir the uppermost layer of soil particles into a thick soup that settles to form a seal or waterproof layer on the soil surface. Unable to infiltrate this impermeable layer, 95-98 percent of the falling precipitation may be lost as runoff. It takes 2,000 pounds of short sodgrass, or 3,500 pounds of bunchgrass, or 6,000 pounds of weeds growing on an acre to reduce the force of rainfall upon soil by 95 percent. Runoff and erosion increase markedly when bunchgrass plants are spaced more than 4 inches apart or when annuals, such as cheatgrass, are more than 2 inches apart. On lightly grazed land, water absorption is twice as much and soil erosion only half as much as on heavily grazed land.

Ultimately, the end result of trampling is soil displacement or erosion. Each year in the 48 contiguous states, about 4 billion tons of soil are lost to water erosion and about one billion (850 million tons in the West) to wind erosion. Losses caused by water erosion tend to be highest on certain agricultural lands, where as much as 100 tons per acre may be lost in a year. Grasslands and forests, however, if in good condition, are highly resistant to erosion, and soil losses seldom exceed 0.03 tons per acre. But on rangelands of the arid and semiarid West, where original soils were shallow and scant at best, overgrazing has produced some drastic consequences.

Bill Meiners, formerly with the BLM and later a private resource consultant and well-informed critic of federal rangeland policies, cites an unreleased report prepared by the BLM in the early 1950's as follows: "It is estimated that the average annual runoff from Federal Ranges in the major river basins of the West is 23 million acre feet of water, or only about 5 percent of the total annual flow of the streams in the States west of the Mississippi. On the other hand it is estimated that the Federal Rangelands produce 320,000 (acre) feet of sediments annually—exceeding the combined volume of sediment discharged by the Mississippi and Colorado Rivers. Converted to a weight basis, the annual sediment loss is equivalent to nearly 500 million tons of soil. To transport this volume by rail would require 244,846 trains of 50 cars each, with each car carrying a load of 40 tons. From a watershed standpoint, we find the Federal Rangelands yielding a minor volume of usable water but producing a major portion of the sediment in western river basins."

In the 1870's, the 3.9 million acres of the Rio Puerco Basin in New Mexico supported 240,000 sheep and 9,000 cattle, owned primarily by two ranchers. Also, numerous prosperous agricultural communities had sprung up along rich floodplains bordering the river, and at the turn of the century, the highly productive basin was known as "the bread basket of New Mexico." Then between 1885 and 1962, an estimated 1.1 to 1.5 billion tons of soil washed from the basin. In 1937, the U.S. Soil Conservation Service estimated that the area could support the equivalent of only 4,300 cattle—about half the number that grazed in the area that year. By the late 1950's and early 1960's, the deep, rich alluvial soils were cut by arroyos (deep gullies) and the agricultural communities had vanished. In the 1930's, the average arroyo was 35 feet deep and 121 feet wide, but by 1979, although the depth remained about the same, average width had increased to 300 feet. In a single year (1972-1973), one arroyo increased in width from 38 feet to 50 feet.

In 1975, when the BLM surveyed its grazing lands in the Rio Puerco Basin, the agency reported that forage capacity was inadequate to support the number of livestock authorized to graze the land. The report stated further that 55 percent (270,170 acres) of the BLM lands in the basin were suffering moderate to severe soil erosion, and it predicted that the percentage of such lands would increase to 73 percent under current grazing practices. Several private investigators contended that these BLM estimates understated the actual extent of erosion. Other agencies found annual water erosion in the basin to be removing 2 to 8.7 tons of soil per acre, and noted that the sediment contribution from the Rio Puerco River accounted for half of the sediment load in the Rio Grande. In addition, estimates of annual soil losses from wind erosion were put at 2 to 4 tons per acre, with highly susceptible areas losing as much as 10 tons per acre.

Livestock numbers in the Rio Puerco Basin have generally declined since the turn of the century. But faced with continuing degradation of soils and vegetation, the BLM has cut livestock use further and instituted a program of "range improvements." The BLM's program of range repair will cost the taxpayers $2 million, yet in 1974, Rio Puerco stockmen netted only $9,527—at that rate, it would take 200 years of livestock profits to repay the cost of the rangeland repair bill! Well-informed skeptics say the grazing cuts are insufficient to do the job. While the Rio Puerco Basin has continued to degrade, a few scientists, apparently unable to believe that cattle could be responsible for such widespread devastation, have sought other possible causes for the drastic soil losses. Although changes in climate and other factors have been mentioned, no one has been able to show with any degree of certainty that significant changes in climate have indeed occurred.

In 1977, a violent windstorm struck the southern San Joaquin Valley in California and in a 24-hour period removed 25 million tons of soil from 373 square miles of largely over-grazed rangeland. As much as 23 inches of soil were removed from some areas, and the average loss from the rangeland was 167 tons per acre. Scientists studying the aftermath commented upon the contrast between the massive damage on grazed land as compared to light damage on ungrazed lands, the difference being an intervening fence.

Silver City, New Mexico, is located at 6,000 feet elevation and gets about 16 inches of precipitation a year (mainly torrential rains in July, August, and September). The town straddles San Vincente Creek, which drains a nearby watershed of 28 square miles. When silver was discovered in 1870, the vicinity of the town was extensively mined, and the forest was removed from the watershed. Furthermore, cattle, sheep, goats, mules, burros, horses, and even swine were grazed indiscriminately throughout the area, and as many as 1,500 cattle foraged right to the edge of town.

Before 1895, Silver City's main street was a busy hub of commerce and social activity. Although the street's level was 2 or 3 feet lower than the surrounding ground, no one seemed to mind. Then on 21 July 1895, torrential rains fell in the denuded watershed and the much abused land was overwhelmed. By the next afternoon, main street was 35 feet below its previous level. In August of 1903, another flood cut the "Big Ditch" down to bed rock—55 feet below the original street level—and extended the excavation 15 miles downstream. Afterwards, when wells in Silver City failed to meet the town's needs, the town and Forest Service agreed to stop all timber harvests and grazing and devoted massive

"THEN WHAT?"

efforts and funds to restoring the watershed to a healthy state.

In general, both wind and water erosion tend to be more severe on rangelands in the arid Southwest. Low precipitation, by supporting only sparse vegetation, favors both wind and water erosion. Topographic irregularities and vegetation reduce wind velocities and severity of wind erosion. On the other hand, slope tends to increase water erosion. Eugene Odum, one of the country's most prominent ecologists, believes that landscape ecology in large areas of the United States has been determined by beef cattle. In an absurd effort to justify massive changes in landscape caused by cattle, an article in the *American Cattle Producer* declared that erosion of soil was good because it leveled rough terrain and produced fertile valleys. The author went on to warn stockmen that range managers and scientists, for reasons of their own, were trying to alarm stockmen unnecessarily about erosion and overstocking.

When soil erodes from rangelands, the damage to range productivity can be devastating. But losing soil is only part of the problem—it has to go someplace! Of the 4 billion tons of soil lost to water erosion each year in the United States, about 25 percent ends up in oceans, but about 75 percent goes into streams, rivers, reservoirs, and lakes. The annual damage caused by these sediment deposits is estimated to be $500 million. Sediments are detrimental to fisheries, clog irrigation systems, fill harbors, impoundments, and reservoirs, and bury assets ranging from towns to agricultural lands. Because of excessive sedimentation, 21 percent of the nation's water-supply reservoirs are expected to have a useful life span of less than 50 years, and another 25 percent are expected to last only 50 to 100 years. In 100 years, only 54 percent will provide storage capacity to meet today's requirements—not to mention increases in demand between now and then. Rangelands in the western United States account for about 28 percent of the total sediment load.

Once the impact of grazing has significantly disrupted soils throughout most of a watershed, major changes begin to occur. As water fails to percolate into soils, the water table drops. As water tables drop, streams cease flowing in the dry season and may eventually dry up, except for brief but lively floods during violent storms or at the time of spring runoff. As the vegetation at streamside and elsewhere deteriorates, stream channels are excavated more rapidly during periods of heavy runoff. Arroyos appear and grow. This entire sequence is well-illustrated in the following example: Before the Civil War, the San Pedro and Santa Cruz rivers, and their tributaries in southern Arizona, coursed along through grassy valleys dotted with marshes and pools. Beaver dams were numerous, and large trout were abundant. Today, these rivers flow intermittently, and much of the time the beds are dry, sandy wastelands with sparse vegetation. Vertical banks along the channels drop 5 to 30 feet below the surrounding terrain. During the summer rainy season, flash floods sometimes fill the channels with a raging, muddy torrent. Recent information has pinpointed the 20-year period between 1875 and 1895 as the beginning of this erosional cycle. That period corresponds closely to the time when livestock grazing was building toward a peak in the area. Similar accounts could be given for hundreds of localities throughout the West.

Originally, little more than a third of the earth's surface was semidesert or desert, but by the late 1970's that amount had grown to 43 percent, because more than 3.5 million square miles of man-made desert had been added to the original—that's an area larger than Brazil. Today, most of the earth's deserts are growing at the expense of adjacent agricultural and grazing lands. This spread of deserts has generated worldwide anxiety and spawned the horrible word, *desertification.*

Between 1968 and 1974, the Sahara Desert marched southward into the Sahel, an extensive transcontinental zone that includes portions of six African nations. Television's vivid reports of suffering and hardship in the Sahel were seen by millions. The devastation was appalling—as many as 250,000 human deaths, livestock losses reaching 90 percent in some areas, and disruptions of biological productivity that may last for decades, even centuries.

Contrary to popular notions, desert expansion is not merely sand drifting from one place to another. It's much more insidious. Areas adjacent to deserts are annexed as human misuse and harsh climate destroy the useful productivity of fragile arid lands. Today, about 14 percent of the earth's population lives in desert and semidesert regions. During the next 25 years, according to some scientists, as much as 25 percent of all arable lands may be converted to desert.

What does all this have to do with the subject of this book? In 1977 in Nairobi, Kenya, the United Nations convened a conference of scientists and experts from 100 nations—the subject was desertification. The participants had no problem agreeing that the most important cause of modern expansion of deserts is the grazing of domestic livestock.

Furthermore, the United Nations' conference specifically pointed to the western United States as a prime candidate for future desertification and noted a high to moderate susceptibility to desert encroachment in the area. Unfortunately, they were talking mainly about the public rangelands—by far the largest landholdings in the West.

Today, desertification in the arid West is described as being flagrant, which is an understatement considering that the total acreage of "severe desertification" exceeds that found in Africa—where the Sahel disaster took place. In all, about 225 million acres of land, mainly in the West, is undergoing severe or very severe desertification—an area roughly the size of the 13 original states. In addition, an area of similar size is currently *threatened* with desertification. And as is true elsewhere, overgrazing has been the most potent desertification force, in terms of total acreage affected, within the United States.

Today, desertification is gobbling up public rangelands because these lands continue to be grazed beyond their carrying capacity. The damage already done is appalling—many desert areas being only one-tenth as productive for livestock as they were when white men first came on the scene. Although modern stockmen attempt to blame all range deterioration on the era of the great stampede, indisputable evidence demonstrates that the damage is still going on. Perhaps the most criminal aspect of current desertification is that the federal government, by giving enormous subsidies to western stockmen, encourages them to continue their attempts to extract something of value from sick and degraded rangelands. The federal bureaucracy and greedy stockmen are not going to stop this disgraceful atrocity—sooner or later, the American people must intervene.

The destruction and loss of soil resources and all the attendant ills on public rangelands in the West can be blamed on too many livestock being placed on the range, too early in the season, and for too long. To protect remaining soil resources on public ranges, only one soil conservation measure is required: Reduce the number of grazing cattle to the carrying capacity of the land. The seemingly harmless old cow has rendered millions of acres of western rangeland to a state of virtual worthlessness, and what is most distressing, the damage cannot be repaired in a reasonable length of time—for all practical purposes, the damage is permanent.

When a poverty-stricken herdsman or peasant in some third world nation overgrazes the land and destroys the soil on which his livelihood depends, it is done in the name of necessity. Nevertheless, Americans, being more enlightened, are apt to point to these examples of environmental destruction with a condescending attitude of surprise, pity, even loathing. But we have done and are still doing precisely the same thing, not out of necessity—for no one would starve without the miniscule contribution of beef produced on public ranges—but out of pure greed and ignorance.

If someone were to take a sledgehammer and begin pounding away at the Washington Monument, the offender would quickly be apprehended and dealt with harshly. But billions of dollars worth of soils, vegetation, and other valuable resources on public rangelands have been squandered, abused, wasted, and destroyed—and no one has been held accountable.

VANISHING STREAMS

The fact that water is indispensable to life is taken for granted. But in the arid and semiarid West, the notion goes beyond textbook declarations, for in the West water *is* life and no one is allowed to forget it. Back in the days of the great stampede, when stockmen rushed in to monopolize sources of water, they knew what they were doing. Controlling the water was tantamount to owning the surrounding public land—would-be competitors were just out of luck. But considering that stockmen recognized the importance of water from the beginning, their subsequent disregard for water resources is somewhat appalling. With 83 percent of the 11 western states in forest and range, the cow—that bovine bulldozer—has made a shambles of water resources across the West. The extent of damage defies comprehension, and consequently, today water is a more precious commodity in the West than ever before.

Throughout the vast interior region of the West, only a tiny percentage of the land has surface waters. But the riparian zone, the generally narrow strip of land bordering streams, lakes, and other surface waters, is biologically the most productive and valuable of all lands in the area. Deep and usually rich soils, abundant ground and surface waters, lush and diverse vegetation, often including the only shade trees for miles around, provide food, water, and shelter for a multitude of animal species. Fishermen, hunters, picnickers, and other recreationists are drawn to the interesting and useful surroundings of riparian zones.

Besides being productive, supporting exceptional biological diversity, and being the most critical wildlife

73

habitat on public rangelands, riparian zones perform other natural, indispensable functions. For example, riparian zones, by intervening between surrounding uplands and surface waters, are in a position to act as a filter, preventing pollutants, sediments, and other materials from reaching water supplies. Streamside vegetation provides shade and moderates temperatures. In addition to being rich, riparian zones physically disrupt the monotony of vast dry uplands and provide avenues and cover for animal movements and migrations. Streamside plants, especially their root systems, reinforce stream channels and resist erosional modification of channels. Also, riparian zones store water, thereby regulating streamflow—reducing the severity at flood stage and augmenting flow during dry periods.

Unfortunately, cows favor riparian zones too—and for the same reasons. With plenty of palatable and nutritious forage, shade, and nearby water, cattle gravitate to riparian zones and simply stay there—ignoring drier and less-inviting surroundings. Because riparian zones represent relatively small areas of land and because they are quite fragile, concentrations of cattle quickly take their toll. In Nevada, where streams are scarce to begin with, a BLM report states, "Stream riparian habitat where livestock grazing is occurring has been grazed out of existence or is in a severely deteriorated condition. Within the state, the habitat along 883 miles of streams is either deteriorated or declining." Given the BLM's propensity for underestimating range problems, riparian conditions in Nevada must be grim indeed, for "grazed out of existence" are strong words for an agency that is derisively called the "Bureau of Livestock Management" by many westerners.

Cattle cause several types of damage to riparian zones and associated streams. Unfortunately, many of these damages trigger chain reactions leading to further undesirable effects. Consider the following sequence: As cattle walk at streamside, wade into streams to drink, or cross streams, their hooves cause the disintegration and collapse of banks, exposing them to erosion. As the banks recede, the stream becomes wider and shallower, with more water surface exposed to the sun. In Utah, streams in grazed areas were 173 percent wider than in ungrazed segments of the same stream. As a result, water temperatures in the stream increase. And as water temperatures rise, the oxygen-carrying capacity of the water diminishes. With the water becoming warmer and containing less dissolved oxygen, cold-water fishes, such as trout, are unable to compete effectively and will eventually disappear to be replaced by "rough fish," such as chubs, squawfish, carp, and suckers, which can tolerate higher temperatures and less oxygen. When fishermen complain about what has happened to a favorite trout stream, state game and fish biologists will treat the stream with rotenone and replant it with hatchery trout, which may survive until the rough fish return. The entire episode has cost the taxpayers a bundle (paid from "wildlife" funds)—meanwhile the cows are still stomping around as though nothing has happened. And that's only the beginning!

Sediments derived from disintegrating banks tend to deposit in calm, deeper pools where currents are less forceful. Not only does this deposition of sediments destroy the essential mix of riffles and holes required by trout and other game fish, it also buries spawning gravels, suffocates incubating fish eggs and embryos in nests, and inundates the habitats of aquatic insects and other important fish foods living in gravels or on the stream bottom. Field studies reveal 37 to 59 percent decreases of biological productivity in streams as a result of increases in fine sediments.

At streamside, excessive grazing diminishes the vital filtering action of the riparian zone, allowing excrement and sediments from surrounding areas to wash over the land and into the water. Removal of vegetation exposes moist soils to evaporative losses and to the baking action of the sun. Soil compaction reduces the amount of water entering soils, diminishes the ability of soils to store water, and places additional stress on the vegetative cover. In Montana, soils along an ungrazed portion of stream retained 772 percent more water than did soils in a grazed segment of the stream.

As cattle move about in the riparian zones and loaf in the shade, trampling is especially injurious to important streamside trees and shrubs, such as willow, quaking aspen, red osier, and others. Seedlings and other forms of plant regeneration may be devoured, crushed, or sustain lethal damage to root systems. Larger plants, which are browsed and used for shade by cattle, sustain root injuries or exposure, while above-ground portions of the plants are frequently broken down by cattle scratching on them or crashing through them. As these larger plants begin to die, their roots no longer resist channel erosion and large chunks of bank begin to collapse into the stream. Undercut banks supported by root systems provide vital trout habitat, primarily essential shade and protective shelter. Removal of overhanging trees and shrubs permits more sun penetration and contributes further to the problem of rising water temperatures. Furthermore, streamside plants, by providing food and shelter to insects, are the source for much of the fish food falling into streams. Finally, the loss of streamside shrubs and trees is critical for many nesting birds, beaver, and a long list of other riparian animals—many of which are fully dependent upon the riparian habitat.

An ungrazed segment of Rock Creek (Montana) produced 268 percent more trout (336 percent more by weight) than did a grazed segment of the same stream. In addition, streamside cover was 76.4 percent greater, the channel was deeper and narrower, and there were more deep holes and runs in the ungrazed segment; the grazed segment had a greater percentage of riffles. Similar studies have confirmed and expanded these findings in several western states.

Streamside vegetation in arid and semiarid rangelands is extremely important for shading and providing tolerable water temperatures. For most species of trout, temperatures below 65° F are necessary for adults, and even lower temperatures are required for successful reproduction. Water temperatures in small rangeland streams, where vegetation has been destroyed by grazing, commonly exceed 80°F.

Simply reducing the number of cattle using a riparian zone is not adequate to protect sensitive streambanks. Just one summer's grazing can result in heavy streambank damage. But habitat improvement and increased trout productivity follow rapidly, once cattle are removed or excluded.

At Big Creek, Utah, riparian vegetation, particularly sedges and grasses, made an excellent recovery when a portion of the stream was fenced in 1970. Within 5 years after fencing, biologists found a 570 percent increase in the number of trout compared to the adjacent grazed area. In 1975, however, trespassing cattle (for 6 weeks in May and June) eliminated woody vegetation and reduced grasses and sedges to the level existing prior to fencing. Stabilized streambanks were refractured and again began collapsing into the creek; overhanging banks were caved in. Also vegetative cover and soil-stability ratings declined. After the trespassing cattle were removed, the sedge-grass community and the streambanks resumed recovery, and by 1978, had returned to the status obtained before the trespass occurred.

In eastern Oregon, 77 percent of the fish population within a fenced portion of stream consisted of game fish, but only 24 percent outside the fence.

Before fencing in 1969, there were not enough trout in Otter Creek, Nebraska, to make population estimates meaningful, and only stocked rainbow trout were present. By 1970, both stocked and naturally reproducing trout were found. From 1971 through 1976, all trout were derived from natural reproduction. After only 18 months of protection from livestock grazing, natural reproduction of trout was well-established. Rough fish (dace, suckers, chubs) made up 88 percent of the population before, but only 1 percent after fencing. Similar results have been obtained elsewhere in the West by fencing trout streams.

Grazing is probably the chief factor responsible for the decline of native trout in the West. In Nevada, the Bureau of Indian Affairs resorted to fencing cattle out of a portion of Mahogany Creek, a tributary of Summit Lake, which supports the largest naturally reproducing population of the Lahontan cutthroat trout (once designated "endangered"; now "threatened").

Although the BLM and Forest Service are changing over to grazing programs involving rest and rotation, these systems were designed to alleviate problems resulting from overgrazing of range plants—they offer no relief whatsoever for the problems peculiar to riparian zones. Currently, fencing is the only effective method of protecting riparian zones. Fences are expensive—usually $2,000 to $6,000 a mile—as is fence maintenance. Furthermore, cattlemen object to stream fencing—they don't like to be excluded from the most productive portions of their grazing allotment.

In 1981, the Oregon Legislature acknowledged the importance of riparian zones by passing a law granting tax exemptions and credits to private landowners willing to preserve, enhance, or restore riparian zones. Fencing streams will be one of the principal methods employed. In eastern Oregon (the portion of the state having most of the public rangeland), fencing cattle out of riparian zones produces the following advantages: 1) reduces peak water temperatures in the summer by 3-12°F on small to mid-sized streams; 2) provides more food and cover for salmon and trout, thereby increasing production from 2-7 fold; 3) increases water retention and summer flows on smaller perennial and intermittent streams; 4) reduces streambank erosion and loss of productive bottomlands; 5) reduces stream sedimentation and improves fish habitat; and, 6) provides critical habitat for wildlife (75 percent of the species of wildlife in eastern Oregon are dependent upon the riparian zone). And what's more important, most of these benefits apply to other western states as well. Despite high costs, fencing riparian zones is obviously a bargain.

Cattle are a major source of water pollution in the West and cause serious reductions in water quality in virtually all surface waters.

On rangelands, sediments, manure, urine, and dead cattle are principal sources of stream pollution, often indicated by unusually high bacterial counts in water. The three groups of bacteria indicating pollution by cattle and other large herbivores are the coliform group, fecal coliform bacteria, and fecal streptococci. In Colorado, each of these reached a daily peak of abundance in a high mountain stream in early evening when falling temperatures reduced the evaporation rate and the rising stream washed daily accumulations of excrement from the streambanks into the water. In areas grazed by cattle, coliform bacteria reach a peak during spring runoff, but fecal streptococci are highest during periods of low flow in the summertime. Summer rainstorms increase the counts of all three types, and overland flow from summer rainstorms is the most important agent causing bacterial contamination of streams.

During the heat of summer, when water in small lakes, ponds, and impoundments is warm, its oxygen-carrying capacity drops significantly. When cattle wade into these waters to cool themselves and to drink, they stir up organic bottom sediments and release large volumes of excrement, both of which require substantial amounts of oxygen for decomposition. This added demand in waters already deficient in oxygen frequently triggers kills of fish and other aquatic life as oxygen levels plunge to near zero.

Although cattle are responsible for much pollution of surface waters on rangelands, which represent vast areas of land, the total impact is relatively mild as contrasted with the pollution generated by feedlots.

Private lands of the West have thousands of cattle feedlots. A 1969 survey found 1,391 in Oregon, Idaho, and Washington, with 154 having capacities exceeding 1,000 cattle, and several exceeding 50,000 cattle. Each head of cattle in a feedlot produces about 34 cubic feet of manure a year, thus a feedlot steer is equivalent to 6 people in terms of the amount of oxygen needed for decomposing daily waste. Because a thousand cattle are often kept on a 10-acre feedlot, wastes equivalent to that of a city of 6,000 people accumulate on a very small area. Urine (which contains large amounts of ammonia—a substance toxic to fish), manure (which depresses oxygen levels in surface waters), and pesticides (used for dipping and spraying cattle) account for numerous fish kills each year in public waters. Because of readily available feeds, feedlots tend to be located near irrigated croplands and close to stream courses. During wet weather, feedlots become quagmires of mud and excrement, and polluted water may seep into ground-water supplies. Heavy rains and melting snow wash feedlot pollution into adjacent surface waters.

Because cattle waste is rich in nitrogen, phosphorous, potassium, and other elements, it fertilizes surface waters, makes huge amounts of nutrients available to aquatic algae, and encourages massive algal "blooms," which may turn the water to green soup. When the nutrient supply is depleted, the algae die and decompose, placing heavy demands upon available oxygen supplies and often triggering fish kills.

Astronomical bacterial counts occur in feedlot runoff; for example, coliform counts as high as 130 million in 100 milliliters (about ⅓ cup) of water. What is more disturbing, runoff water from feedlots may contain pathogenic bacteria—types capable of causing disease. In the state of Washington, 61 cases of leptospirosis in humans resulted from swimming in water contaminated by infected cattle. Other diseases, such as salmonellosis, may be transmitted to man from contaminated cattle waste. Also, numerous water-borne diseases of cattle, such as black leg and hoof rot, may be spread to big game species living downstream from contaminated feedlots.

Although cattle are responsible for drastic reductions in water quality, their most severe harm has been to the *quantity* of water. Thousands of watersheds throughout the public rangelands of the West have been destroyed or rendered virtually worthless by the insidious impacts of the grazing cow. In these streams, rains and spring runoff form raging torrents, and afterwards, flow decreases to a mere trickle or ceases altogether as abused watersheds are unable to store water and regulate streamflow. Vast sums of public money have been spent to "channelize" these streams or to riprap their banks in an effort to keep rampaging flood waters from washing away additional riparian lands and valuable bottomlands. To make matters worse, during the growing season, when water is scarce, ranchers divert tremendous amounts of irrigation water from available sources to produce hay and other winter feed for cattle. Because ranchers acquired "water rights" earliest and cattle operations on public lands usually include the headwaters of streams, cattlemen are first to take their "share" of water. As a result all other users downstream are forced to make do with what is left, consequently, throughout the arid West, downstream users, such as cropland irrigators, utilities generating hydropower, biologists concerned with anadromous salmon, cities, and all others, are constantly suffering the effects of water shortages created by the cows and cowboys back in the headwaters and watersheds. What is most perplexing, these various constituencies constantly feud and bicker among themselves over water demands, but never direct their anger to the real culprit responsible for their problems—the rancher.

If it were possible to examine the abundant and high-quality water resources of the West before cattle and to compare them with the pitiful remnants of today, the comparison would be shocking and cause for profound grief. Literally thousands of permanently flowing streams have been converted into intermittent streams that flow only a few weeks or days a year. For all practical purposes, a large percentage of these streams are now nonexistent. Undescribed species of fish were discovered in some western streams that are now dry—what better testimonial to the destructiveness of the cow.

The remedy for healing and restoring a stream destroyed by overgrazing is embarrassingly mundane—a cow-proof fence. Using this simple expedient of excluding cattle, researchers in several western states have created year-round flows in once dry streambeds. Harold H. Winegar, formerly a biologist for the Oregon Department of Fish and Wildlife, has done some of the pioneering studies in this exciting field.

A description of Camp Creek (Oregon) in 1875 pictured the valley floor as meadowland with scattered marshes. Only 28 years later, because of cattle grazing, the valley contained gullies and arroyos 15 to 25 feet deep and 25 to 100 feet wide. The stream carried violent flood waters, but flowed only intermittently at other times, and the lush meadows disappeared and were replaced by sagebrush and rabbitbrush. In the mid-1960's, Winegar fenced about a mile of the eroded and gullied stream bottom. Between 1969 and 1974, an additional 3 miles were fenced. Some grass and clover were seeded inside the fence, and willow and Russian olive seedlings were planted.

By 1976, 45 species of plants were found in the fenced area, where only 17 had occurred before fencing. Water samples taken in February 1972, February 1973, and November 1973 showed a reduction in sediment load of 79, 48, and 69 percent after flowing through 3.5 miles of fenced channel. At one point in the stream, 36 inches of sediments had been deposited. The first beaver was seen in 1971, and 8 dams were present in 1973. Waterfowl were rarely seen before fencing, but since 1969, four to six pairs of nesting ducks have used the area each year. Also, 12 species of mammals have been found within the fenced area.

Thus, the benefits of fencing are essentially a complete reversal of the damages caused by cattle grazing. Willows, riparian shrubs, and other vegetation reestablish and rebuild the biological diversity. Root systems stabilize banks, capture sediments, and begin the process of narrowing and deepening the stream channel. But what is more important, as the surrounding water table rises and water storage is renewed, the stream begins to flow and eventually flows year-round—providing water for dozens of downstream uses. (At Camp Creek, flow began 225 yards inside the upstream fence, and about one-half cubic foot of water per second flowed, cool and clear, through the four miles of fenced stream, but disappeared 30 yards outside the downstream fence!) As cover and shade are restored, summer water temperatures drop as much as 10° F. Lower temperatures, developing pools, overhanging banks, reduced sediments, and abundant insects lead to the reestablishment of a thriving population of trout. Beaver, waterfowl, deer, songbirds, raccoons, and all the other riparian animals return and thrive. The danger of downstream flooding is abated, soils rebuild and stabilize, water quality improves, and in short, the stream system is reborn in full health.

In the West, the cry for water never ceases. Billions of dollars of public funds have been spent in the region for dams, impoundments, and other systems to augment and distribute precious water supplies. In the 11 western states, where 48 percent of all the land is publicly owned, livestock graze about 70 percent of the total land area. Forest Service and BLM lands in the 11 western states (361 million acres) include 2.8 million acres of lakes and reservoirs, 1.03 million miles of fisheries streams, and 2.8 million acres of riparian lands and wetlands. For a hundred years cattle have had free run of the watersheds and riparian zones of the entire region, and still that reckless practice continues, with critical water resources being tremendously misused for the benefit of a tiny minority. Today, fewer than 35,000 cattlemen on public rangelands are contributing the equivalent of slightly less than 2 pounds of beef per person to the nation's beef supply. As Dave Foreman of Earth First! points out, the nation could produce more beef on road rights-of-way in the eastern states than is being produced on all the public rangelands in the West. Only 12 percent of the forage used by livestock in 11 western states comes from public land (only 2 percent in Washington, but 49 percent in Nevada).

Allocating so much of the available water resources to the livestock industry has created hardship for all other dependencies upon water—wildlife, fisheries, sportsmen, electric utilities and their customers, farmers, cities, and dozens more. Although water shortages are truly critical in some parts of the West, in most places, current shortages amount to little more than inconveniences and minor economic disruptions. But if the region continues to grow and fails to strictly husband its precious water supplies, critical shortages will eventually threaten the economic fabric of the entire region. Sooner or later, the West, and in fact the entire nation, must choose between granting cows highest priority in vital watersheds and riparian zones or having abundant and healthy water supplies for all other needs. Current management of water resources throughout the West is a costly and wasteful extravagance and invites certain disaster. It's really not a very difficult choice.

TUMBLEWEEDS, CHEAT, AND SAGE

To appreciate the impacts of livestock grazing upon the pristine vegetation of the West, we must first examine the numbers of domestic livestock involved, determine how the numbers have changed with time, and recognize some factors affecting the severity of grazing on available rangelands.

From the time of earliest settlement, the number of cattle in the 11 western states has grown continuously. The sharpest increase, however, took place since about 1940, when the number of cattle increased nearly 150 percent. Today, the cattle population in the West stands at an all-time high. In 1870, sheep were already twice as numerous as cattle, and their numbers peaked around 1910 and then began to decline. Although the sheep industry enjoyed a moderate resurgence between about 1925 and 1945, the number has since dropped nearly 75 percent. Today, sheep are about as numerous in the West as they were in 1870, but cattle are now more than 8 times as abundant. Although the largest *numbers* of livestock were grazing western rangelands while the sheep industry flourished, the large increase in number of cattle during the past 20 years has brought the total numbers of livestock to a level exceeding that of all the years prior to about 1910. In other words, despite all the fuss about the great stampede and the surge of livestock into the West before the turn of the century, peak numbers of livestock did not even occur until well after that time. Furthermore, once those peak numbers were reached, they were maintained fairly constantly for more than seven decades, right up to the present.

But in an assessment of grazing impacts, numbers tend to be deceiving. For example, there is a big difference between the amount of forage consumed by a cow and a sheep; in fact, *one cow eats as much as five sheep*. Even at their absolute peak of abundance, sheep did not come close to rivaling cattle in terms of total forage demand. Today in the West, the cattle population requires almost 17 times more forage than sheep. In spite of cattlemen's contentions to the contrary, the conclusion is inescapable—the principal cause of deterioration of western rangelands is now and has always been the cow—not sheep.

Besides numbers of livestock, other factors must be taken into account in comparing today's grazing impacts with those at the turn of the century.

Because of the recent growth of the cattle population, forage demand in the West is at an all-time high. That demand, however, is actually much greater than numbers alone would suggest, for the average cow today weighs about 1,000 pounds compared to the 800-pound cow at the turn of the century. As a result, each modern cow requires about 25 percent more forage than its smaller predecessor. Also, because large acreages of rangeland have gone into highways, towns, farms, parks, airports, and other developments, there is less range to support today's livestock. Each year in the contiguous 48 states, about a million acres of land are diverted to such uses. Finally, because of past abuses, modern rangelands are not as productive as they once were. In 1976, for example, it was estimated that 75 percent of western rangelands were producing forage at less than half of their potential.

When America was discovered by Europeans, the vegetation of the new continent was in a condition described by plant ecologists with the word *climax*. Beginning with basic rock or derivative materials, pioneering plant communities establish themselves, start building soils, and eventually prepare an environment suitable for a more advanced community of plants, which will then invade and occupy the site. This process, called succession, continues with succeedingly more advanced communities of plants until it reaches the climax vegetation—a final stage of succession dictated by the prevailing climate and other biological and physical factors. Although the climax vegetation can be removed by disturbances, such as fire, a stage of succession consistent with the aftermath of the disturbance will occupy the disturbed area and again initiate successional changes leading to the reestablishment of climax vegetation.

Before the arrival of Europeans in the United States, the East was dominated by various types of broad-leaved forests, with the species composition of the climax forest (e.g., beech-sugar maple, oak-hickory, etc.) reflecting regional differences in climate. In the Great Plains, where less rainfall favored grasslands, species of dominant grasses formed the climax vegetation of extensive zones distinguished by amount of annual rainfall and other climatic factors.

In the West, the diversity of climax vegetation far surpassed that found in other parts of the nation and reflected a diversified climate strongly influenced by regional differences in elevation and the barrier effects of mountain ranges intercepting marine sources of moisture destined for the arid interior. Although vegetative zones ranged from shrub deserts to arctic-alpine plant communities, most mountain ranges were clothed in types of evergreen forests. But a large portion of the West, especially the extensive interior valleys, lowlands, plains, and plateaus, supported an assortment of climax grasslands or combinations of grassland and shrubland.

Although fires (set by lightning and Indians), landslides, lava flows, and other disturbances may have destroyed some climax vegetation, such incidents were restricted to relatively small areas. While Indians may have been responsible for minor and localized alterations of the pristine vegetation, it is highly significant that they lived on the land for millenia without damaging the soil. Furthermore, in the area now occupied by the 11 western states, an estimated 20 to 30 million large mammals, including bison, pronghorns, bighorn sheep, elk, and deer lived. Most of these animals fed upon climax vegetation, but did so without causing major changes in vegetation type. Then came the cow!

The immediate effects of grazing upon plants are trampling and injuries sustained when a portion of the plant is cropped and eaten. Trampling, described in preceding chapters, is generally more destructive than damages caused by actual grazing or browsing. Furthermore, many of the less desirable range plants, such as shallow-rooted annuals and forbs (an herb other than grass) with taproots, tend to be less susceptible to trampling than are some of the esteemed native perennials, such as bunchgrasses, that have fibrous or bushy root systems.

When a plant is *lightly* grazed or browsed, it may respond by growing at a more rapid rate as missing portions are replaced. Ranchers and some of their better-educated apologists have used this fact as a justification for all grazing in general and as a specific excuse for having cattle on waterfowl refuges, big game refuges, and other sites where cattle really shouldn't be. The contention is that grazing actually makes vegetation more productive. But that word "lightly" is the crux of the matter. In practice, if lightly grazed public ranges can be found at all, they are likely to be in remote places where cattle refuse to go. Overgrazing is still the rule rather than the exception.

The rationale for proper grazing is the fact that plants produce a surplus of leaves and stems that can be safely removed without endangering the future growth and survival of the plant. Even if it were possible to remove all of the above-ground portion of a plant, as is true of annual grasses because they die anyway and regenerate from seed the next year, good stewardship demands that a minimum amount of leaves and stems be left to protect soil and contribute to the litter layer. When excessive grazing removes more than the surplus portion of the plant, the plant begins losing tissue reserves needed for the manufacture and storage of foods for growth, repair, and other vital biological functions. Overgrazing reduces the growth of roots and above-ground portions of forage grasses, and causes some species to produce fewer seed heads. Bunchgrasses may develop dead centers and eventually separate into smaller clumps. If a plant is repeatedly overgrazed, it becomes weak and eventually dies.

The ability of plants to withstand grazing varies according to species of plant, time of year, and other factors. Some plants succumb to even light grazing, while others can be clipped nearly to the soil and survive. Most plants are stressed if 30-50 percent of the above-ground portion is cropped. Crested wheatgrass, an exotic bunchgrass extensively planted on public lands to provide forage for cattle, is well-known for its ability to withstand 60 to 80 percent cropping. In contrast, if 70 percent of the current year's growth of winterfat (an important desert shrub eaten by cattle and sheep) is consumed during the growing season, the plant will die, and if plants are grazed year-round, they may require 10 years of rest to regain original size. In pine forests of the West, removal of only 30 to 40 percent of the annual growth of forage is recommended, but all such generalizations are risky, and grazing pressure should reflect on-site study, local conditions, and sound multiple use principles.

Palatability is an important consideration. All herbivorous animals have favorite food plants, which are sometimes called "ice cream plants," because they are actively sought, taken first, and often eaten to the ground before other plants are used. In riparian zones of the Northwest, cow parsnip is a favorite of cattle, as is lead plant in the northern prairies. On arid rangelands, many of the native bunchgrasses are "ice cream" plants and disappear rapidly when overgrazed.

When a logger walks into a virgin forest with a chainsaw and great trees begin crashing to the ground, the sense of loss and magnitude of the impact upon the ecosystem can be overwhelming to a casual observer. But when that insidious creature, the cow, ambles across the landscape munching here and there on plants, an observer sees little reason for alarm—yet the end results may be the same. As grazing continues in an area, the cumulative effects of trampling and eating plants bring about changes—at first subtle, but eventually drastic—in the plant community. These vegetational

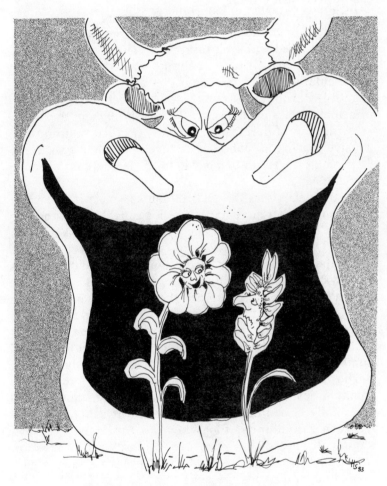

"MY LIFE INSURANCE COMPANY?
WHY DO YOU ASK?"

changes happen in tiny increments that tend to go unnoticed by ordinary observers, but the before and after comparison can be truly astonishing.

Under an improper regime of grazing, plants most susceptible to trampling and those grazed selectively are quickly stressed and soon disappear. These species, called *decreasers*, are first to succumb and their decreased representation in the community is an early sign of overgrazing. Perennial bunchgrasses, which once were the principal species in climax grasslands throughout the West, are examples of decreasers. As early as 1910, burning and abusive grazing in Idaho had reduced perennial grasses by 85 percent, the result being a 40 to 75 percent loss of range carrying capacity.

As the decreasers die and relinquish space in the plant community, other more hardy species capable of contending with the current level of grazing pressure begin taking their places. These plants, the *increasers*, may be less susceptible to trampling because they have a taproot instead of a fibrous root system, they may hug the ground, making it more difficult for cattle to overgraze them, or they may be less tasty, armed with thorns, or otherwise equipped to resist grazing. Increasers are usually native plants that were part of the climax community, but represented by relatively small numbers. Big sagebrush, an increaser originally forming perhaps 20 percent or less of perennial bunchgrass communities, has become the dominant plant and formed essentially closed stands on thousands of square miles of western rangelands. Elsewhere in the West, yarrow, shadscale, mesquite, creosote, and several others are increasers that currently dominate overgrazed ranges once populated with native grasses.

Once the increasers are established and holding a site, if intensive grazing continues, even they may be displaced by a group of even more hardy plants known as the *invaders*. Many of the invaders are not native to the region, but are exotic species introduced from the Old World. Ordinarily, when invaders move in, range conditions have begun to deteriorate seriously—topsoil may have been lost, gullies may be present, water tables may have dropped, and much of the native plant cover may be gone. Among the dozens of invaders, cheatgrass, Russian thistle, several species of mustards, filaree, halogeton, and several kinds of thistle are prime examples. Many invaders are able to hold a site for long periods of time, but others are transitory. If grazing pressure is reduced, invaders like filaree and mustards may be displaced by native plants as normal succession takes over, however, in worse case situations, this process may require decades or even centuries. For example, in Arizona, perennial grasses failed to recover 30 years after grazing ceased. And in California, exotic weeds and grasses that arrived with the Spanish still dominate extensive areas of rangelands and have formed a sort of secondary climax, impervious to normal succession toward native grasses even in the complete absence of grazing.

Under the influence of grazing, the vegetative changes described in the foregoing paragraphs have completely altered millions of acres of climax vegetation in the western states. What is most disheartening, in every instance, the change represents a loss of rangeland resources—even for the cattle that were instrumental in causing the change. Today, native grasses have been virtually eliminated from large portions of the West. Shrubs and exotic forbs and grasses currently dominate vast acreages. On California grasslands, where the Spanish began grazing large numbers of livestock in the early 19th century, much of the change took place before range scientists could properly document the precise composition of the original vegetation. Some examples of these monumental vegetative changes are instructive.

In the Cache Valley of Utah and Idaho, explorers and early settlers found abundant grass and little sagebrush. But excessive livestock grazing has drastically reduced grasses and led to increases in sagebrush. Although sagebrush dominates heavily grazed areas, some tracts that have not been grazed, plowed, irrigated, or frequently burned continue to support much the same vegetation described by early travelers.

In other desert grasslands, pure stands of grass are rare, and most of the arid and semiarid West is currently dominated by shrubs, with remnant native grasses tucked here and there, and more often, the shrubs share the landscape with alien grasses and forbs.

Cheatgrass, an annual native to the Old World, was first detected in 1861 in Pennsylvania. Mainly by following in the aftermath of disturbance or loss of native grasses, cheatgrass spread so rapidly through the West that its presence often escaped notice. By 1900, cheatgrass apparently occupied most of its present range—being most common in the Northwest, but abundant and highly visible throughout much of the West from Alberta south to Texas. In Idaho, where cheatgrass apparently arrived around 1890, it was considered the most important plant on spring ranges by 1932, and by 1949 was the dominant species on more than 4 million acres of rangeland.

Initially, many stockmen applauded the arrival of cheatgrass and considered it to be superior to the native grasses it replaced, however, such euphoria soon proved to be unwarranted. Cheatgrass greens up early in the season, but quickly sets seed and dies, therefore, providing nutritious forage for only a brief portion of the year. Dead cheatgrass has low nutritive value, the awned seeds often lodge in the jaws of cattle and cause chronic injury and irritation, and the plant remnants and roots are too spindly and sparse to provide adequate protection against soil erosion. Furthermore, cheatgrass is highly flammable—almost incendiary—being 500 times more likely to burn than any other grass. Today, where cheatgrass is extensive, five times as many fire crews are required to suppress range fires, and the fire season may be extended by as much as 1 to 3 months. In many instances, cheatgrass carries fires into other vegetation that would not otherwise burn. Although cheatgrass does not normally invade healthy stands of native grasses, a few plants do become established here and there, and will quickly occupy the site in the event of disturbance, such as heavy grazing or fire. Once a solid stand of cheatgrass is present, it can perpetuate itself, at least on many sites, and continue to dominate almost permanently. Many other invaders, such as Russian thistle and mustards, may thrive on a badly abused site for a few years and then be replaced by cheatgrass.

Halogeton, a native plant of Russia, is an especially appropriate irony on western rangelands. It was first recorded near Wells, Nevada, in 1934. Halogeton quickly invades poor, disturbed soils, especially in heavily grazed areas where rainfall is scant and soils highly alkaline. It shuns cultivated lands and competes well with native plants. By 1958, halogeton had spread over 11 million acres, and today it occurs throughout most of the West where conditions are appropriate. The irony is that halogeton, while largely a creation of the western livestock industry, stores large amounts of oxalic acid in its succulent leaves, contains abundant minerals and more crude protein than alfalfa, but is highly poisonous to cattle and sheep, especially in late summer through early winter. As little as 6 ounces of the plant can be fatal to a sheep.

In Idaho, halogeton first arrived in the 1940's, invaded various rangeland habitats, killed hundreds of sheep, and eventually put 11 sheep operators out of business in the Raft River Valley. In 1954, the U.S. Congress passed the *Halogeton glomeratus* Act and appropriated funds to fight the existence and spread of halogeton on western ranges. Because each plant may produce as many as 50,000 seeds, which are spread when the plant breaks off near the ground and blows over the landscape, and because some seeds are able to germinate up to 10 years after being produced, the act proved to be a futile gesture. Most of the money was eventually spent to plant crested wheatgrass on other rangelands so that livestock would not have to use ranges infested with halogeton.

Today, pinyon pine and juniper, often in mixed stands, cover about 75 million acres in the West. In most places, juniper was originally confined to rocky ridges and rimrocks where soils were poor and shallow, but now it has spread and grows in dense stands on deeper soils previously occupied by grasses or mixed shrubs and grasses. For example, in

Texas, junipers covered about 18 million acres in 1949, but invaded more than 3.5 million additional acres by 1965. In Utah, where juniper populations expanded 500 percent between 1864 and 1934, the principal cause of the expansion is believed to have been heavy grazing by livestock. Elsewhere in the western states, overgrazing and fire suppression, both prime fetishes of ranchers, have permitted junipers to expand into other vegetative zones. Livestock disperse juniper seeds, while trampling tends to reduce competing vegetation and favors the establishment of juniper seedlings. Juniper is highly sensitive to fire and is eliminated on sites burned at 15-year intervals. Overgrazing and fire suppression have also favored the spread of pinyon pine. Although cattlemen are disturbed by invasions of juniper and pinyon pine on public lands, wildlife managers and recreationists may applaud the process as providing interesting and useful diversity.

In the West, periodic droughts are a certainty. Nevertheless, agencies and ranchers are eternally optimistic and in stocking rangelands gamble that every year will be a good one. But when drought does strike, even normal stocking rates are likely to lead to severe overgrazing, and the combination of overgrazing and drought can be devastating to range vegetation. In Kansas, the 1934 drought—the worst one on record—killed 74.8 percent of the plants on an overgrazed site, but only 64.6 percent on a moderately grazed site. And in Montana, it took 8 years for conservatively grazed range to return to good condition after the 1934 drought.

In 1934, Idaho rangelands supported millions of acres of exotic annual weeds, which served as breeding habitat for the beet leafhopper. During the drought, when even these weeds were stunted, leafhoppers abandoned the ranges and moved onto croplands. As a result, 90 percent of the sugar beet crop was destroyed in six counties in southern Idaho, two sugar factories had to close, and 500 people lost jobs. When the drought ended, range productivity in Idaho had been reduced to 25 to 32 percent of its original level, and only about 25 percent of the native stands of perennials persisted on important rangelands at lower elevations.

Although cattlemen steadfastly refuse to acknowledge the possibility of drought when stocking ranges, they are quick to seek public assistance when drought strikes. From 1933 to 1939, Idaho stockmen received $321 million in disaster relief. The federal government loaned stockmen funds for feed and even bought excess livestock that ranchers were unable to feed. Afterwards, when the cheatgrass turned green, ranchers said the range had recovered and proceeded to restock at high levels in an effort to recoup losses caused by the drought. Even today, ranchers continue to deny any contribution of overstocking to the severity of the 1934 drought. What happened in Idaho was no exception—the story was much the same throughout the West—and little has changed. As recently as 1977, western cattlemen were again crying "drought," requesting federal aid, and getting it.

An interesting point, often overlooked in assessing the condition of range vegetation, is that the first national range survey was completed in the early 1930's during a period of critical drought. The findings in that survey have been used as a "baseline" for all subsequent comparisons. Thus, range studies done in a non-drought year should *automatically* show some degree of improvement, and if range conditions are found to be static, that may actually represent a decline in condition. Cattlemen have argued that the survey was biased—being done at a time of drought, it showed range degradation that did not represent permanent damage—and when it rained and the exotic annuals turned green, they pointed to the green as proof of range recovery. Critics of the industry, however, point out that subsequent range surveys only look good in comparison with 1934 data and that current conditions are cause for alarm.

Historically, fire played a vital role in nature's scheme. Stockmen have always feared fire and objected to burning anything that might possibly be eaten by a cow. On rangelands, absence of fire often combines with severe overgrazing to favor plants like juniper, pinyon pine, and sagebrush, which may be useful to wildlife, but shunned by cows. Without the revitalizing effects of fire, decadent stands of shrubs crowd out understory forbs and grasses and expose bare soil around and between plants. Once the herbaceous ground cover disappears, old-growth shrubs become virtually fireproof, except in strong winds, when fire becomes an unacceptable risk.

Burning vegetation too frequently or at the wrong season can damage valuable range plants and favor invaders, such as cheatgrass, Russian thistle, and others. If burns are grazed too soon or too heavily, the benefits of burning are often lost. For example, when sagebrush is burned and then grazed heavily, an even denser stand of sagebrush will reinvade the site. Because burned sites are especially vulnerable to soil compaction and erosion, they should be given a couple of years of rest before being grazed. Unfortunately, even the Forest Service does not always practice this precaution. While fire is indispensable on rangelands, grazing is not a substitute for it, and the combination of fire and overgrazing is exceedingly disastrous.

It doesn't take a very astute student of rangelands to recognize that vegetation is the basic resource of the livestock industry. Despite the obvious truth of such a statement, cattlemen have always looked at cows—not the vegetation. How else could Idaho ranchers have welcomed the arrival of cheatgrass and Russian thistle and declared these exotic plants to be valuable additions to the rangeland forage? Range scientists have done extensive studies of range vegetation and developed sophisticated methods for determining and measuring carrying capacity and trends of rangeland vegetation. But science and sophistication are wasted on the typical rancher who looks upon all plants simply as "forage." As a result, range scientists and land managers can complain about the poor condition of the range and plead for better grazing techniques, but suspicious, greedy ranchers stubbornly ignore such talk—and if there is something green growing out there and if the cows are eating it—the rancher is perfectly content to go about business as usual. This attitude has led to shameful devastation throughout much of the West. Pristine communities of climax grasslands have been destroyed and replaced with low-quality stands of shrubs and alien weeds and grasses on millions of acres of public land. Today, there are no public or private grasslands in pristine condition. Although it has often been pointed out that no rancher ever went broke from *undergrazing* the range, but plenty have gone broke from *overgrazing*—there is pitifully little evidence that stockmen actually believe the message or its lesson.

Today, management agencies contend that range abuse has diminished on public lands and point out that less acreage is currently in a declining condition than was true in the 1930's. Steve Gallizioli, a wildlife biologist with the Arizona Game and Fish Department, has likened such "improvements" to those of a burning building—"If the firefighters succeed in reducing the level of the flames from 20 feet to 5 feet, that is an improvement, I guess, but if they cease efforts at that point and decide that they have improved the situation by 75 percent, this is not going to help that burning building very much. It is going to burn down anyway even though it's going to take it a little longer to do so."

RUFFLING FEATHERS

From sea level to above timberline, millions of acres of western rangeland are used primarily for livestock grazing. These lands are, to a very large extent, managed specifically for the maximum benefit of domestic grazing animals. Under these circumstances, if grazing or its associated range practices were to benefit any of the dozens of species of birds inhabiting the rangelands, the benefit would represent serendipity rather than foresight or planning. Unfortunately, on rangelands as elsewhere in life, free benefits resulting from pure accident are rare. And as a consequence, the livestock industry on public lands is a colossal burden to bird life throughout the West.

Like most animals, birds require habitat containing suitable food, water, and cover. Unlike most animals, however, many birds migrate and need a specific habitat on the breeding grounds, another on the wintering grounds, plus patches of suitable habitat at stopping places along the migration route. Although birds are quite mobile, all their vital resources must be closeby—the proper spatial relationship is essential. For example, some small insectivorous birds make as many as 900 trips a day to feed nestlings—obviously, nesting sites must be close to food sources.

The habitat requirements of each species of bird are specific and fairly inflexible. It's not enough to say that a species of bird eats insects, for it may actually eat only certain insects found on the leaves of a particular type of plant. Furthermore, the diets of young and adults may differ, and during the winter, the population may switch to different foods altogether. And cover is not just a bush to hide in—

different birds may need specialized cover for nesting, roosting, feeding, escape, concealment, protection from adverse weather, and so forth. Given the specific nature of bird habitats, it is little wonder that they can be easily damaged by herds of voracious herbivores the size of cows.

In general, the most detrimental types of grazing to birds are systems intended to get maximum use from available vegetation. Year-long grazing and grazing the same land with two types of livestock (e.g., cattle and sheep) that eat different plants are especially destructive. Also, grazing during the nesting season tends to be more harmful than grazing at other times. But in the long run, any grazing or intensity of grazing that destroys food sources, removes understory vegetation, or damages essential cover will have a detrimental effect upon species dependent upon those resources. Given the long reign of the livestock industry and its cumulative impacts upon western ecosystems, the deleterious effects upon bird life have been substantial.

Upland game birds are ground nesters. Several species inhabiting rangelands and grazed forest lands have suffered marked reductions in range and abundance attributable to livestock grazing. Montezuma quail have declined or been extirpated on much of their former range in Texas, largely because of overgrazing. Surviving populations are primarily restricted to national forests and other regulated grazing lands in Arizona and New Mexico. In the case of Montezuma quail, grazing may actually increase major food plants, but destroys perennial grasses required for nesting and cover.

Modification and destruction of semidesert grasslands have eliminated the scaled quail from peripheral portions of its range in Arizona and other localities. Also, overgrazing is viewed as the principal cause of the demise of the masked bobwhite in Arizona and Sonora. In California, A.S. Leopold blames overgrazing for a marked reduction in California quail populations during the past 75 years.

In Arizona, a comparison of survival of young wild turkeys on heavily grazed and ungrazed lands revealed 580 young per 100 hens on ungrazed plots, compared to only 150 young per 100 hens on grazed plots. The difference was attributed to a reduction of nesting and escape cover caused by grazing. After participating in the fall turkey hunt, one Arizona hunter wrote, "Never saw or heard a turkey in 4 days time. Areas all overstocked with cattle. Very little turkey habitat remains."

Other species of upland game birds reported to be adversely affected by livestock grazing include the lesser prairie chicken, the greater prairie chicken, blue grouse, and sharp-tailed grouse. Also, the ruffed grouse, an inhabitant of riparian zones in forested areas of the Northwest, suffers severe habitat degradation in many locations. Livestock conversion of mixed sagebrush-grassland habitat to pure stands of decadent sagebrush is detrimental to sage grouse.

In 1978, Carroll Littlefield, a waterfowl biologist with the U.S. Fish and Wildlife Service and authority on sandhill cranes, noted that 55 scientific investigations of the effects of livestock grazing upon waterfowl revealed decreased production or other detrimental effects. In contrast, only one study reported higher success of nesting ducks on moderately grazed land than on ungrazed land. In California, 42.2 percent of 116 waterfowl nests on idle land hatched, but none of 7 on grazed land hatched. In Iowa, nesting success of waterfowl on idle or lightly grazed land was 24.4 percent, but only 10.5 percent on moderately and heavily grazed land. In a Utah study, the effects of cattle grazing were considered to be as serious as a lack of water. Numerous investigators have emphasized the importance of residual vegetation (plant cover left over from the preceding growing year) as a deterrent against predation of waterfowl nests. Because dense nesting cover is so essential to refuge operations, the Director of the U.S. Fish and Wildlife Service in 1972 stated that, "haying and grazing are incompatible with upland nesting duck and ground nesting bird objectives. . ." Unfortunately, his message has gone unheeded on many refuges.

Among waders and shorebirds, numerous species suffer reduced nesting success in the presence of grazing. At Malheur National Wildlife Refuge in Oregon, the success of nesting greater sandhill cranes was 54.6 percent in mowed-grazed, 63.6 percent in mowed-ungrazed, and 84.2 percent in unmowed-ungrazed habitats. Upland sandpipers in North Dakota enjoyed 71 percent nesting success on ungrazed prairie, but only 48 percent on grazed prairie. In a 12-year study, also in North Dakota, 38 nests of American bitterns were found in tall, dense vegetation, but the species avoided nesting on nearby annually grazed grasslands. In contrast, in Colorado, killdeer nested in heavily grazed sites on bare ground with sparse vegetation, and mountain plovers sought overgrazed areas and often nested alongside piles of cow dung, which may have served as windbreaks or possibly as sources of insect food. Cattle egrets, an Old World species that has invaded the United States, follow grazing cattle and capture insects disturbed by them. Finally, at Grays Lake National Wildlife Refuge in Idaho, where an effort is being made to assist the endangered whooping crane by hatching eggs in nests of proxy sandhill cranes, two chicks were allegedly trampled or "sat" upon by cattle!

Among raptors, northern harriers and short-eared owls prefer ungrazed habitat for nesting. Meadow voles and other mice are numerous in the cover of ungrazed meadows and are a major food item of the rough-legged hawk and northern harrier, both of which spend a greater percentage of their feeding time hunting over ungrazed terrain. Northern harriers are also believed to have suffered from the overgrazing of riparian zones. Although some reports have stated that jackrabbits and certain rodents are more numerous on overgrazed lands, and therefore, may provide an increased food supply for golden eagles and other raptors, other investigators believe such increases to be temporary and contend that prolonged grazing abuses eventually reduce the numbers of jackrabbits and rodents too.

In addition to the direct effects of grazing, the livestock industry has had a number of indirect impacts upon raptors. Predator control intended to protect sheep from coyotes has resulted in the poisoning of golden eagles by compound 1080 (sodium monofluoroacetate). In a widely publicized case, about 50 golden eagles were killed in Wyoming—illegally killed pronghorns were laced with poison, and the pilot of a small plane was hired to shoot eagles on the wing. In this instance, the eagles were slaughtered in an area not even used by domestic livestock! Also, where poison grain has been used to reduce populations of prairie dogs and other rodents competing with livestock for forage, burrowing owls, which use abandoned burrows as nesting sites, have declined. In many instances, the mass killing of rangeland rodents has created food shortages for raptors and exposed them to possible secondary poisoning from eating poisoned rodents. Grasshopper control on rangelands has also caused severe losses of songbirds and others, such as American kestrels.

Numerous scientific studies have revealed adverse effects of grazing upon songbirds and other nongame species. On Kofa National Wildlife Refuge in Arizona, Crissal thrashers and brown towhees were less abundant in grazed than in ungrazed desert shrubland. In Oklahoma, there were 50 percent fewer Bell's vireos and dickcissels on grazed land. In a 10-year study in Ohio, breeding birds were four times more abundant in ungrazed woodlands than in an adjacent grazed woodland, and the ungrazed site supported more than twice as many species of plants. Also, a larger percentage of the species of birds in the grazed woods were hole-nesters. Although before and after studies are lacking, it is apparent that the wholesale destruction of riparian zones on public rangelands has had a major impact upon songbird populations. As with fishes, fencing these areas has the effect of restoring bird populations to a healthy state.

Various studies show reduced diversity and diminished density of songbirds with increasing severity of grazing. Certain types of ground nesters and species that feed primarily in understory vegetation are particularly susceptible to effects of grazing. Other species, such as horned larks (called the beach lark in Europe) and nighthawks, normally select bare ground for nesting—these may increase on overgrazed sites. One investigator noticed that captive horned larks were especially fond of tearing apart dried cow chips and examining them for food items. Cowbirds, a parasitic species that lays its eggs in the nests of other birds, feed on insects around grazing cattle and seem to be unusually successful and numerous in overgrazed habitats. When rangelands deteriorate and songbird populations are sharply reduced, the remnant vegetation is left exposed to increased damage by insects.

Although relatively little hay is cut on public lands, national wildlife refuge managers permitted 589 private stockmen to cut hay on about 41,300 acres in 1974-75. Limited mowing can be a good management practice, for example, when swales and low spots are mowed to discourage early nesting waterfowl from nesting in places that will flood later in the spring. Also, some species, such as sandhill cranes, Canada geese, and some ducks, may feed and loaf in mowed areas, but select unmowed sites for nesting. At Malheur National Wildlife Refuge, flooding native hay meadows to increase hay yields for permittees frequently results in waterfowl nesting areas being flooded and nests destroyed. Also, because the refuge has been heavily grazed, the banks of ditches and canals often collapse and fill the channels with silt, causing high water to overflow the banks and inundate surrounding nesting areas.

The most serious impact of haying, however, is the large numbers of birds and other animals killed by mowing machines and other equipment, especially when hay is cut too early in the season. In 1976 in southeastern Oregon, two ranchers estimated that they had killed between 400 and 600 birds during two weeks of mowing (July 1 to 15). Most victims were shorebirds, but numerous waterfowl nests, ducklings, and sandhill crane chicks were reported destroyed. One operator stated that he killed two young pronghorns with a mower in 1975. Many birds tend to crouch and hide when the mower approaches, thus making themselves easy victims to the approaching sickle bar. On refuges where haying is permitted, the cutting of hay should be delayed until young birds have fledged and moved out of areas to be mowed.

At Malheur Refuge for many years, much of the hay was raked into windrows and left on the ground until fall when cattle were put on the land for the winter. This practice encourages the growth of fungi in the wet hay and favors as-

"A BALE OF HAY FOR YOU,
SHREDDED TWEET FOR ME."

pergillosis, a fungal disease fatal to waterfowl. Finally, it should be pointed out that prolonged haying and removal of hay from refuge lands creates a critical drain upon essential plant nutrients and can only lead to a declining productivity of the lands for wildlife uses.

Numerous so-called "range improvements" have become standard practices on public rangelands in an effort to increase cattle production, especially on lands that have been severely overgrazed and are currently producing little forage. Although many of these practices are supposedly done in the name of multiple use, such claims are thinly concealed efforts to justify benefits to livestock, and if it were possible to view such amateurish deceit with emotional detachment, the claims would be cause for much mirth.

An especially destructive range improvement, one that has occurred on thousands of square miles of BLM land, is the killing of sagebrush, usually by spraying with an herbicide, such as 2, 4-D. Usually, sprayed areas are later re-seeded with a monoculture of exotic grass, such as crested wheatgrass. These seedings are intensively grazed. Among birds, only horned larks use such seedings consistently, and they prefer bare ground anyway. Burrowing owls and meadowlarks may use seedings during the nesting season. Sage sparrows, Brewer's sparrows, and sage thrashers prefer sagebrush, and in Wyoming, Brewer's sparrows declined 67 percent the first year and 99 percent by the second year after sagebrush was sprayed. No nesting occurred on the sprayed plot. In Montana, Brewer's sparrows declined 54 percent one year after spraying and 5 years later had barely begun to return; other species of birds had not returned to the area. Both species diversity and relative densities of nesting and non-nesting birds are significantly lower on crested wheatgrass seedings than in overgrazed sagebrush. Sage grouse, which feed almost exclusively on sagebrush leaves in the winter, are severely damaged by sage removal.

Other commonly practiced types of brush control on public lands include the killing of pinyon pine, mesquite, and various species of juniper with herbicides, fire, or mechanical methods, such as bulldozing or chaining (i.e., dragging a large anchor chain across the land between two large tractors). In Texas, where the golden-cheeked warbler depends upon *mature* Ashe juniper for nesting, removal of junipers as a range-improvement measure caused such a serious reduction in numbers of the warbler that it was declared a threatened species by the U.S. Fish and Wildlife Service. Although brush control is generally harmful to a number of species of birds, it can actually be beneficial if strips, rather than huge blocks of land, are cleared. In general, if clearing must be done, burning is cheaper and produces more benefits to the vegetation and to wildlife.

Grazing systems involving deferred-rotation or rest-rotation are currently a fad with the Forest Service and BLM and require the construction of thousands of miles of additional fences. Although grazing critics are supposed to be placated by these systems, because certain pastures may be in non-use at a given time, there is little solace in knowing that other pastures are therefore bearing the full brunt of grazing pressures in the interim. Such schemes are not likely to benefit bird habitat. Barbed-wire fences, while treacherous to big game animals, are not normally dangerous to birds, except on some waterfowl refuges. An unfortunate exception was a juvenile whooping crane killed in Colorado in a collision with a fence.

Range managers and stockmen are particularly apt to emphasize the potential benefits to wildlife of newly constructed stock-watering sites. However, it must be pointed out that many small birds living in remote arid sites do not have to drink daily, but get sufficient water from foods, dew, and occasional rainfall. But when a new source of water is created in dry areas, cattle move in, quickly create a bare, denuded sacrifice area around the water, and then proceed to overgraze the surrounding habitat. Certainly these events do not benefit birds, and such species as sage grouse often decline drastically with the arrival of intensive grazing in previously undisturbed habitat. Also, many water developments include watering troughs, which become death traps for the drowning of small mammals and birds, unless escape ramps are built into them (and they rarely are).

Additional adverse effects of range improvements on big game and the purses of taxpayers will be discussed in later chapters.

Although many people, especially those from eastern states, are surprised to discover the extent of livestock grazing on public lands in the West, a reaction closer to shock occurs when they learn about grazing on national wildlife refuges. In 1974-75, private ranchers held permits to graze about 1.3 million acres (4 percent of the total) of refuge land. While grazing occurred on 103 refuges in 36 states, almost 70 percent of the grazed refuge lands were in 3 states: Montana (8 refuges), Nevada (5 refuges), and Oregon (4 refuges). Malheur National Wildlife Refuge, primarily a waterfowl refuge, accounted for nearly 28 percent of the total AUM's allotted by the entire national wildlife refuge system. A detailed examination of the effects of cattle grazing at Malheur Refuge provides an outstanding example of the adverse impacts of grazing in general and on bird life in particular.

Malheur Refuge is in southeastern Oregon's Harney Basin, which is the northernmost extension of the Great Basin. Historically, the Harney Basin, with remnants of a large pluvial lake and extensive marshes, meadows, and other aquatic environments, was a major stopping place for countless flocks of migratory birds. In addition, it supported enormous populations of nesting waterfowl, wading birds, shorebirds, and bird life of most every description. Some 287 species of birds have been recorded at Malheur, and the teeming bird life of the area attracted wide attention, even before the turn of the century.

Eventually, an increasing number of local settlers began to harvest birds for food and other uses. Then plume hunters, seeking the frills of a demanding millinery industry, came to harvest Malheur's wealth of bird resources. The results were devastating—especially to colonies of nesting birds at Malheur Lake, which is the largest freshwater marsh in the nation. Soon, great egrets were exterminated, and other species were diminished or threatened. In 1908, responding to outrage by the press and public, President Theodore Roosevelt created the Lake Malheur Reservation. Additional lands were added in 1935 and 1940 to bring Malheur Refuge to its present size of about 181,000 acres.

In 1948, waterfowl production at Malheur Refuge was 150,950 young ducklings (97 percent of the total) and goslings (3 percent). Then production began to decline, and between 1963 and 1972, total production averaged only 29,600 birds a year. In 1973, an exceptionally dry year, total waterfowl production on the refuge dropped to the dismally low number of only 13,300, then increased to 21,300 in 1974. In 1975, when 18,052 young waterfowl were produced on Malheur's 181,000 acres, 60,000 acres of privately owned lands adjacent to the refuge produced 12,800 waterfowl—proportionately far more.

Mallard production at Malheur dropped from 50,000 in 1944 to 8,000 in 1951, then to 2,000 in 1973, 2,120 in 1974, and 2,898 in 1975. Originally the most numerous duck on the refuge, mallards dropped to fourth place, far behind cinnamon teal and gadwalls—species that nest late enough in the spring to conceal nests in newly grown vegetation and are, therefore, less dependent upon residual cover.

Malheur Refuge had a breeding population of about 235 pairs of sandhill cranes. They reared an estimated 68 young to flight stage in 1970. But the number of young reared to flight stage dropped sharply to 2 in 1973, 2 in 1974, and 17 in 1975. Of 436 crane nests studied between 1966 and 1974, a total of 235 (51.5 percent) was destroyed by predators, chiefly ravens and raccoons. Cranes do not breed until 4 years old. With such low recruitment rates, the breeding population at Malheur was destined to decline, and by 1982, was down to 214 pairs.

What had happened at Malheur Refuge to bring about such cataclysmic reductions in bird populations? The answer is cows! Before 1940, annual cattle grazing on the refuge amounted to fewer than 40,000 AUM's. When mallard production peaked in 1944, the number of AUM's had grown to

"...MAYBE THERE'LL BE A PLACE
TO LAND ON THE FREEWAY !!!"

49,000. By 1951, AUM's were up to 100,000, and they continued a general increase, reaching an all-time high of 125,000 AUM's in 1972. From the mid-1960's to the mid-1970's the average was 117,167 AUM's. By the 1971-72 grazing season, the refuge was carrying 65 grazing permittees, which represented slightly more than 30 percent of the cattlemen in Harney County. (Note: Harney County has almost 6.5 million acres and is larger than eight of the individual states.)

Early nesters—mallards, Canada geese, and sandhill cranes—select a nest site long before vegetation begins a new year's growth, consequently, these species depend upon residual nesting cover from the preceding year. Malheur's grazing, which occurs through late fall, winter, and early spring, was leaving little residual cover—and not much of any type of vegetation for that matter. With nests poorly concealed or exposed in plain view, predators had a heyday. With 40,000 AUM's in 1940, duck-nesting success was 65 percent, but by 1964, with AUM's up to 111,600, duck-nesting success had fallen to only 24.7 percent. Thus in the early 1970's, instead of lush expanses of residual cover, early nesting species found scant cover and bare ground.

In the mid-1970's, Malheur Refuge had 450 miles of barbed-wire fences, and just the interior fences would have formed a single strand of barbed wire extending from Portland, Oregon, to Los Angeles, California. Many flying birds died each year from colliding with fences concealed by rank growth of cattails and bulrushes (which the cows didn't eat). Numerous temporary fences were erected to protect waterways from cattle, and these often bisected nesting territories of large birds, such as cranes, and forced them to fly back and forth across the fence. The refuge maintenance crew did little besides chase cows, mend fences, irrigate hay fields to be mowed, and dig the silt and eroded mud out of irrigation canals.

Through all of this the refuge manager talked about geese using the browse of grazed meadows, continued to speak of grazing as a "vegetational management tool," and fretted about his "moral commitment to the ranchers."

There was even an attempt to justify grazing as a means of opening up "dense" stands of vegetation so that ducks could take their ducklings to water. According to official policy of the U.S. Fish and Wildlife Service, grazing is to be permitted on refuges only if the practice enhances or does not conflict with wildlife management objectives. But the situation at Malheur was best described by Earl Sandvig, a retired Forest Service range specialist and a frequent critic of range abuses on public lands, when he wrote, "Malheur is no longer a waterfowl refuge, it is a badly over-used cow pasture."

In the spring of 1976, refuge visitors, many of whom had driven hundreds of miles to reach the refuge, were greeted with scenes of total devastation—cow manure as far as the eye could see, emergent vegetation trampled and reduced to filthy mats, dead cattle and cattle skeletons littering refuge waterways and canals, cattle wading and urinating in streams soon to be opened to public fishing, trenches worn several feet deep into ditch banks and levees, willow thickets broken and scattered, and vegetation eaten to bare ground. All this for the benefit of about 60 ranchers, many of whom owned airplanes and drove Cadillacs. In contrast, refuge visitors numbered about 25,000 per year—most of them bird-watchers.

In 1976, a massive letter-writing campaign took place and resulted in substantial reductions of grazing at Malheur. By 1980, grazing had been cut to 42,056 AUM's, although 4,090 tons of hay (one ton of hay equals about 2.65 AUM's) were being cut and hauled off the refuge. Total waterfowl production had climbed to 51,600, including 7,580 mallards, and sandhill crane production was up to 34. In the early 1980's, production had fallen again, presumably because of improper irrigation and a build-up of certain predator populations. In any event, the refuge is no longer just a cow pasture.

At Malheur Refuge, bureaucrats, charged with protecting and managing public lands and resources, yielded to local political pressure and livestock interests. The land and resources suffered. Stockmen and their associations have a history of exerting pressure on federal employees, and it takes strong resolve and courage to resist these pressures and serve the wider public trust.

Birds are a part of that public trust. Birds perform essential societal roles, such as insect control, but there is really much more to it. Millions of us find everyday pleasures and delights in the songs and antics of birds— whether we admit it or not, just having them around is an elixir. All of us are grateful each spring when the first robin shows up in our yard. In a way, birds are unwitting companions in a great experiment in survival taking place on planet Earth. When the miner's canary ceases singing, falters, and falls from its perch, it signals danger. Birds on western rangelands are sending us a similar message—an aroused and indignant public must respond.

BUFFALO TO BEEF

Originally, the 11 western states were inhabited by an estimated 20 to 30 million big game animals. These species evolved *with* western grasslands and other range habitats, and the vegetation and large herbivores were mutually adapted and coexisted in natural harmony. This is not to say that huge herds of bison never overgrazed the rangeland—they surely did. If an area was abused, however, it was temporary, the herd moved to other forage supplies, and until the area was restored to an attractive level of productivity, there was no incentive for the herd to return. Furthermore, these large herbivores, unlike domestic livestock, were basically at the mercy of natural mechanisms of population control—they were not winter fed, inoculated against disease, protected against natural predators, nor multiplied to excessive numbers because a market trend promised high profits. In other words, before white settlers moved into the western states, wild ungulates (hooved herbivores) grazed compatibly with the carrying capacity of natural ecosystems.

Today, cattle alone exert more grazing pressure on western rangelands than did all the pristine populations of native ungulates. Currently, the total grazing pressure from all domestic livestock and remnant populations of big game animals on western rangelands is probably half again as much as it was when Europeans first discovered America. The story of the effects of livestock upon pristine populations of wild ungulates in the West is one of the most sordid and disgraceful episodes in American history.

Numerous authorities have estimated pristine numbers of wild ungulates in the United States. Although such estimates are obviously "guesses," there is sufficient factual information to insure that the estimates are reasonable. The most recent (1978) and probably most accurate of these estimates are those of Frederic H. Wagner (College of Natural Resources, Utah State University, Logan) for the 11 western states. We have used Dr. Wagner's estimates in the following discussions.

Originally, between 5 and 10 million bison roamed the plains of Montana, Wyoming, Colorado, and the intermountain valleys and mountains of the West. Today, the 11 western states (excluding Montana) support 495 bison—less than one ten-thousandth of the original number. Of course bison were intentionally slaughtered in wholesale numbers to keep them off railroad tracks, to starve Indians onto reservations where they would have to grow their own food, and for hides and meat. Nevertheless, these causes of decline in numbers of bison become somewhat academic because the total forage demand of pristine bison populations (plus a great deal more) is currently allocated to cattle. While it would be pure folly to advocate restoration of anything like original numbers of bison, it is still difficult to accept the notion that such a magnificent natural resource has been destroyed only to make room for Herefords and profit-seeking cattlemen. Surely the principle of multiple use entitles modern Americans to at least see an occasional bison on public lands. There is a dangerous precedent and a shocking lack of logic in sacrificing a species of native wildlife for nothing more than a few hamburgers.

Original pronghorn populations in the 11 western states numbered between 10 and 15 million compared with about 271,000 today, which is about 2 or 3 percent of the original number. Bighorn sheep have dropped from an estimated 1 to 2 million to 20,400 (perhaps 1 percent of the original number). Original populations of mule deer and blacktail deer are estimated at about 5 million (which may be high) as compared to about 3.6 million today. Finally, pristine populations of elk, which probably numbered about 2 million, have dwindled to about 455,000, a decline of about 75 percent.

In considering these numbers, it is only natural to think of overshooting, habitat diversion to farms and cities, and other blatantly deleterious factors. If, however, an animal species has plenty of high-quality habitat, it can tolerate a great deal of adversity and continue to maintain large, vigorous populations. Out of 622 million acres in the 11 western states, 48 percent is public land, administered predominantly by the BLM and Forest Service. Obviously, this land could sustain magnificent populations of wild ungulates, if we wished, but no such policy is being pursued.

For example, in 1976 the Forest Service managed 188 million acres in the 50 states, but employed only 158 professional biologists (staff spending at least 50 percent of their time on fish and wildlife)—that's one biologist for each 1.9 million acres. The Forest Service allocated $11 million to its fish and wildlife budget—1.6 percent of the total budget. The BLM in the same year managed 470 million acres (including lands in Alaska) and employed 140 biologists—one biologist for each 3.36 million acres of land (an area larger than Connecticut). The BLM's fish and wildlife budget of $5 million was 1 percent of their total budget. In 1979, when the Forest Service and BLM budgeted $25.1 million for fish and wildlife in the 11 western states, the two agencies, after collecting grazing fees, reported a net loss of $27.8 million from grazing programs in these same states, and that loss did not include cost of personnel, administration, and other related costs, such as fire suppression. The BLM spends about 10 times as much on grazing programs designed to benefit livestock as on wildlife, and this does not include special funds, such as those from the Rangeland Improvement Act. In other words, livestock interests are faring very nicely on public lands, but management agencies are not making even a halfhearted effort to build up populations of wild ungulates (or any other wildlife for that matter).

Cattle are primarily grazers, preferring grasses, but taking forbs or even shrubs when conditions dictate. In diet, cattle are direct competitors of bison and bighorn sheep, although desert bighorns tend to take larger amounts of browse. In preferring forbs and shrubs, but eating some grasses, pronghorns have a diet very similar to that of domestic sheep. Mule deer feed on a wide range of foods—shrubs and forbs are staples—but more grasses are taken in the spring, and the winter diet consists largely of browse. Domestic goats have similar food habits. Elk resemble horses in diet and prefer grasses, woody vegetation, and forbs, in that order. Although it is customary to speak of grazers eating grasses and forbs and browsers eating woody species of plants, these preferences are practiced only when a choice is available. On poor range, cattle compete severely with all other large ungulates. For example, in Idaho, bighorn sheep suffered disease, parasitism, reproductive failures, and low densities, all attributed to effects of malnutrition caused by cattle overgrazing the bighorn's winter range.

Most wildlife biologists believe that wild ungulates are more selective and finicky in their feeding than livestock. As a consequence, these species may be adversely affected by subtle changes in vegetative composition. Domestic livestock, on the other hand, have been selectively bred to exist in nearly all parts of the world, feed on a wide selection of plants, and survive on whatever is available. This fact alone gives livestock a decided advantage on public rangelands in their currently abused condition.

As the most palatable plant species disappear from depleted ranges, competition for food becomes critical between big game and cattle. At least two species, bighorn sheep and elk, are so incompatible with livestock that they will often abandon an area when cattle appear. In Utah, desert bighorns disappeared from Red Canyon in the southern part of the state in 1887 when cattle arrived. Cattle were removed in 1974, and within 6 months, bighorns returned. In another Utah study, 30 cattle were introduced into an area inhabited by bighorns. Although the cattle were removed in a month, no bighorns were seen in the area for 8 months. In eastern Oregon, bighorns originally occurred throughout and at all elevations. Today, they are largely confined to steep rocky rims and rugged scarps—about the only places inaccessible to cows. In Nevada, twice as many desert bighorns were found on ungrazed areas, and most western populations of bighorn sheep inhabit sites with little or no livestock grazing. Diseases introduced by livestock and destruction of the native perennial grasslands have been prime causes of the decline of western bighorn populations.

In Montana, elk vacated lands occupied by large numbers of cattle, and similar elk behavior has been observed in Oregon, Utah, and Arizona. In Arizona, elk moved into an area fenced against cattle and continued using the site for 5 years, but left when cattle were readmitted. Steve Gallizioli, in a popular article on how to be a successful elk hunter, contends that finding a hunting area devoid of cows may be the most important key to a successful elk hunt. He emphasizes that cattle should not have been on the grounds for at least 5 or 6 months.

As the West was settled, elk vanished from most of their historic range, and by 1900 only remnant herds occurred in scattered places in the Rocky Mountains and Pacific Northwest. Besides the adverse effects of competing with too many cattle on summer ranges, elk have suffered severely from having much of their winter range taken up by settlements and private ranch lands. For example, in Utah a State Board of Elk Control was established in the early 1900's to deal with nuisance elk. At one point, control efforts, overshooting, and competition with livestock nearly extirpated the Utah elk herds, and the state had to be restocked with elk from Yellowstone National Park. Today, Utah has only 13,000 elk, but about 2 million livestock on its 80,000 square miles of land, and that's the way the cattlemen want it. What is most astonishing about such disparate numbers is that Utah sportsmen are willing to accept them!

The livestock industry has been instrumental in keeping elk herds low throughout the West, and in recent years, the Forest Service has often participated in such efforts. For example, in 1980 a group of ranchers in northeastern Oregon asked the Oregon Fish and Wildlife Commission to authorize a sharp reduction in the area's elk herd. The ranchers complained that elk were getting into alfalfa fields, munching haystacks, and competing with cattle for forage on leased *public* lands managed by the Forest Service. The Forest Service supported the ranchers, and warned that if the elk herd was not reduced, then cattle grazing would have to be curtailed. That's multiple use? In this instance, the ranchers should have been given a choice: Either they could feed the elk on their private lands and be reimbursed at the same rate per AUM they pay for public grazing for their cattle (Note: in AUM's, 3.1 elk equal one cow), or because the area was overstocked with cattle anyway, accept a reduction of cattle grazing so that the elk range would recover and diminish the necessity for elk to feed on private lands. An Oregon Fish and Wildlife Commissioner flew over the area and observed, "Unofficially, I'm sympathetic. . .but I've got a half million hunters out there."

To protect private lands, many western states feed elk herds in the winter, construct exclusion fences, and pay reparations to ranchers when these measures fail.

Early settlers in the West found mule deer scarce. The lush grasslands in the area were not prime deer habitat—deer prefer shrubs, not grasses. Today, grazing has increased shrubs at the expense of grasses, and some authorities credit livestock grazing with being a cause of marked local increases in deer populations in the first half of this century. But fire and logging may have been more important. Gallizioli states that if overgrazing ever benefited deer, the benefits were short-lived, and contends that in Arizona, ranges are in such bad condition that cattle and deer are in severe competition. Although no data exists to show benefits to deer from livestock overgrazing, at least two studies have shown deer use of lands to have an inverse relationship to cattle use.

Although mule deer may use young tender cheatgrass, they are unable to overwinter on it. Vast areas of foothill habitat throughout the West, once important to overwintering deer herds, have been invaded by cheatgrass and burned at frequent intervals. Repeated burning has killed shrubs, leaving little or no browse for wintering deer herds.

The continued existence of sizeable mule deer populations in most western states has been a saving grace to managers of public rangelands and stockmen, for if deer had declined in the same manner as other big game species, irate citizens and sportsmen would have surely demanded management reform. Instead western hunters seem content to hunt deer and overlook the paucity of other, once abundant, big game species.

Pronghorns theoretically can share rangelands with cattle and do so without competition, provided the range is in good condition. On overgrazed or poor-quality rangeland, of which there is plenty, competition may be severe. At the turn of the century, some authorities were predicting that the pronghorn might become extinct, and the population dropped as low as 26,600 in 1924, but began to recover as conservation efforts mounted. A drastic reduction in the domestic sheep population has no doubt helped, because these two species compete for many of the same food plants, especially in the winter. Some of the highest densities of pronghorn today are in central and northeastern Wyoming on *private* rangelands.

Although numerous examples exist of livestock transferring diseases to big game animals, bighorn sheep have probably suffered most, having been extirpated in Oregon. However, in 1925 to 1927, foot and mouth disease spread from domestic cattle to deer herds on Stanislaus National Forest in California and 22,000 deer had to be slaughtered to eradicate the disease.

In many parts of the West, feral populations of horses and burros compete with various species of big game animals on public lands. It should be noted that free-roaming horses and burros found in the West today are not from original Spanish stock, but are derived from more recent escapees from domestication. In Grand Canyon and other places, burros are unusually detrimental to bighorn sheep—competing for food and fouling water supplies. In Nevada, an estimated 30,000 feral horses require more forage than the state's estimated population of 81,000 mule deer. Both horses and burros feed indiscriminately on most plants and are able to survive even on overgrazed range. In recent years, the BLM has developed an extensive program to capture wild horses and burros on its lands and dispose of them through a public adoption program. Many critics have failed to support these efforts, contending that the AUM's gained by removal of feral horses and burros will simply be transferred to stockmen for additional numbers of cattle. Strong enthusiasm for the program by ranchers seems to support these suspicions.

Management agencies, especially the BLM, tend to allocate meager resources to wild ungulates. One is reminded of the commonly held misconception that if no other use can be found for a parcel of land, it can always be used for wildlife. Wildlife, like domestic livestock, thrives better on rich productive lands. In Oregon, the Ironside Grazing Management District, consisting of 1,001,964 acres of BLM land, allotted 142,118 AUM's to livestock (mainly cattle) but *zero* AUM's to wildlife in 1980. In the Lakeview District (3,342,026 acres), 166,454 AUM's were allotted to livestock, but only 10,916 AUM's to wildlife. Yet both units are major areas for mule deer and pronghorns, with small populations of bighorn sheep in the Lakeview District and some elk in the Ironside District. In the Caliente Grazing District in Nevada, the BLM *planned* a reduction of 128 desert bighorn sheep—guess what will happen to those AUM's!

Barbed-wire fences are a serious hazard for all kinds of big game animals, and as the BLM and Forest Service launch massive programs of fence construction to support rest-rotation and deferred grazing, fences threaten to become a truly alarming cause of wildlife mortality. Instances of deer and elk entanglement in fences are common, especially in densely vegetated habitat. In many cases, the Malheur National Forest being a prime example, old and burned fences are left standing or strewn about even after new ones are constructed nearby. We found a live pronghorn tangled in a barbed-wire fence at Hart Mountain National Antelope Refuge (Oregon) and saw skeletons of several deer and pronghorns hanging in refuge fences. The leading cause of mortality to moose calves on Red Rock Lake National Wildlife Refuge (Montana) is entanglement in fences. Although deer and pronghorns prefer to go under or through fences, they often jump them, and frequently, the front legs clear the fence, but the hind legs catch between the two top strands; the animal is left dangling from the fence to die. At Malheur National Wildlife Refuge, a pronghorn attempted to jump a barbed-wire fence in an area where 6 inches of water stood. When it failed to clear the fence with its hind legs, the pronghorn was left hanging, but eventually tired of holding its head above water and drowned. Obviously, were it not for private livestock grazing, there would be no reason to have barbed-wire fences on national wildlife refuges.

In a study of causes of accidental death of bighorn sheep, 17 (12 percent) were found to have died in fences and other wire. In Arizona, 10 rams are known to have died in rights-of-way fences along Interstate 10 in a 2-year period. These sheep were trying to cross the highway and became entangled in one of the two uppermost strands of wire, with the wire passing above the tips of the horns and between the head and neck. In struggling to free themselves, the bighorns suffered severe lacerations and died of loss of blood. An unknown number of others are believed to have torn themselves free and escaped with serious injuries.

Pronghorns are fleet runners and do not often attempt to leap fences. Although many have learned to go through or under fences, frightened herds will often run a mile or more parallel to a barbed-wire fence, rather than cross it. In many places where deep snow accumulates, pronghorns are unable to negotiate fences and die when they become "trapped" in areas without adequate food and water. On lands where large numbers of pronghorns occur, the BLM has started using 3-strand barbed-wire fences with the bottom strand about 18 inches above the ground. Ideally, the bottom strand should be smooth wire. Most fences on public land are four strands of barbed wire tightly stretched between steel posts—difficult obstacles for man or beast.

Sheep ranchers sometimes build net-wire fences in a largely futile effort to protect sheep from coyotes. These fences constitute impassible barriers to pronghorns. In southeastern New Mexico, ranchers battled to keep net-wire fences on their BLM grazing allotments in a half-million acre region west of Roswell, which once supported the most productive population of pronghorns in the Southwest. In 1940, about 3,000 pronghorns inhabited the region, but by 1976, less than 300 could be located. According to wildlife biologists, the population crash was caused by miles of net-wire fences installed by sheepmen in the 1930's and 1940's. In this semiarid country, pronghorns must be free to search for food and water, and when enclosed in the same pasture with domestic sheep, they suffer severe competition for the same food plants. Also, unlike cattle and sheep, pronghorns cannot survive periods of drought on a diet of hay.

In 1965, the BLM decided to do something about the impact of net-wire fences, and over a period of years, about 300 miles of fence were modified in New Mexico and four other states. Ranchers, however, fought the plan to remove the net-wire fences, claiming that the modified fences would lead to increased predation of sheep, impede control of livestock, and lower the resale value of home ranches. (Note: Public grazing permits are sold as a part of home ranch sales.) The ranchers appealed to the press, the bureaucracy, and sympathetic politicians, and as is often the case when ranchers feel threatened, they argued that the federal government was encroaching upon states' rights, coyotes would drive all of them out of business, ranchers being natural and well-informed conservationists knew what was best for pronghorns, and pronghorns in the area survive only because of the net-wire fences. Thanks to the Federal Land Policy and Management Act, principles of multiple use and sustained yield prevailed and the net-wire fences had to go.

The so-called range improvements done in behalf of domestic livestock on public lands are of little value to big game species, and in fact, are most often detrimental. While pronghorns may share water holes or even troughs used by cattle, most sites become so fouled and devoid of vegetation that they are shunned by wild animals. New water developments serve to extend overgrazing into prime big game habitat.

Numerous studies have documented detrimental effects upon wild ungulates from spraying rangelands with herbicides to remove brush or trees, such as junipers. Because the commonly used herbicides kill all broad-leaved plants (everything but grasses), they destroy the diversity of shrubs and forbs required by most species of big game. Brush removal may totally destroy the value of wildlife winter ranges. Adverse effects of spraying have been shown for deer, peccaries, pronghorns, and desert bighorn sheep. Spraying is especially destructive when done on large blocks of land. Although wildlife biologists recommend that no more than 40 acres of sagebrush be cleared at a time, the BLM sprays as much as 9,000 acres in a single operation. Leaving quarter-mile strips unsprayed, however, may sometimes improve wildlife habitat by providing a greater diversity of vegetation and creating attractive edges between vegetative types.

Fire is a natural factor on wildlands, and no rangeland plant community has developed without its influence. Unfortunately, the early livestock industry developed a negative attitude toward fires, and this has contributed to a general policy of fire prevention and suppression on public rangelands, even though most wildlife biologists acknowledge the value of burning as a management practice. Millions of dollars of public money have been spent controlling fires, and only recently has a more sensible attitude toward burning begun to surface. Because fire recycles nutrients, removes decadent plants, and initiates vigorous resprouting of tender nutritious growth, big game species seek burns for feeding. In Wyoming, for four years after a burn, bighorn sheep and mule deer grazed a burned area more than adjacent unburned sites.

Perhaps the most harmful of the "range improvements" is the planting of huge acreages of public land, especially BLM land, to monocultures of exotic grasses, such as crested wheatgrass. Thousands of square miles of western rangelands have been converted to such seedings. Idaho had about 1.6 million acres in 1978.

Crested wheatgrass seedings are nothing more than a conversion of wildlife habitat into cow habitat. Although BLM workers and others cite some spring use by deer and pronghorns, it must be pointed out that deer and pronghorns are also seen on highways—that doesn't mean highways are a favored or useful habitat. In the spring green up period, pronghorns use seedings, but even then, 60 to 90 percent of their diet is still sagebrush. Neither deer nor pronghorns use seedings regularly in the winter, there are no data showing that any species of wildlife gains weight or thrives on seedings, and pronghorns will not give birth to kids on seedings. While seeding a single species of grass is not recommended for pronghorns, experts do recommend seedings of a mixture of plants, such as a minimum of six species of grasses, six species of forbs, and six species of shrubs.

Many crested wheatgrass seedings are being planted on major winter ranges of big game species, and because these seedings are grazed heavily by cattle (as much as 80 percent utilization is recommended to keep other plants from invading) and are veritable biological deserts for wild ungulates, the practice is exceptionally damaging to wildlife populations. In summary, one can only say that monocultural seedings favor a single use of public lands—grazing livestock—and as such, clearly should be a violation of federal laws specifying management for multiple uses.

Today, public grazing lands of the West are being managed strictly for a cow monoculture, despite the fact that there is a great deal of scientific evidence showing such a practice to be unwise. In this country, we have accepted the rancher's often-quoted contention that rangeland forage is out there, but is wasted if a cow doesn't harvest it. In parts of the Soviet Union and Africa, cattle have been shunned in favor of managing large herds of wild ungulates (game farming?) for food and hides. Mixed herds of wild game are known to be more efficient at using available vegetation and actually produce more useable protein than do cattle.

Given the choice, cows prefer to take certain grasses and leave other plants, but if their numbers are increased to gain better use of the forage, overgrazing and range depletion result. Furthermore, their low mobility favors overgrazing. Cattle also require large amounts of water.

Research in Africa has shown that species of big game, however, tend to specialize and feed on a narrow spectrum of available plants. A mixture of several types of wild ungulates can coexist without serious competition or overgrazing and use a much broader range of vegetation than cattle would use. When forage is in short supply, wild ungulates may travel great distances to reach new food supplies, thus overgrazing is rare. Furthermore, many African species of game have minimal water requirements and high natural resistance to diseases, which may be exceptionally destructive to introduced livestock. Raymond Dasmann did a cost analysis comparing the production of beef and native grazers. Although the native grazers produced only a pound of meat per acre per year more than beef, the annual profit margin was $1,416 for beef compared to $8,960 for native grazers. The difference reflected the high cost of maintenance and production for an exotic animal, the cow, in a natural environment.

While mixed-game ranching has proved more profitable than cattle ranching in parts of Africa, similar potentials have not been properly studied in the western United States. If, however, it were possible to get beyond our blind preoccupation with the cow, tremendous potential might be found. We are not advocating game ranching on public land, but rather are suggesting that the basic principles of successful game ranching might be used to produce and sustain large populations of native American ungulates on certain public lands. For example, at Hart Mountain National Antelope Refuge, a visitor is fortunate to see a pronghorn, but herds of cows wander about, even in campgrounds much of the time. The 275,000-acre refuge is being severely overgrazed by cattle belonging to only a half-dozen local cattlemen. Refuge managers justify grazing by stating that the cattle eat only "excess" forage, beyond the needs of wildlife, and that "controlled" grazing of cattle makes some areas more attractive to wildlife. What they don't explain, however, is why cattle must do the grazing to improve deer, pronghorn, and bighorn sheep habitat. In any event, the refuge is a mess—hundreds of cows stomping riparian zones, devouring and trampling all that "excess" forage, every stream despoiled with cattle excrement, miles of barbed-wire fences (and huge piles of steel posts and rolls of new wire waiting in the equipment yard), dozens of expensive cattle guards, costly watering systems for cows, and more. But the point is, because all this is being done for the benefit of only a half-dozen private ranchers and represents an outrageous affront to thousands of refuge visitors (and millions who don't visit the refuge), why not get rid of the cattle, the fences, and all the other ranching paraphernalia and manage the entire 275,000-acre refuge for a mixed population of native American ungulates—deer, pronghorns, elk, bighorn sheep, bison, and anything else that would live there? Wouldn't most Americans (the people who own the refuge) rather see these species than a Hereford? Why not use a chunk of public land to benefit the public, instead of turning it over to a mere handful of cowboys? And there are other public lands that could be similarly managed.

Steve Gallizioli, Research Chief of the Arizona Game and Fish Department, has said many times that, "the grazing of domestic livestock on western rangelands has probably had a greater adverse impact on wildlife populations than any other single factor." The evidence certainly supports his wisdom. Yet, we have made and continue to make available to cattle an amount of forage exceeding that required by the total pristine populations of 20 to 30 million head of native ungulates. Today, on much of the public land, instead of finding big game, the hunter finds herds of cows crashing around in the canyons and woods, rolling rocks, bellowing, and creating disturbances that alert every game animal for miles.

With the exception of deer, western game animals represent a pitiful remnant of pristine numbers. Hunters, wildlife enthusiasts, and citizens in general have meekly accepted less and less. The modern hunter has convinced himself that it is not the bagging of game that counts, it is the recreation—getting out-of-doors and giving it a try. While containing a grain of truth, this built-in apology for hunting failure amounts to a little more than a colossal concession to 36,000 livestock owners who, for all practical purposes, dictate a shortage of wildlife on public lands of the West. While ranchers are small in number, they are highly organized, pushy, and constantly alert and ready to defend their favored status on public lands. Meanwhile, hunters, conservationists, and other citizens are busy bickering among themselves about gun laws (sportsmen may end up keeping guns, but have nothing to hunt), predators, and such issues. While the rest of us have been arguing about peripheral game matters, the cattlemen have taken the only thing that really counts—the habitat.

What is most incredible is that the people who care about big game in this country outnumber public grazers, probably by a ratio of 100,000 to 1 or more. If these people ever get organized and decide what they want, they yield enough political clout to put stockmen in hasty retreat. The simple expedient of a boycott of western beef until the cowboys are ready and *willing* to accept *real* multiple uses of public lands would turn the trick. Meanwhile, Americans and their wildlife are 4th-class citizens on the nation's public lands, and those lands have been converted into the world's largest pasture for the exclusive use of cows!

SENSELESS SLAUGHTER

Predators have been maligned, tortured, poisoned, wasted, pursued, and killed on sight in a vengeance without precedent. Today, species formerly found throughout much of the nation are confined to isolated pinpoints on the map, and in most places, only the wily and adaptable coyote and man remain as large mammalian predators of any consequence. A rich, unique, and magnificent part of America's wildlife heritage has been shamefully sacrificed for the sake of the domestic livestock industry. Perhaps the most shocking aspect of the predator tragedy is that American taxpayers have financed a substantial portion of the extermination costs and provided federal employees to do the killing. It is a sorry record. Unfortunately, the slaughter is still going on and the livestock industry will not be content until the last predator has been chased down and destroyed.

The earliest attempt to domesticate wild animals and keep them captive for exclusive human use invited confrontation with predators, and no doubt the predators obliged. Despite efforts to minimize losses to predators, those first stockmen must have accepted a certain amount of loss as inevitable and yet cherished whatever was saved for the table. It is significant that the stockmen, their livestock, and the predators survived those early encounters.

Today, popular notions about predators have grown fuzzy, influenced by misconception, folklore, and children's stories. Every child knows that the "big bad wolf" goes around huffing and puffing and blowing down houses, but how many know that there is no known case of an unprovoked attack on humans by wolves? Admit it or not,

"Little Red Riding Hood" and similar tales exert a pervasive influence on attitudes relating to predators and their management. Given these falsehoods and a general lack of factual information, is it any wonder that our public policies regarding predators are a muddled and incongruent mess?

Predators are meat eaters. In nature's scheme, predators are not killers any more than birds are killers for eating insects, rabbits for eating grass, or humans for eating fish. Vital solar energy is captured and converted into food plants (producers), plants are devoured by herbivores (primary consumers), and herbivores are eaten by predators (secondary consumers). It's that simple, yet such food chains are the basis for all life on earth—predators are simply a link in the chain. Problems arise, however, when we view a predator as a thief eating something we would rather have. As secondary consumers, predators perform essential functions that only they can do, and it is utter folly to imagine that we can fill the predator's role. For example, predators help check population explosions of prey species, remove carrion, help keep wildlife populations healthy and within carrying capacity of the environment, provide human recreation, exemplify nature's diversity and ingenuity, give meaning and substance to esthetic values such as wilderness, and provide opportunity for learning and enjoyment for all of us. Most of all, we need predators because we could not bear the void and shame that would come with their extinction.

Bounty systems, paying a reward for the killing of a specified type of animal, date back 2,000 years or more. In this country, public involvement in predator control began as early as 1630 when colonists in Massachusetts offered a bounty for several types of predators. Eventually, bounties for predators became standard procedures in most states, and by 1892 wolves were eradicated in Pennsylvania.

When the Forest Service began charging stockmen a fee for grazing, permittees argued that the agency as landlord should be responsible for protecting livestock from predators. In 1915, congress accepted the rancher's argument and appropriated $125,000 to be used by the

Biological Survey (Dept. of Agriculture) for predator control. In retrospect, this action of congress set a highly significant precedent—it opened the door to using public funds to kill publicly owned animals on public lands for the economic gain of private stockmen. The validity of that decision is still being debated.

In any event, from this humble beginning public involvement in financing and sponsoring the killing of predators grew rapidly, fueled by a willingness of the states, livestock associations, and ranchers to provide matching dollars for cooperative projects. The Biological Survey was eventually transferred to the Department of Interior and put in the Branch of Predator and Rodent Control, which in 1965 was euphemistically renamed as the Division of Wildlife Services within the Bureau of Sport Fisheries and Wildlife. Today, responsibility for predator control rests with the Division of Animal Damage Control in the U.S. Fish and Wildlife Service.

Between 1951 and 1970, about $110 million in federal and contributed funds were spent on cooperative programs of predator control. By 1977, the federal budget for predator control had reached $11 million a year, of which $5.5 million was spent on cooperative programs, with a minimum contribution of three federal dollars for each dollar of state or industry money. In 1978, the total expenditure climbed to about $18 million, with federal expenditures amounting to more than $10 million in 15 western states. The Division of Animal Damage Control employs more than 700 field workers (once called government trappers, currently known as animal damage control agents) and a large staff of supervisory and administrative personnel.

In addition to federal predator control, many states and even some counties operate tax-supported programs of their own. A few states and some counties within other states continue to pay predator bounties of various sorts, although these are largely political ointment, since bounties clearly fail to increase game supplies or to reduce livestock and poultry losses.

THE PRICE OF BEEF:
SENSELESS SLAUGHTER

Today, predator control finds little support among professional wildlife biologists or professional wildlife agencies or societies. Modern wildlife biologists stress the vital importance of good habitat in sustaining desirable populations of wildlife. Without high-quality habitat, wildlife populations cannot flourish, and no amount of predator control can alter that fact. Furthermore, as scientific studies have revealed the enormous reproductive potential of predators, biologists have come to view predator control as simply harvesting the annual surplus without really forcing a decline in the overall population. In fact, investigation has shown that when predator numbers are reduced, the remaining predators respond by producing larger than normal litters. In other words, predator control is a sustained-yield harvest—a costly, futile, and self-perpetuating boondoggle. Also, as public interests in the out-of-doors and natural resources have grown, wildlife biologists have decreased the emphasis upon managing for shootable game—today, game, nongame, and predators are given a more equal status and managed as *wildlife*—a complete biological system. Although a few sportsmen, who are self-proclaimed armchair biologists, may continue to advocate predator control, the practice is currently nothing more than a public subsidy to the livestock industry, especially to public grazers who are already highly subsidized.

At first, government trappers used guns, metal leg-hold traps, snares, denning (digging out and killing young from family dens), and other relatively crude devices. Initially, control efforts were generally directed at protecting livestock. Just before World War I the use of strychnine baits became standard practice. Although certain control efforts continued to be aimed at specific predators molesting livestock, the fundamental goals of the programs shifted, becoming indiscriminate and directed at all predators in general. Suddenly, the measure of success was a large body count, even if the predators killed had never seen a sheep or calf.

Then in the 1940's the pace quickened when the "coyote getter"—a cyanide gun powered by a pistol cartridge—

came into wide use. Coyotes (or any animal attracted to the scent) set off the mechanism by tugging on a scented wick, causing sodium cyanide dust to be blown in the animal's mouth. The device was later replaced by a model known as the M-44, which is spring-powered. Thallium sulfate, a deadly poison, also came into general use, but was eventually forbidden in federal control programs because it was too toxic and nonselective. Toward the end of the 1940's, sodium monofluoroacetate, commonly called Compound 1080, an extremely hazardous chemical affecting the nervous system and cardiac functions, was placed in meat baits. Because 1080 is highly stable, animals frequently are secondarily poisoned by feeding on other 1080 victims.

With such an arsenal of toxic chemicals, federal predator control quickly turned into an absurd and senseless orgy of killing with minimal regard for life in general and scant relationship to the original goal of reducing predation on livestock. It was predator genocide—not predator control.

In a 10-year period (1961-70) 141,029 baits of meat containing 1080 were used (as many as 15,692 in a single year), mostly in a gigantic grid of bait stations at 6-mile intervals throughout western rangelands and forests, even where no livestock grazed. Although intended for coyotes, these baits were equally attractive and lethal to badgers, foxes, golden eagles, magpies, and numerous other carrion eaters. In the same 10-year period, 7,190,206 tallow pellets containing strychnine were scattered over the western landscape from planes, automobiles, horseback, and other conveyances. Nearly 840,000 were put out in 1965 alone. Any animal attracted to tallow could become a victim of the baits, including dozens of animals ranging from songbirds to hunting dogs. Because the pellets were widely scattered, often in remote places, the extent of the actual kill was impossible to determine. Also, in this same 10-year period, federal employees distributed on millions of acres of land 1,361,375 pounds of grain poisoned with 1080, not to kill predators, but to kill rodents competing with livestock for vegetation. Much of this poison grain ended up on public land. Finally, during the last 9 of those same 10 years, federal predator control agents racked up 470,938 "coyote-getter years" (=one coyote-getter set for a full year) and 293,365 trap years (=one trap set for a year). And in addition, these industrious fellows were digging out dens, fishing pups out of dens on lengths of barbed wire, pumping poison gas into burrows, using flamethrowers on dens, shooting predators from the ground, airplanes, and helicopters, and no doubt attempting to smash with government pickups any predator encountered on highways!

In 1972, a committee of experts chaired by Stanley A. Cain (University of Michigan) reviewed the federal program of predator control in a government-sponsored report. Basically, the report was highly critical of the program, and among a number of fundamental recommendations, was one calling for a ban of all toxic chemicals used in the federal program. Within a month, President Richard Nixon banned the use of toxicants on public lands and in federal predator control. The Environmental Protection Agency then cancelled or suspended all uses of 1080 carrion baits, strychnine tallow pellets, and sodium cyanide in the M-44. Because M-44 devices could still be used in "experiments," these were soon back in general use. Although Cecil Andrus, Secretary of Interior in the Carter Administration, halted all research and development of poisons having secondary effects, notably 1080, the Reagan Administration soon let it be known that it favored reinstituting the use of 1080. In 1982 an administrative law judge ordered the EPA to lift its ban on 1080, but specified that 1080 be used only in single lethal dose baits applied by experienced federal predator control specialists or in rubber collars attached to necks of sheep or goats. Ranchers could use the collars, but not the baits. In other words, 1080 is now available to the same people who made such a disgraceful mess of it in the first place!

Much of the federal program of predator control has involved poisons, which did not permit an accurate accounting of what and how many animals were actually killed. Certainly the numbers would be impressive—even shocking. With other methods, however, predator control agents have kept a body count, at least of major animals killed. In one 34-year period (1937-70) the *known* number of animals killed by federal employees include 23,803 bears, 7,255 mountain lions, 477,104 bobcats and lynx, 2,823,056 coyotes, 50,283 red wolves, and 1,574 Lobo wolves. (Note: Taxpayers should go back and read the preceding sentence again—just to ponder the value received for tax dollars spent!) In this list of known kills, the total for red wolves represents only 28 years of effort, because after that, the red wolf, plus grey wolves, grizzly bears, and two forms of mountain lions had to be put on the *Endangered Species List*. Ironically, the nation's endangered species are also under the care of the Department of Interior, which handles predator control and prints the following notice on its publications: "As the Nation's principal conservation agency, the Department of Interior has responsibility for most of our nationally owned public lands and natural resources. This includes fostering the wisest use of our land and water resources, protecting our fish and *wildlife*, preserving the environmental and cultural values of our national parks and historical places, and providing for the enjoyment of life through outdoor recreation . . .(italics ours)." What bureaucratic deceit! In fairness to the agency, however, it must be pointed out that the Branch of Animal Damage Control (known as the gopher chokers) represents a source of embarrassment to most professional employees and to other branches having true conservation missions.

In additon to the count of "target" predators killed, the U.S. Fish and Wildlife Service also keeps a list of certain other large animals. In one year (1963) the known body count for these animals included 6,941 badgers, 1,170 beaver, 24,273 foxes, 7,615 opossums, 6,685 porcupines, 10,078 raccoons, 19,052 skunks, and 601 miscellaneous (?).

Finally, many other nontarget animals killed or caught in traps are not considered worthy of reporting or counting. These species are usually labeled "trash" animals. Even so, in 1977, the U.S. Fish and Wildlife Service admitted to catching nearly 10,000 nontarget animals, mainly in steel traps. The list includes such animals as feral cats and dogs, javelina, deer, rabbits, ringtails, ground hogs, armadillos, vultures, crows, but strangely no hawks, owls, or eagles. Other trappers report catching domestic livestock, wild turkeys, quail, various songbirds, several species of hawks and owls, and even gopher tortoises. Although a few of these trapped animals are well enough to be released, others are found dead or have to be killed, and even if released the animals may be so seriously injured as to be unable to survive.

Many stockmen have criticized our public efforts to rid the nation of predators—they feel that we have not approached the task seriously, and consequently, the results have not met their expectations. In other words, they are still losing livestock. As recently as 1978, the Fish and Wildlife Service said, "Limited case study evidence is convincing that coyote control can reduce livestock loss, but there are too few such studies to permit statistically meaningful generalizations on a Westwide basis." What this means in plain English is that if a coyote is killing sheep and is killed, then sheep losses will decline. But after spending millions of dollars, thousands of man years, and indiscriminately slaughtering every predator that our technology would permit, there is still no evidence that the effort has reduced livestock losses on a regional basis. In fact, sheep losses may actually have increased during the period of heavy use of poisons. After more than 65 years of publicly supported predator control, there is little evidence as to whether massive predator control does any good.

What specific benefits has the livestock industry derived from predator control? Presumably cattlemen should be pleased, for the large predators—grizzly bears, wolves, and mountain lions—capable of killing cattle have been virtually exterminated from most of their original ranges, are now confined to a few remote locations, and are prominent on the list of rare and endangered animals. But this has not placated cattlemen, who have now turned their attention to the coyote. Much of the killing of coyotes in the West today, although ostensibly done to protect sheep, is actually done in cattle country where no sheep occur. Although numerous

studies show that adult cattle are eaten only as carrion, the same studies show that coyotes do kill some calves. In 14,289 coyote stomachs, calves occurred in less than 1 percent, and some of those calves were probably already dead when consumed. On the other hand, field studies consistently show that 50 to 75 percent of the coyote's diet consists of rabbits and rodents that compete directly with cattle for forage. It is a mistake to attempt to analyze cattlemen's attitudes about coyotes from the standpoint of logic. The majority of them drive around in pickups with rifles stored in a rack behind the driver's seat and shoot at every coyote they see. Cattlemen are willing to pay from their own pockets more than $120 an hour to have coyotes gunned from helicopters. In parts of the West, many ranchers kill coyotes and hang them from barbed-wired fences, presumably as a warning to other coyotes in the neighborhood. All this has little to do with ranching or economics, but is, instead, a stubborn vestige of macho frontiersmanship, identifying the ranchers as practicing westerners out of the old mold. The calves saved would not even pay for the ammunition and gasoline, not to mention the time.

Officially, sheep are the justification for most predator control in the West. In the 1940's, the total number of sheep in the nation reached about 55 million, but has declined to about 10 million. Western sheepmen would have us believe that this decline was forced upon them by coyotes—"they drove us out of business." However, the decline took place during the time when predator control was at an all-time high—including widespread use of poisons. Furthermore, the decline in sheep numbers has actually been greater in 31 eastern states than in the West, where coyotes abound. Obviously, the increased use of synthetic fibers and reduced demands for mutton and lamb have had a greater impact upon the industry than coyotes.

A major obstacle to assessing coyote damage to the sheep industry has been the paucity of accurate and realistic statistics on kills. Associations of sheepmen and agricultural organizations have relied upon questionnaires sent to sheep ranchers to obtain data. Such surveys, however, provide grossly inflated estimates of coyote kills. For example, in 1974, postcard surveys of sheepmen showed an 8.8-percent loss of lambs and a 3-percent loss of ewes to coyotes in the 15 western states. But that same year field studies done by U.S. Fish and Wildlife Service biologists in Wyoming showed only 2.1 percent of the lambs and 0.2 percent of the ewes being killed by coyotes. When the study was expanded to 3 years, it continued to show 2.3 percent of the lambs and 0.2 percent of the ewes being killed by coyotes. Congressman John D. Dingell of Michigan and his chief of staff, Frank M. Potter, accurately summed up the situation: "According to the sheepmen to whom we have talked, it is doubtful if any sheep has died a natural death in the past century; extermination of all coyotes, whatever the environmental costs, is their battle cry."

Field investigations by federal biologists show the major causes of lamb mortality to be premature birth, starvation, and disease; ewes die mainly from birth complications, infections, stress, and disease. Many sheepmen refuse to acknowledge these findings, as illustrated in the results of questionnaires sent out by the U.S. Department of Agriculture in a survey of losses of lambs and ewes in 15 western states in 1974. Nevada reported a 29.0-percent loss of lambs and an 11.9-percent loss of ewes to coyotes; the other 14 states reported a 7.4-percent loss of lambs and 2.3-percent loss of ewes to coyotes. In reporting losses due to all other *known* causes, Nevada sheepmen attributed to these causes only 2.2 percent of the lambs and 1.4 percent of the ewes lost, while sheepmen in the other 14 states blamed these causes for 9.0 percent of the lamb and 5.5 percent of the ewe losses. Even with such disparate numbers, the survey showed only 27 percent of the lamb losses and 37 percent of the ewe losses to have been caused by coyotes. Obviously, if sheepmen could reduce significantly the 73-percent loss of lambs and the 63-percent loss of ewes caused by factors other than coyotes, we could all get off the predator-control treadmill! Only a few sheepmen suffer severe losses to coyotes, a fact suggesting that human negligence may play an important role.

During the years when the use of poisons was in full swing, sheepmen reported drastic declines in predation losses, but during those same years they reported no reduction in total losses. Either the decline in loss to predators was exaggerated, or for some mysterious reason, more sheep die anyway when coyotes don't get them! Nevertheless, when the use of poisons was banned in 1972, the sheep industry objected immediately and reported an explosion in coyote populations. What they didn't realize, however, was that 1080 baits placed in the field in 1971 were still effective and would continue to kill until 1973!

In assessing the value of total sheep losses, the industry regularly provides the popular press with estimates ranging from $20 to $27 million a year. In contrast, authorities outside the sheep industry have tended to estimate the total value of annual sheep losses as $4 to $10 million. Such wide differences are obviously not explainable as errors in arithmetic.

Several investigators have reported higher rates of predation on livestock, both sheep and cattle, on overgrazed ranges. When livestock are undernourished, they are less able to care for themselves, and in many instances predators are merely removing doomed animals that are already destined to die of malnourishment. Also, overgrazing, provided it is not too severe, favors rabbit and rodent populations, encouraging a buildup in coyote populations that brings coyotes into contact with livestock. Research on taste preference shows that, if given a choice, coyotes actually prefer mutton to rabbit, especially if the mutton is carrion. Coyotes have greatly benefited from range abuse, and to a large extent, stockmen have created their own predator problem by overgrazing. If that weren't enough, there is even a study showing that peg-legged coyotes (those that have lost a leg from being trapped or from chewing it off to escape from a trap) feed about a third less on rabbits and rodents, but feed about a third more on sheep and goats!

More than 60 percent of the federal funds for predator control are spent on coyote control, presumably for the benefit of the sheep industry. Yet 63 percent of all the sheep raised in the West are owned by only 6 percent of the producers. Furthermore, public lands provide only 15 percent of the forage for sheep in the West and only 8 percent of the forage used by all sheep in the nation. Obviously, the taxpayers in supporting a nationwide predator program for the benefit of sheepmen are being extremely generous to a tiny minority engaged in a business having little general impact upon the nation's economy!

There is a clear and urgent need for public reassessment of the nation's predator control program. For almost 7 decades, public funds have been spent for presumed benefits to a small number of stockmen. There is no evidence showing that the effort has been successful. However, we have ravaged our pristine populations of magnificent carnivores and pushed some species to the brink of extinction. From every indication, the entire program has been ill-conceived and cause for national shame.

The system of federal control agents fosters intramural competition (one trapper attained hero status by taking 600 coyotes in one year) and high body counts. These employees are not professionally trained biologists, live in communities where stockmen are neighbors, and because portions of co-operative funds are provided by stockmen, are subject to the whims and pressures of local politics. Even vast undertakings, such as the 1080 bait debacle—which may have killed only coyotes that eat carrion, not the active predators that prey upon living animals—have been poorly designed and carelessly conducted. Overall, the system is indiscriminate, self-perpetuating, and not properly aimed at reducing livestock losses.

Public involvement in predator control has had a damaging effect upon the national psyche and attitudes. Large numbers of rural children grow up hating eagles, coyotes, magpies, hawks, owls, and other animals. A teen-ager can blast a magpie without remorse, because someone once told him that magpies peck the eyes out of domestic livestock! Current attitudes relating to predators and many other animals as well date back to frontier days when biological knowledge of animals was superficial. But today we number 233 million, are better-informed (at least the information is available), and our national ecosystems simply cannot sustain such waste, ignorance, and antiquated notions about our fellow creatures.

Predator control is a triple subsidy—we pay in dollars, in lost wildlife resources, and in lost national pride. Stockmen are a small minority and already enjoy numerous subsidies—miniscule public grazing fees, range improvement programs, drought relief, tax advantages, etc. The cycle is vicious—livestock overgraze public lands, invite rabbit and rodent populations, and attract coyotes; then we hear pleas to kill coyotes with public funds, and finally, rodent and rabbit control is needed when the coyotes are gone. Overgrazing is one of the industry's largest subsidies—the costs in soil, water, wildlife, and other resources are inestimable. Every stockmen goes into business knowing that predators exist, but someplace along the way, the burdens of that private decision are shifted to the public.

Knowledgeable groups have pleaded for predator control to be limited to the offending animals. Others have asked for a system of extension trappers to teach stockmen how to handle their own problems on private land. Still others have suggested that the stockmen create their own insurance system—a small tax on each head of livestock to pay for individual losses to predators. Furthermore, various nonlethal methods have been developed to protect livestock (e.g., taste aversion, lethal collars, specially trained dogs, special fencing, etc.). But none of these suggestions is going to get anywhere as long as the public is willing to foot the entire bill.

This nation is founded on the fundamental concept of business being a private, free-enterprise system. All businesses have pitfalls, and the cost of doing business is included in the price of the commodity at the marketplace. Predation is one risk of being in the livestock business—it is not a public responsibility. Public lands belong to all the people, and all the resources on these lands are by law to be managed by the federal government as a public trust. That includes predators. There should be no predator control on public lands, with the possible exception that healthy populations of fur-bearing animals might be taken for recreation and profit—but only to wisely use the resource—not to protect privately owned domestic animals. If stockmen wish to shoot or trap predators on their own private lands, that would seem to be their business and their decision.

Several groups of professional scientists have studied the issue of predator control and made excellent suggestions for improvements. These suggestions have largely been ignored. Stockmen got the public into predator control by exercising political clout. And the wanton slaughter of our nation's animals is going to continue until the public finally exercises its clout and simply refuses to tolerate any further insanities.

GRAZING SLUMS

Few of us would put a bull (or any other cattle for that matter) in a china shop. Unfortunately, our respect for the well-being of china shops does not extend to nature's pantries. If a fragile and delicate environment will support cattle, or even *looks* like it will support cattle, custom dictates that it be promptly and fully stocked and not a blade of grass "wasted." Never mind that nature be unwilling, or that the land may have higher values than forage production. Then when nature rebels, as is usually the case, everyone seems surprised and unwilling to accept the consequences.

Natural environments are complex, but incredibly functional—precisely the right organisms take part, vital roles are filled perfectly, the work is always done, interrelationships are exact, diversity is encouraged and conserved, natural limits are respected, the components survive, and the whole is perpetuated undiminished. For example, investigations have shown a single acre of grassland to support 3.6 to 4.8 million invertebrate animals of a size large enough to be seen with the unaided eye. Add to these the numerous vertebrate animals, the diverse plant community, and the billions of microscopic organisms, mainly in the soil. Miraculously, this heterogeneous assemblage of living organisms is able to function as a harmonious unit. Just among insects, the diversity is enormous—root eaters, sapsuckers, predators, carrion feeders, parasites, and dozens more. But they all fit in, and the system works.

What happens when a herd of hungry cattle is turned loose in a natural ecosystem? Obviously, the impacts are many. The physical disruptions of grazing and trampling decrease cover, destroy food sources, compact soils, increase evaporation rates at the soil surface, permit high soil temperatures, reduce shade, change the structure of vegetation, and much more. Each impact reverberates in a chain reaction through the system, making it unlikely that any species will escape totally unaffected. Ultimately, the combined impacts weaken the community superstructure, and once initiated, the ecological disruption grows and spreads. Each year the cattle will return and nudge the decaying system a bit closer to poverty.

Ecosystems having rich biological diversity tend to be highly stable; less diverse ecosystems lack stability and tend to experience wide fluctuations in population densities, severe disease epidemics, and other variables. Grazing destroys diversity and sets in motion a progressive simplification of ecosystems. In general, the more intensive the grazing, the more rapid the loss of diversity. And when range improvements, such as brush clearing and seedings, are made on overgrazed ranges, diversity suffers further, as when a monoculture of a single species of plant, such as crested wheatgrass, is created. In Idaho, an ungrazed stand of big sagebrush supported 31 species of plants, a grazed stand of big sage supported 9 species, ungrazed crested wheatgrass supported 3 species, and grazed crested wheatgrass supported 5 species (the latter included halogeton, a poisonous exotic).

As grazing degrades an environment and reduces the diversity of plant life, the changes eventually affect animal diversity as well. With increasing impairment of the environment, many species experience difficulties in finding food, cover, and other essentials—these species (the decreasers) diminish in number and finally disappear. But a few species may actually thrive in simplified and impoverished environments created by grazing. In fact, populations of these animals (the increasers) often explode and occur in extraordinary numbers. Because increasers survive impoverished rangeland conditions, they usually compete with cattle for available forage, and, consequently, are often considered to be pests by ranchers and range managers.

All animals require a suitable habitat, and the grazing of domestic livestock deprives many species of this critical resource. When overgrazing is severe, few species survive. Other species prefer degraded environments, invade them, and flourish. In this way, grazing produces animal slums— old residents requiring a high-quality environment are extirpated and replaced by a few species able to survive in an impoverished environment. It's a bad trade—many species of interesting animals exchanged for a few species of less interesting pests. Unfortunately, vast areas of public rangeland have been converted to animal slums by overgrazing. In fact, some regions have been so badly abused that not even animal slums can prosper—just cows!

Harvester ants, common insects throughout arid rangelands of the West, build mounds as tall as 2.5 feet, remove all vegetation from a disc as large as 30 feet in diameter surrounding the mound, and forage on plants, especially seeds. When 25 or more mounds per acre are present (more than 80 per acre is common), the ants may remove vegetation from as much as 20 percent of the land and cause ranchers to launch poisoning campaigns. In some instances, harvester ants spoil range seedings by gathering the sown seeds and cutting newly sprouting plants. At a density of 20 colonies per acre, harvester ants may collect 20 pounds of forb seeds and 10 pounds of grass seeds per acre per year. One of the principal factors favoring high densities of harvester ant mounds is intensive livestock grazing.

In plant communities dominated by various species of sagebrush, plant-eating insects, primarily aphids and beetles, were more abundant on grazed plots than on ungrazed plots. When overgrazed sagebrush was killed and the range planted to an introduced crested wheatgrass, populations of a plant bug previously of no economic importance erupted and sharply reduced the productivity of the wheatgrass.

According to the U.S. Department of Agriculture, grasshoppers are the most important insect competitor for forage on western rangelands. Throughout the world, open semi-arid regions having sparse vegetation produce magnificent grasshopper populations. Several ecology textbooks and dozens of scientific papers based on studies in North America, Africa, and Australia cite overgrazing of rangelands as a major cause of severe grasshopper infestations. In 1935, a team of investigators observed "clouds of grasshoppers in heavily grazed areas and only an occasional hopper in lightly grazed areas." One researcher concluded, "Where judicious grazing occurs, grasshoppers do not or cannot permanently injure the range," and another warned, "Judicious management of cattle within selected grazing limits is the keynote of success in grasshopper control on the range." A uniform grassy cover is often recommended to reduce grasshoppers and discourage reproduction, and several authorities have even prescribed a three-strand barbed-wire fence as the best protection against grasshoppers! On over-grazed land, grasshopper eggs tend to hatch earlier because the sun is better able to reach and warm the soil and hasten the rate of egg development. Bare soil offers ideal sites for egg deposition.

In 1979, 7.2 million acres of the West were sprayed, mostly with malathion, an organophosphate insecticide, to kill grasshoppers. The war against grasshoppers is waged by the Animal and Plant Health Inspection Service (APHIS), a branch of the U.S. Department of Agriculture. Blocks of land having 10,000 or more contiguous acres are sprayed, if all landowners within the block agree to participate. On private land, half the cost is paid by the federal government and half by the private landowner. When public lands are sprayed, APHIS, using public funds, bears the entire cost, which was $1.50 per acre in 1980. APHIS, state departments of agriculture, and the cooperative extension service actively hustle landowners to participate in the program, which has become an "insecticide treadmill"—keeping a large number of bureaucrats gainfully employed while ignoring overgrazing as a basic ecological cause of grasshopper infestations.

Although malathion is less toxic than some other insecticides, it is nevertheless a broad-spectrum poison—killing all insects, not just grasshoppers. Spraying destroys the insect food sources of many birds, lizards, fish, and other animals and kills large numbers of important pollinating insects, such as bees, bumblebees, and butterflies. In several documented instances, grasshopper spraying has killed aquatic insects, crayfish, various species of fish, and other aquatic life, even though streams are supposed to be avoided by spray planes.

Ranchers holding grazing permits on public lands are especially fond of APHIS's grasshopper control program, because if the ranchers can persuade the Forest Service or BLM to spray grazing allotments, the taxpayers pick up the entire bill. Consequently, at the first sign of a few grasshoppers, ranchers call meetings, write congressmen, complain to the press, and exert enormous pressures to coerce agencies to spray.

In most instances, the benefits derived from spraying grasshoppers fail to justify the costs. For example, in southeastern Oregon it takes 7.8 acres of good to excellent BLM grazing land to feed a cow for a month. In 1983, when a rancher will pay $1.40 for a month's forage, it would cost $11.70 (at the 1980 rate of $1.50 per acre) to spray 7.8 acres for grasshoppers—thus the public would pay a subsidy of $10.30 a month for every cow grazing sprayed land. On poorer, less productive range, where as many as 29 acres are required to produce a month's forage for a cow, the cost of spraying would be $43.50 and the taxpayer's loss would be $42.10 *a month for every cow* using the sprayed range. What is worse, such unproductive rangelands are actually sprayed!

Studies done by the U.S. Department of Agriculture show that about 301,395 grasshoppers will eat as much forage as a cow. APHIS sprays when grasshopper infestations reach 8 grasshoppers per square yard (38,720 per acre). At that point, the grasshoppers on one acre are consuming only 12.8 percent as much as a cow, and it would cost $11.68 to kill 301,395 grasshoppers to prevent them from consuming

$1.40 worth of forage. Furthermore, 301,395 grasshoppers represent 680 pounds of high protein food, which if fed to chickens would produce much more human food than a cow—even after she had stomped around on the range for years. The point is, the entire program is a boondoggle—ranchers create the grasshopper problem by overgrazing and then expect to be rescued at public expense, no matter how absurd the cost-benefit ratio.

Frogs and salamanders are unusually vulnerable to the adverse effects of livestock grazing. Although egg and larval stages are spent in water, adults and young migrate considerable distances over land. Being slow and spending long periods concealed in patches of vegetation or in shallow burrows in the soil, many individuals are exposed to trampling. Excessive removal of vegetation by grazing livestock deprives frogs and salamanders of vital cover and resting sites and may adversely affect insects and other invertebrates used as food. Although many rangeland water holes are potentially useful breeding sites for amphibians, excessive use by livestock often destroys essential vegetation at the water's edge, churns up sediments in the water, and thoroughly tramples the area, thus rendering it unsuitable for amphibian use. Being insect eaters, frogs and salamanders are useful animals on rangelands, but are poorly adapted to survive the rigors of overgrazing.

Desert and semidesert shrublands of the West support a rich assemblage of lizards. Virtually all such land is grazed, most of it excessively. In comparing lizard populations on ungrazed and grazed desert shrubland, researchers have found twice as many lizards on ungrazed land. Furthermore, the total weight of lizards per unit area was 3.7 times greater on ungrazed plots. While desert horned lizards and leopard lizards did not occur at all on the grazed area, zebra-tailed lizards, which often run on the hind legs only and prefer scant vegetation, hardpan, and open terrain, were nearly twice as abundant on the grazed area.

In another study, lizards were more abundant and displayed greater species diversity on 6 of 7 lightly grazed sites than on comparable heavily grazed sites. The one exception was desert scrub habitat, which was the only site to retain its original vegetative structure after being heavily grazed, the reason being that cattle did not destroy the dominant shrub layer. Widely foraging species were more abundant on lightly grazed than on heavily grazed sites, and two species were not found at all on heavily grazed desert grassland. Also, lizards that forage by sitting and waiting in open spaces were more abundant in lightly grazed habitats. But species that forage while sitting and waiting on rocks, trees, tree limbs, and other objects tended to be more abundant in heavily grazed areas, presumably because cattle break off limbs, push over trees, and create litter that provides an abundance of perching sites. In general, heavy grazing reduces lizard abundance and diversity by destroying low-height vegetation, primarily perennial grasses and palatable shrubs. A similar physical alteration of vegetation would seem to account for the striking scarcity of lizards in crested wheatgrass seedings.

Snakes fare poorly on rangelands that are severely overgrazed. Most large seedings are devoid of suitable cover and offer exceptionally sterile surroundings for snakes. Some moderately grazed crested wheatgrass seedings, especially at lower elevations, may provide an adequate supply of rodents for food, but lack permanent populations of snakes because concealment cover and shade are unavailable.

In the Southwest, desert tortoises are unique and fascinating inhabitants of desert landscapes. Tortoises feed on plants, may live 100 years or more, and have a relatively low rate of reproduction. In recent decades, populations of desert tortoises have declined precipitously because of various human activities, especially livestock grazing. Grazing livestock consume the same plants used by tortoises for food, and when areas are heavily grazed, especially in the spring, tortoises are left with an inadequate diet for months at a time. Even without livestock, tortoises find scant food outside the brief period of spring abundance—and that abundance is not guaranteed every year in the desert. In addition to competing for food, livestock trample burrows, destroy vegetation used as temporary shelter, and trample individual tortoises, especially young whose shells remain soft and vulnerable until about 4 inches long. When livestock grazing deprives a female of proper nourishment, she may lay fewer eggs (if any) and may require 2 or 3 years to replace the fat reserves lost in egg laying. In southwestern Utah between 1935 and 1945, tortoise populations were estimated at about 150 per square mile, but by 1977 had declined to only 25 per square mile. Obviously, desert tortoises are incapable of competing effectively with domestic livestock and are at the mercy of the BLM on whose land most populations occur. In failing to protect desert tortoises, the BLM is disregarding its highest responsibility, which is to safeguard the public trust.

The best known examples of animal slums created by live-stock overgrazing involve rodents and rabbits. Many rodents, such as voles, prefer dense stands of stable, perennial vegetation. These animals, an important food source for various birds of prey and predators, decrease as grazing intensity mounts. Many other rodents are increasers, and as perennial vegetation gives way to annual grasses, forbs, and shrubs, these rodents flourish. Thus, as climax range vegetation reverts back to earlier stages of succession, pocket gophers, ground squirrels, kangaroo rats, pocket mice, prairie dogs, and other "animal weeds" are favored. For example, when overgrazing permits large numbers of forbs to invade dense stands of grass, the habitat for pocket gophers is enriched, and while the rancher blames the pocket gophers for deteriorating the range, the gophers are, in fact, only taking advantage of ideal conditions created by livestock grazing.

Although huge sums of public and private money have been spent in efforts to control many of these range pests (about 1.4 million pounds of grain laced with 1080 was used by animal damage control agents in 10 years—1961 to 1970), the benefits are short-lived and expensive. Poisoning campaigns directed at the black-tailed prairie dog have driven the black-footed ferret to the brink of extinction. Also, poisoning of rodents on rangelands exposes many valuable predators and birds of prey to the danger of secondary poisoning. Because the problem of rodent increasers is brought about by grazing, poisoning is not ecologically sound. Instead, the obvious way to control these unwelcome range pests is to decrease grazing pressures of livestock sufficiently to allow a good stand of grass to return—in other words, proper range management. Kangaroo rats and pocket mice, which are nocturnal seedeaters, even thrive on some crested wheatgrass seedings.

Jackrabbits are the most conspicuous and ubiquitous range animals (except for livestock) in the arid West, and when native grasslands are opened up by livestock overgrazing, jackrabbits move in and take over. Probably because they are so large and conspicuous, jackrabbits rival the coyote as a cause of mental anguish among ranchers. Once jackrabbits invade rangelands overgrazed by livestock, they may sustain large enough populations to perpetuate the overgrazing, even if livestock grazing is reduced.

Jackrabbit populations are cyclic, ranging from extreme scarcity to extreme abundance about every 5 to 10 years (average about 7 years), consequently, the newsworthiness of jackrabbits as range pests waxes and wanes with the cycle. Because jackrabbits provide as much as 75 percent of coyote diets, coyote control amplifies the abundance of jackrabbits during peak years, when populations in eastern Oregon alone have been estimated at 20 million rabbits. When populations reach peak numbers, jackrabbits abandon their normal habitat on overgrazed rangeland and invade alfalfa fields and other croplands. At these times, ranchers become frantic—they shoot rabbits, club thousands of rabbits to death in organized drives (as recently as 1982, about 100,000 jackrabbits were slaughtered in such drives in southeastern Idaho), and inundate the media with pleas for federal assistance. In 1915, Harney County, Oregon, responded to the rancher's plight by offering a 5-cent bounty for each jackrabbit, but after forking out $51,459.10 (a large sum in those days), the county's solvency was threatened and the offer was withdrawn.

Obviously, simultaneous campaigns to control coyotes and

jackrabbits at public expense are counterproductive and absurdly illogical.

When grazing becomes too severe, even jackrabbit populations decline. Although jackrabbits use the edges of seedings at night, they avoid venturing far into seedings or using them during the day because of the absence of protective cover and shade.

When grazing lands are abused by domestic livestock, occasionally there is a happy ending. In Africa, when cattle overgrazed the land, it became virtually worthless for further grazing and a huge invasion of Tsetse flies occupied the countryside. Because the flies carried a trypanosome parasite (a protozoan) to which cattle were highly susceptible, the cattle were quickly eradicated. With the cattle gone, the range vegetation recovered and grew rank and healthy. In the western United States, no such thing could happen, because when stockmen overgraze public lands and create range pests, there are no consequences to pay. Instead, the federal government exercises its immense generosity with public funds and rushes to the rescue with a large selection of free or inexpensive poisoning programs. Politically, it is a lot easier to poison vast acreages of public lands than to tell a western rancher that he must reduce his cow herd to the carrying capacity of his allotment. Until that situation changes, grazing slums will continue to be a part of the West.

RANGE IMPROVEMENTS?

A large percentage of the public grazing lands lie beaten and stripped of productivity by decades of abuse. Setting out to improve these lands is a national obligation—we owe it to the land and to generations unborn. Guided by the concept of multiple use, respect for ecologically balanced plant communities, and a modicum of common sense, we should be able to bring these public rangelands back and convert them into a source of national pride. Perhaps congress entertained such thoughts when it passed the Rangeland Improvement Act, with the support of several well-intentioned conservation organizations. But why did other conservation groups and many better-informed critics of federal range policies denounce and oppose the legislation? The answer is simple. Opponents of the act were people familiar with western rangelands—people who knew from experience that "range improvements" is a bureaucratic euphemism, a slick disguise for deceit, bad ecology, and corrupt economics. Although the notion of range improvements may have started with high purpose and promise of sound public benefits, it evolved quickly into a political ploy to avoid cutting livestock grazing to the carrying capacity of the land. Unfortunately, that has not changed, and on public rangelands today, "range improvement" can usually be defined as producing maximum forage for an increasing number of cows, sticking the taxpayers with the bill, and pretending that multiple use doesn't exist.

Sagebrush, several species of junipers, pinyon pine, and a few other species of plants have invaded millions of acres of western rangeland. It's still happening. In behalf of the livestock industry, some range spokesmen argue that these plants are inhabiting areas where they are not native and don't belong. These people avoid discussing why the plants have spread, who is going to pay the bill for removing them, or what the costs will be to wildlife, soils and other resources—they simply emphasize that these plants are competing with forage plants useful to livestock. An often repeated slogan of the industry states that for every 1 percent increase in sagebrush, cattle forage declines 3 to 5 percent. Biologically, this should come as no surprise, for historically, no cattle-like herbivore lived in the Great Basin region, thus, the vegetation of the area evolved without mechanisms for dealing with the impacts of the likes of cattle. When cattle were introduced into the region, shrubs increased, native grasses and forbs decreased, and plant communities were opened up to invading exotic weeds, annual grasses, and certain shrubs and trees.

Despite legitimate questions about the causes of brush invasion, the will of the livestock industry has prevailed, and millions of acres of land invaded by shrubs and trees have been sprayed with herbicides, plowed, chained, bulldozed, burned, or otherwise *treated* (an interesting euphemism) to kill the offending plants. So far, about 11 or 12 percent of the original land dominated by sagebrush has been cleared.

But when the invading shrubs have been eradicated, it soon becomes apparent that competition with forage plants wasn't really the problem after all. Now new complaints surface—no native plant is able to fill the vacuum left by shrub removal, the land has too little cover and needs protection from erosion, cheatgrass and other weeds are taking over the site, the native vegetation will probably come back, but it will take too long, the range is still not contributing to the local economy, if something isn't done, grazing cuts may be unavoidable, if the area could be made more productive, grazing pressure could be reduced on other overgrazed sites that have more potential for natural recovery, and so forth. All of this, of course, is leading up to the fact that the agency just happens to have the perfect solution—crested wheatgrass—it's fast, cheap, and according to its admirers, a miracle grass. When the proceedings reach this point, there is no time to discuss why crested wheatgrass is the choice, who is going to benefit, who is going to suffer, who is going to get stuck with the bill, or what the long-term consequences will be. When cows are hungry, ranchers antsy and grumbling, and the public a willing patsy, you get on with the seeding. By 1980, this type of range management had yielded 12.5 million acres of crested wheatgrass seedings, and when the federal money spigot begins flowing again, millions of additional acres of public rangelands are just waiting to be "improved" in the same manner.

Crested wheatgrass, a native of Turkestan, was introduced into the United States in 1898 and became popular in the northern plains and Montana in the 1920's. By the late 1930's, the grass was being planted in various places in the intermountain West, and after 1950, seeding crested wheatgrass became a rangeland mania.

Beginning in 1963 in the Vale BLM District of eastern Oregon, an 11-year project resulted in the seeding of 267,193 acres (about 10 percent of the federal rangeland in the district) at an estimated cost of $20 million (including roads, fences, cattle guards, water systems, etc.). The actual amount spent is a mystery because no separate accounting was kept of project funds. The project funds were simply added to regular funds for range improvements (which totalled about $127.6 million in the district during the 11 years), time spent by BLM personnel was not charged to the project, and other special funds spent simultaneously on other range improvements were apparently mixed and shuffled. The entire project seems to have been a gigantic boondoggle to reward the ranchers who had reduced the land to a state where seeding was necessary. Some people probably should have gone to jail!

In 1961, before the Vale Project began, the district supported 332 grazing permittees, 89,273 horses and cattle, and 40,077 sheep. By 1974, when the project was completed, the district had only 235 permittees, 75,893 horses and cattle, and 8,000 sheep. By 1980, the numbers had dwindled to 218 permittees, 70,627 horses and cattle, and 5,945 sheep. Obviously, these data reveal no benefits justifying a $20 million expenditure. Even if all present and past BLM expenditures for grazing since the initial investment of $20 million are ignored, it is still a shock to find that the Vale District will collect only about $590,000 in grazing fees in 1983. Of that amount, 50 percent will go for range improvements in the district, 12.5 percent goes to local governments, and 37.5 percent ($221,250) will be returned to the U.S. Treasury. Obviously, that amount doesn't even begin to pay the interest on the Vale Project, not to mention the principal!

In 1974, at the completion of the Vale Project, 235 permittees grazed in the *entire* Vale District, thus the federal expenditure for the project amounted to about $85,106 per permittee. But most of the money was spent on only 40 of the 147 allotments in the district, and these 40 allotments were probably grazed by no more than about 65 permittees, thus the federal expenditure amounted to about $307,692 each. Regardless of how the dollars were apportioned, the Vale Project was a spectacular public rip-off—a professional job of public embezzlement. What's worse, that special project represents only a fraction of the tax dollars spent in one small area by a single agency in 11 years, and it's a drop in the bucket compared to the public funds lavished on ranchers using public rangelands throughout the West.

By 1980, 740,042 acres (about 5 percent of the total) of the BLM rangelands in Oregon had been seeded to crested wheatgrass. Oregon's acreage, however, pales compared to that of some other states, like Idaho, which had seeded 1.6 million acres by 1978.

Crested wheatgrass seedings cost $15 to $62 per acre. The BLM sets costs at $20 to $30 per acre to prepare and seed the site, adds an additional cost of $10 to $20 per acre for watering systems, fences, and other facilities, and acknowledges substantial continuing costs for maintenance and administration; the initial cost seems to average about $40 per acre. Although it may seem strange, ranchers pay

the same fee (currently $1.40 per AUM) for grazing seedings as they do for grazing any other "unimproved" public rangeland.

Seeding is somewhat risky. Many fail to develop and turn into solid stands of cheatgrass and Russian thistle. When a seeding is successful, BLM policy requires a 2-year halt in grazing to give the new clumps of grass an opportunity to grow and become firmly established. Depending upon use and a host of other factors, the life span of seedings is usually 15 to 25 years, but others may last 30 years or longer. Sooner or later, sagebrush and other invading brush species reclaim the site and necessitate starting over with a new seeding. Once an area has been seeded, the combination of herbicide kill, intensive physical trampling, and competition with crested wheatgrass virtually eradicates native grasses and forbs, thus there is little choice but to reseed when brush reinvades. Furthermore, high-yielding stands of crested wheatgrass deplete soil nutrients, while dominating available soil moisture, thereby discouraging the re-establishment of desirable native species. Old worn-out seedings are less productive than the original overgrazed native vegetation. In other words, once a decision is made to seed, other alternatives of management are greatly diminished or forsaken, and the management agency is stuck with crested wheatgrass.

In their eagerness to excuse the fact that crested wheatgrass seedings are a sterile monoculture, many supporters of the livestock industry have started referring to communities of overgrazed sagebrush as a "sagebrush monoculture." They argue that seedings merely replace one monoculture with another. This is, of course, absurd. To begin with, it doesn't cost American taxpayers $40 an acre to get a stand of sagebrush! Furthermore, even the most pitifully overgrazed sagebrush community has much greater plant diversity than a wheatgrass seeding. More than 100 species of birds are known to forage and nest in sagebrush communities, but only the horned lark consistently uses seedings. It is biological nonsense even to suggest that one species of plant in an extensive seeding can meet the diverse food, cover, nesting, concealment, and other requirements of a diverse animal population. One authority stated, "A full stand of crested wheat is probably the most exclusive and least dynamic plant community found on western rangelands." Nevertheless, stockmen are not content to call crested wheatgrass a good cattle forage and let it go at that. Instead they continue their unconvincing argument that crested wheatgrass is actually a universal manna.

Conservationists have opposed extensive crested wheatgrass seedings because they are exotic monocultures and amount to little more than biological deserts. In contrast, small irregularly shaped seedings (e.g., 40 acres or so) create a maximum of biologically rich interfaces with other vegetation, increase vegetational diversity, and are, therefore, generally acceptable. But agencies, especially the BLM, have preferred large blocks of land simply because such areas are more cost-effective and provide more acceptable cost-benefit ratios. Of course, forage production is the only economic benefit considered. In Oregon, a 36-square mile seeding was recently proposed! Seedings of 600 to 2,500 acres are most common, but others have exceeded 10,000 acres. Again, the argument has been put forth that crested wheatgrass should be no more objectionable than cheatgrass, since both are exotics. True, but cheatgrass, another contribution of the livestock industry, is usually not a monoculture, doesn't cost $40 an acre, and if left alone, will often be replaced by something better. In Oregon, the BLM has recently recommended that seedings be kept at 600 acres or less and that irregular shapes be considered. Even agency personnel admit that seedings larger than 1,000 acres are difficult to manage properly.

Many of the crested wheat seedings throughout the West were unplanned. The BLM has available emergency funds for use in fire rehabilitation. When rangeland burns, the BLM moves in quickly and seeds the burned area to crested wheatgrass on the pretense of reducing soil erosion. This program has numerous severe defects.

Crested wheat is planted on burned sites, not because it is the best defense against erosion, but because it is a favored cattle forage. Even the Soil Conservation Service has a low opinion of crested wheat as an all-purpose plant for protecting soil from erosion. The normal procedure of seeding a summer burn in the fall yields only tiny sprouts of crested wheatgrass the next spring, when soil protection is most critical. Furthermore, heavy equipment used in seeding may actually encourage soil erosion by disrupting the protective surface of the soil, disturbing the ash layer, and injuring root systems of surviving plants. In semiarid climates, natural revegetation by a combination of annuals and native perennials will adequately cover a burn in the same time or more quickly than a seeding. Because seedings are expected to sustain heavy use by large numbers of cattle, the soils of the area are destined to suffer intense trampling and disturbance for the life of the seeding. Heavily grazed crested wheat offers minimal soil protection.

But the most serious fault of the rehabilitation program is that it openly invites range arson. Grazing permittees are aware that planting crested wheat seedings is usually a standard procedure after burns. Thus, a rancher disatisfied with an unproductive and overgrazed allotment needs only to drop a match and presto—he has a seeding! One rancher walked into a country store and reported that he had noticed a range fire on some BLM land down the road. He remarked, "If it's still burning next week when I'm in town, I may go by and tell the BLM about it." In the Burns (Oregon) BLM District, where all seedings average only 1,500 acres, fire rehabilitation seedings have been so numerous and closely spaced that the district now has two blocks of relatively contiguous seedings of 24,300 and 46,000 acres! Is this an act of God, or simply another example of the cowboys raiding the public till?

Although many claims are made for crested wheatgrass, most of these appear to be seriously flawed. Because crested wheat greens up about 3 weeks earlier than native ranges, seedings were supposed to be used early and permit a delay in turn-out on native range, thus reducing trampling damage. Also, seedings were supposed to take pressure off native range and give it a chance to recover. In practice, however, no one, not even ardent fans of the wonder grass, has attempted to demonstrate improvements of native range attributable to crested wheat seedings. In fact, where seedings are enclosed in an allotment with native range, the native range tends to suffer because of the heavier stocking rates on seedings.

Intensive use of seedings by wildlife is an imagined myth. Deer will sometimes use seedings during brief periods, but only if the crested wheat has been heavily grazed to remove dead stubble, but that, of course, renders the seeding un-attractive to most other forms of wildlife and vastly diminishes the already minimal role of crested wheat in protecting soil. Pronghorns prefer sage. And even though millions of acres have been planted to seedings, the experts are still arguing about seeding management—some say seedings are overgrazed, others contend that they aren't grazed enough. Most seedings are grazed but a few weeks a year. In a few instances other plants have been seeded with crested wheat to increase the attractiveness of the seeding to wildlife, however, the other plants (e.g., clover) tend to be selectively eaten out. In fact, given a choice, even cows prefer native perennial grasses. Native grasses are not seeded because of their low seed yield, low viability, and low germination rates. Critics argue that acceptable strains of native grasses could have been developed long ago if agencies had taken an interest when crested wheat seed first became commercially available in 1929.

Crested wheatgrass has become a dangerous fad, for it is thought of as a one-shot panacea to range problems. It is cheap, fast, and gets bureaucrats off the hook. But crested wheat seedings have no purpose beyond creating cow forage—they have no public benefits, only rancher benefits. Multiple use and long-range ecological concerns are totally ignored. No doubt seedings will continue, just because the BLM is embarrassed by 85 percent of its range being in an unsatisfactory or worse condition. But in the long run, total dependence on a single species of plant will backfire, just as would happen if we converted all croplands in the nation to corn fields.

From the beginning, stockmen had free run of all public grazing lands from sea level to the tops of the highest mountain ranges, and a precedent was set for livestock use of *all* public lands. The entire West became one huge, unfenced pasture on which the free-enterprise livestock industry cavorted. Early on, a virtual absence of fences nullified any agency intentions to seriously manage grazing lands. Later, when a policy of management could be delayed no longer, agencies were either unable or unwilling to insist upon cutting numbers of livestock to bring them into conformance with range carrying capacities. That decision carried with it two vitally important corollaries. First, it meant that if livestock numbers were not to be contained, then forage production had to be the prime concern in range management—all other resources and all other considerations automatically became secondary. Secondly, the agencies had to do something—something to convince the rest of the nation that troubled rangelands were receiving attention. Ideally that something should have an aura of scientific respectability (at least enough to hoodwink the general public) and should smack of modern technology (that would help the public forget the past abuses, which were simply testimony of a former period of ignorance). Range improvements were just what the doctor ordered, but it would not create the proper impression to scatter these about in random fashion. What was needed was range improvements incorporated into a *program*—a range management program accentuating the production of livestock forage, but salable to the public. Then came rest-rotation grazing and *voila*—the wish was granted.

While range management agencies were unwilling to reduce livestock numbers on large units of land, they were perfectly willing to fence these large units into myriad smaller pastures, each to be intensively managed for livestock grazing. Thousands of miles of new barbed-wire fences, thousands of expensive water developments, new roads, cattle guards, and all the other paraphernalia meant grandiose budgets for the agencies, increased personnel, and all the trappings of a rapidly growing bureaucracy.

Again, the ball was tossed to the taxpayers. Furthermore, people concerned about soil, water, air, wildlife, and other resources of rangelands were stunned. What about multiple use? The livestock industry and their supporters were absolutely floored by this lack of appreciation. "What about all those *wildlife* water holes?" And the clincher—some of those little pastures in a system of rest-rotation grazing are going to be "resting" every once in a while, and the cattle are going to be moved around from place to place. Yes, sort of a gigantic publicly financed shell game. Cattle are going to be used to tromp seed into the ground, intensive grazing will remove the stubble and dead vegetation and make it available to wildlife, rangeland vegetation will be more effectively converted into useful red meat, fire hazards will be reduced, intensive grazing will stimulate plant vigor— these and other benefits were promised. But who wanted them besides stockmen?

Is there no end to what the public is expected to pay for the 3 percent of the nation's beef produced on public rangelands? Rest-rotation grazing has grown into a form of madness. Agencies, especially the BLM, are counting on such systems to solve grazing problems. The decision to implement this controversial and expensive panacea has drawn shouts of derisive criticism from every segment of the conservation community. Skeptics have wisely asked the BLM to reconsider its commitment to rest-rotation, at least long enough to determine whether or not the presumed benefits are real or illusory. But the bureaucratic wheels were already in motion, and more than $2 billion is authorized for rangeland improvements on BLM lands in the next 20 years— that's $95,238 for each grazing permittee.

Rest-rotation grazing fails to address the problem of riparian zone abuses, and since the system demands intensive use, it promises to aggravate an already serious concern. A few months of rest now and then is not going to benefit wildlife habitat, especially when during years of use, the vegetation will be thoroughly stripped from the same land. No doubt, a pair of killdeer or an occasional pair of mallards will use some of the water holes, but with intensive grazing, most water holes will be fouled by livestock and laid bare to the elements. In Colorado, rangelands near overused water holes absorbed only a third as much rainfall as good grasslands some distance away. Furthermore, the water holes will encourage cattle to concentrate in areas formerly used exclusively by wildlife. Also, thousands of miles of fences will eventually make it impossible for big game to move freely, and the peril of entanglement in fences will statistically increase to unacceptable levels. Finally, the system of roads and other structures used to service the small grazing units will open up back country to increased erosion, disturbance, and hunting pressure—especially road hunting and poaching in places that cannot be adequately patrolled by law enforcement officers. For example, Malheur National Forest already has 7,102 miles of roads—and is building more. Bill Meiners, formerly a range specialist with the BLM, has best described rest-rotation grazing—he says it's a "bummer."

Perhaps the most objectionable of all forms of range improvement is the practice of allowing grazing permittees to make desired improvements on public lands with their own funds. This practice has generally been discouraged by federal agencies, but a certain amount of it has been overlooked or even encouraged. But the Reagan Administration, with its strong sympathies for private enterprise, has openly invited ranchers to invest in rangeland improvements on public grazing lands. The danger of permitting such a policy is that it bestows upon the rancher a quasi-legal ownership in the land. Once the grazing permittee considers himself a co-owner of federal grazing property, the managing agency is rendered powerless in enforcing the provisions of the grazing permit. Furthermore, when a permit expires, it is virtually unthinkable for it not to be renewed if the rancher owns stationary fixtures on the land.

In the early 1980's, the Reagan Administration, which favors converting all public lands to private ownership, has gone a step further in giving grazing permittees a foothold in the ownership of their grazing allotments. Water rights on public lands are currently reserved for public use by an executive order signed by President Coolidge in 1926. But the Solicitor General in Secretary of the Interior James Watt's office has issued an opinion questioning the validity of the public's claim to waters on public lands! Urged by ranchers and several members of the Sagebrush Rebellion, the Nevada Cattlemen's Association passed a resolution calling for Coolidge's order to be annulled. The National Cattlemen's Association quickly chimed in with a similar resolution. Although copies of these resolutions were sent to President Reagan, who supported the Sagebrush Rebellion in his 1980 campaign, the principal assistance is expected to come from Nevada's Senator Paul Laxalt, who is one of Reagan's closest friends, Reagan's 1980 campaign manager, and recent Republican National Chairman. Should this attempt to steal public water rights prove successful, it would virtually eliminate any voice or influence the public might have in the management of public rangelands—and the public has pitifully little influence as it is.

Also, in 1983, as a part of his "Good Neighbor" policy, Secretary of the Interior James Watt announced plans for a 10-year "stewardship" program for selected ranchers. Under the program, ranchers using BLM land would pay for capital improvements, such as fences and water holes. In return, the BLM would grant these ranchers greater freedom of operation—fewer examinations of range condition, fewer checks of numbers of animals using an allotment, and possibly no designated grazing season! To make certain that the BLM grants ranchers increased freedom, Watt's proposed BLM budget for 1984 calls for a $7.4 million cut in range management and a massive reduction in range personnel. Although only ranchers with a "good" record of stewardship would be eligible to participate, this program revives most of the abuses found on public rangelands a century ago.

So, what is left to be said? Range improvements are nothing more than a massive public subsidy to livestock ranchers. If it were only a matter of public dollars being squandered on a minority commodity interest, that would be one thing, but range improvements are accomplished at the total expense of all other constituencies and resources of rangelands. The public's right to the benefits of multiple use is being gradually diminished for notions of questionable ecological validity. Recklessness has been substituted for sound stewardship. In short, current policies governing public rangelands are an outrage—a sort of wayward and self-serving juggernaut that views contemptuously any values or interests beyond those of its approximately 36,000 ranching clientele. Surely, the time is long overdue for the other 233 million of us to express some indignation and insist upon some drastic changes.

MULTIPLE USE—A CHARADE

Multiple use has been defined in many ways. One popular definition states that multiple use is managing the resources of the land for the maximum benefit of the largest number of people. Regardless of definition, multiple use implies that lands and their resources are to be used according to relative importance, but in a manner that protects and perpetuates them. Public lands, except for wildlife refuges (where wildlife is supposed to be given highest priority) and a few lesser holdings, are to be managed according to the principles of multiple use—it's the law, clearly and unequivocally.

The charge given to land management agencies by congress in the Federal Land Policy and Management Act (1976) is worth quoting, ". . .management of the public lands and their various resource values so that they are utilized in the combination that will best meet the needs of the American people. . .a combination of uses that takes into account the long term needs of future generations for renewable and non-renewable resources, including, but not limited to, recreation, range, timber, minerals, watershed, wildlife and fish, and natural scenic, scientific and historical values. . .harmonious and coordinated management of the various resources without permanent impairment of the productivity of the land and the environment with consideration being given to the relative values of the resources and not necessarily to the combination of uses that will give the greatest economic return or the greatest unit output.''

In practice, on the nation's public rangelands, multiple use is merely a charade, a convenient smokescreen used by management agencies to justify the exploitation of public lands and resources by favored commodity interests. Calling the BLM the Bureau of *Livestock* Management is not just sarcastic humor, for if the agency were to abandon its grazing program, in most of the West, it could close shop, disappear, and hardly be missed. The BLM exists for ranchers and cows. While the Forest Service is less narrow in perspective and somewhat less blatant in its favoritism to commodity interests, the agency makes few bones about it—lumbermen come first, stockmen second, and everyone else can exercise their rights to multiple use by picking through the residue that is left.

It's not a case of other constituencies being denied access to public rangelands—far from it. The BLM and Forest Service encourage citizens to seek multiple uses of the lands, string counters across access roads, and tally the resulting body counts in annual reports. Nevertheless, citizens interested in multiple uses and the resources most cherished by these citizens are merely tolerated, denied the same attention given dominate users, and expected to manage with the impacts and remnants of commodity exploitation.

Thus, the weekend camper using the BLM campground at Jackman Park on Steens Mountain in southeastern Oregon finds a herd of Herefords milling about in the campground, stands in fresh cow manure while preparing meals at campground tables, and drinks water piped from an unfenced spring, which is stomped and fouled by cattle. Fishermen in the Malheur National Forest are forced to abandon a favorite trout stream as the banks collapse, the stream becomes shallow with silt and gravel, the riparian vegetation disappears, flow diminishes, and trout vanish. Before launching, boaters at Owyhee Reservoir at the mouth of Leslie Gulch on BLM land must chase cattle from the boat ramp and may be unable to move their vehicle and boat trailer off the launch ramp because cattle excrement has turned it into a slick and filthy quagmire. During terrible winters when bighorn sheep at Leslie Gulch are driven by weather to seek refuge in the protected canyon, they find only beaten sagebrush, scant cheatgrass, and a few scattered tumbleweeds left by the herd of cattle that overgrazed the narrow canyon through the summer. And on the Umatilla National Forest, hundreds of cattle occupy the land into November, slicking off every twig of forage or browse, and when snow piles up 2 feet deep and temperatures plummet to 20 below zero, herds of hungry elk search the denuded land for enough nourishment to stay alive. And these are just a few examples of multiple use as practiced on public rangelands—examples are legion, as most western outdoorspersons can testify. Salmon fishermen, downstream water users, flood victims, bird-watchers, photographers, hunters, fishermen, trappers, and just about everyone else have learned to play second fiddle to cows. It's disgraceful, but until livestock numbers are reduced to the carrying capacity of rangelands, a valid policy of multiple use is physically and biologically impossible. Meanwhile, valuable and irreplaceable rangeland resources will continue to suffer, and agencies will grasp at every wild scheme promising a quick fix for grazing problems.

How do management agencies justify such public contempt and open defiance of the law's intent? There are several explanations. Although the concept of multiple use encompasses values that cannot easily be measured in dollars, agencies have, nevertheless, used economic considerations as a basis for decisions and actions. In justifying its massive program to convert rangelands into crested wheatgrass seedings, the BLM states, "Benefit-cost ratios tend to favor projects which generate high market values. Thus, projects having significant environmental, social, political, or scientific benefits which are difficult to value economically are at a disadvantage when compared to developments which have high market value."

High market value indeed! What utter nonsense. In 1983, the Forest Service and BLM *combined* will collect about $25 million in grazing receipts for use of the public rangelands entrusted to them. Of the $25 million, about $9.4 million will go to the U.S. Treasury. In contrast, each year Americans spend $517 million on *birdseed*—more than 55 times the income the public receives for permitting western stockmen to monopolize 361 million acres of public rangeland.

"Multiple Use is one thing...
But this is Ridiculous!!"

Furthermore, the annual livestock values derived from grazing federal rangelands in the 11 western states are estimated to be about $390 million—far less than the national birdseed bill.

American hunters and fishermen spend about $15.8 *billion* (not million) annually in pursuit of their sports, yet the BLM has the audacity to tell us that they plant crested wheatgrass, a biological desert having lousy watershed values, because of high market value. Obviously, the BLM has become so mesmerized by cows that it has completely lost sight of what constitutes values in other sectors of society.

The refusal of rangeland management agencies to put into effect an equitable and balanced program of multiple use is difficult to comprehend. Congress has issued a clear legal mandate. Furthermore, the American people have, for more than a quarter century, steadfastly supported environmental protection and shown a willingness to pay for it, even through recessions, times of high unemployment, and adverse political climates. Clearly, the public expects more from its vast holdings of public lands than 2 pounds of hamburger per person per year. One needs only to examine the life-styles and everyday values of our citizenry to see evidence of these higher expectations.

According to data gathered by the U.S. Census Bureau in 1980, each year 100 million Americans (more than 50 percent of all adults) participate in outdoor recreation relating to fish and wildlife. About 42 million fish, 17 million hunt, and 83 million observe wildlife, hike, photograph nature, or enjoy other "nonconsumptive" uses of the out-of-doors. These people spend an incredible $40 billion a year in pursuit of their recreation and sport. (Note: In 1983, the value of *all* U.S. cattle was $46.7 billion.) As a group, they tend to be unusually well-educated, a high percentage of them are active and young, and they tend to be politically aware. Furthermore, outdoor recreation and its supporters are growing faster than the general population. In 1955, outdoor recreationists spent about $155 each on their activities, but today, that expenditure has climbed to $500. In 1965,

Americans made 27.2 million recreation visits to public lands, but in 1978, recreation visits had soared to 196 million. Hunters alone spend more than 300 million days in the field, and a large percentage of those days are spent on public lands. Yet in 1979, the BLM spent nearly $69 million on range improvements for its 21,000 grazing permittees, but only $21.4 million on recreational programs, and $9.9 million of that went for wilderness review—an administrative task!

Obviously, if agencies examine economic realities, no legitimate economic justification can be found for sacrificing true multiple use of public rangelands to livestock domination. Furthermore, by ignoring, or at least giving low priority to the multiple use interests of 100 million citizens having substantial claim to the public land and its resources, management agencies seem to be committing political suicide. After all, public agencies should be interested in cultivating the goodwill and support of such a formidable block of voters. Why are management agencies willing to take such bold political risks in behalf of the western livestock industry?

Western politicians, livestock associations, and stockmen maintain a solid and unified front and have conspired to provide a secure political umbrella under which management agencies can operate. In contrast, the myriad groups interested in other aspects of rangeland environments have never spoken in unison. Because of internal bickering, competition for members, differing goals, and lack of communication, out-of-doors groups, while representing a powerful but sleeping giant, have been ineffective in making use of their potential political clout. Meanwhile, free-wheeling expenditures of public funds in grazing programs have fueled the rapid growth and expansion of management agencies and have made them bold. Ranchers, associations, federal agencies, and sympathetic western politicians have found effective allies in the range departments of most western land grant universities and in county agents and other employees of the cooperative extension service. These groups, being vigilant and industrious, with regard to rangeland issues, despite their minority status, have out-gunned multiple use advocates almost every time.

Day-to-day operating procedures are rigged to benefit commodity interests. For example, BLM district managers appoint advisory boards to assist them in management decisions. These boards, however, are stacked with grazing permittees and their allies. For example, Secretary of Interior Watt has favored members of his own political party (Republican) and has even appointed industrial lobbyists and ranchers to represent wildlife interests. In the past, a token "environmentalist" was appointed to represent all interests beyond grazing. Just sitting with such a board is an intimidating experience if you aren't wearing cowboy boots. Although multiple use charades may be played at these meetings, the cows always win.

Both the Forest Service and BLM have been instructed by congress to examine their landholdings for potential units to be considered for possible designation as wilderness. Ranchers vehemently oppose wilderness, especially BLM wilderness, despite the fact that such lands are open to grazing—ostensibly because they won't be permitted to drive pickups on wilderness lands to deliver blocks of salt to livestock. Also, the BLM is preparing environmental impact statements for all its grazing districts. Many other important decisions are being made, and all of these, by law must be subjected to public scrutiny in public hearings. The hearings, however, are customarily held in small western cow towns or logging communities, where the meeting halls are packed with cattlemen, loggers, and local supporters of commodity uses. A Sierra Club member in this atmosphere would feel like a Christian among the lions. In other words, it takes immense courage and a reckless disregard for personal health to attend one of these meetings and to get up and speak in behalf of any resource other than forage and livestock. Obviously, the decisions made in such meetings deal with issues of *national* concern, yet the meetings are conducted in a manner to insure control by local and commodity interests. No doubt, the outcome of such meetings would be quite different if they were held in

Boston, New York, or Chicago, where citizens have a legitimate interest in *their* public lands, yet the procedure excludes them and their opinions. With such a system, multiple uses don't have a chance.

Agency budgets virtually eliminate all possibilities of true multiple use. To begin with, non-commodity programs are given only token funding. But even these miniscule amounts are generally used to remedy intolerable conditions created by dominant uses. Thus, when the Donner and Blitzen River, originally one of Oregon's finest trout streams, was virtually destroyed by cattle overgrazing (a ravaged riparian zone, collapsing banks, siltation, high water temperatures, etc.) the BLM expressed concern, but could do nothing until "wildlife funds" were appropriated to fence out the cattle once every few years! Strange logic. Almost nothing is done exclusively for the benefit of wildlife. For example, wildlife funds are often used for fences, water holes, seedings, and other "wildlife improvements" that end up being beneficial principally to the grazing program. Thus, even the pittance budgeted for non-commodity uses ends up lining rancher's pockets. Surely, this type of sham violates the spirit of the law, if not the letter.

Among employees of the Forest Service and BLM are many sincere, bright, and dedicated advocates of realistic multiple use. Most often, these are specialists trained in wildlife or fisheries management, recreation, archaeology, or other noncommercial disciplines. Underbudgeted and eclipsed by their cowboy-boot-bedecked colleagues in grazing programs, most of these employees live in frustration, and many become candidates for ulcers, transfer, or early retirement. Conservationists should identify such employees and encourage them to stick it out—the nation needs their talents. But that isn't enough—the political climate of federal agencies must be restructured to encompass multiple use and its advocates.

Perhaps significant changes are forthcoming. Opposition to public grazing subsidies and unacceptable environmental costs, such as soil erosion, diminished water supplies, deterioration of wildlife habitat, and others, is growing. As more and more of the nation's population lives in metropolitan and urban areas, resentment of the costs and problems created by a rural and ever-demanding livestock industry is bound to intensify. Strong support for the concept of multiple use exists in urban centers, as illustrated in a recent statewide poll in California showing strong approval for efforts to protect and manage resources of the state's deserts. With increased growth of urban centers and more leisure time, greater recreational use will be made of public lands. The day may come when urban citizens are unwilling to share a campground with a cow. Because the fastest growing demands on public lands are for nonconsumptive uses, it is only a matter of time until urban voters and nonconsumptive users gain a stronger voice in determining policies of public land use. In California, our most populous state, 90.9 percent of the population lives in urban areas—in Nevada it's 80.9 percent, 80.4 percent in Utah, 79.6 percent in Arizona, and 78.5 percent in Colorado. Because the population of the 11 western states is growing at a rate more than double that of the rest of the nation, urban growth is rising swiftly.

As the nation becomes more sophisticated and better enlightened through rapid communication and the "information explosion", poor land stewardship, degradation, pollution, and unpleasant aesthetics may become increasingly unacceptable. The value of stable and healthy environments is gaining esteem. Already many conservationists are pointing out that wilderness *is* multiple use, in other words, healthy watersheds, reservoirs of clean air, a diversity of plant habitat, flourishing animal communities, pools of genetic diversity, and opportunity for various types of recreation have immense public worth that need not be translated into dollars to be justified. Once such thinking gains widespread acceptance, it will no longer be possible to convince the public that the only value on rangelands is forage or that a blade of grass is wasted if a cow doesn't eat it.

Today, the BLM manages some 400 million acres of land in Alaska and in the lower 48 states. About 326 million acres are classified as big game habitat, 353 million acres as small game habitat, and 82 million acres as waterfowl habitat. These lands include 47 million acres of wetlands, 30 million acres of riparian lands, 669,000 miles of perennial streams, and more than 4.8 million acres of lakes and reservoirs. No agency in American government manages more wildlife habitat than the BLM. One out of every 5 big game animal in the United States lives on BLM lands—50 percent of the moose, 65 percent of the mule deer, and 45 percent of the pronghorns. More than half of the West Coast catch of salmon and steelhead comes from spawning beds within these lands, and more than 93,000 miles of fishable streams are included. In addition, BLM lands harbor most of the nation's important archaeological sites, paleontological deposits, and habitat for more than 200 species of threatened or endangered wildlife. The list goes on and on. But the point is, can an agency entrusted with so much of the nation's natural wealth and heritage be permitted to only espouse multiple use, or must it actually *practice* multiple use? To date, the BLM has routinely breached most management principles inherent in the concept of public trust.

Put another way, for the sake of a few cows, does the American public really want these lands to be poisoned for grasshoppers, rid of predators, chained and sprayed with herbicides to kill plants, converted to crested wheatgrass seedings, and insulted in all the other ways necessary to sustain the western livestock industry at a maximum level?

Multiple use, at best, is a faulty concept. Obviously, swimmers, waterfowl, hunters, fishermen, fur-bearing animals, water skiers, and speed boats cannot simultaneously use a small body of water. Some parcels of land have special or unique values and cannot be submitted to every rangeland use. For such lands, uses that damage the resource are inappropriate—noncommercial uses must be given highest priority if the resource is to be protected and preserved.

With multiple use, there will always be conflicts among the various users and uses of land. But on public rangelands, multiple use is all we have. Therefore, the general public is

"THAT AIN'T THE KIND OF RENEWING
THIS RESOURCE NEEDS !///"

obligated to insist that it be properly and fairly administered—precisely as the law of the land specifies. Today, that
is certainly not the case.

In September 1982, Robert Burford, Director of the BLM
in the Reagan Administration, in speaking to the National
Public Lands Council whose members are ranchers holding
BLM grazing permits, stated: "When I came to the Bureau
of Land Management about 18 months ago, I found that our
public lands were being 'managed', not as public lands belonging to all the taxpayers of this nation, but as private
playgrounds for a number of special interest groups whose
primary concern was the preservation of those playgrounds.
That's a lousy way to run a railroad—and we've all suffered
for it. Locking up, or regulating, public resources so excessively that they can only be used by a chosen few is not
management. It's heresy."

THE CLOUT OF A FEW

In the early West, stockmen grew accustomed to taking what they wanted—power, land, water, or whatever. After all, everybody's land is nobody's land. Thus, while public rights were suppressed or nonexistent, individual rights flourished without meaningful restraints. In the power shakeout, stockmen battled settlers, cattlemen battled sheepmen, and big operators battled little ones for supremacy. Individualism, one of the West's favorite illusions, was virtually synonymous with personal greed and ambition, and it fit perfectly into the national design, which was to reap an enormous wealth of resources from a wild and forbidding frontier and convert the dollars into a strong and vigorous nation. Exploitation of the West was an urgent task—obstacles could not be tolerated and weren't. In this frenzied atmosphere, western stockmen seized power and learned how to wield it. They learned well.

Today, the West and the nation have changed drastically, but stockmen haven't. Upon attaining a state of middle-aged maturity, the nation no longer feels compelled to exhaust every goody in nature's pantry and has consented to setting aside some forests, parks, watersheds, and other resources for the future. Through the years, the people have entrusted the federal government with safeguarding these and other public resources, with insuring their wise and proper use, and with managing the public heritage in perpetuity. This has placed constraints on the western livestock industry— and it doesn't like it.

Today, western stockmen strive to capitalize on their role as pioneers in the settlement of the West, and in every confrontation argue their "right" to special consideration because of what their ancestors did for the developing nation. No credit is given to homesteaders and all the others who also contributed. Furthermore, today's stockmen retain a lust to liquidate, to get cows on every acre, to confiscate the commons. This burning desire to exploit would be bad enough, but is augmented by ranchers having inherited sufficient political power, sense of superiority, dogged boldness, and pure temerity to *insist* upon having their way. Stockmen have kept the West in constant turmoil.

From the time the federal government undertook to manage and regulate grazing on public lands, ranchers have had a field day. Most of the battles have centered around efforts to cut back on numbers of cattle and length of grazing season, or to increase grazing fees. But these issues are only the tip of the iceberg, for the real objective of stockmen has been to convert privileges granted them on public lands into basic personal rights—rights that come without government or public regulation or intervention.

Volumes could be written about the stubbornness, cussedness, ploys, chicanery, gyrations, deceit, ruthlessness, viciousness, and skulduggery employed by western stockmen to impose their will on public lands. William Voigt, a former Executive Director of the Izaak Walton League, has done a masterful job of documenting and describing these tantrums in a superb book, *Public Grazing Lands—Use and Misuse by Industry and Government.* Voigt's book should be required reading for all citizens having an interest in public lands.

From the time of its inception in 1905 until the start of World War I, the Forest Service accomplished little in gaining control of grazing. During the war, when patriotic fervor filled the forests with record numbers of livestock, ranges were severely damaged. In the ensuing years, some progress was made towards reducing grazing pressure, and by 1925, the Forest Service had resolved to bring grazing within carrying capacity of the range. (Note: By 1983, it still hasn't happened.) Then came the Great Depression and severe drought years—the Forest Service relented and pushed grazing cuts into the future.

Finally, in 1945, with World War II ending, the Forest Service decided to move—to take control of grazing— livestock numbers were to be reduced and grazing seasons altered as needed to put overgrazed ranges on the road to recovery. Except in emergencies, cuts were to be gradual, explained thoroughly to permittees (often with on-site tours of affected allotments), and as fair as possible. Normal channels were open to permittees wishing to appeal decisions. The program was reasonable and necessary. For example in 1948 when in full swing, proposed cuts would have reduced sheep grazing by 0.2 percent and cattle grazing by only 0.03 percent. Nevertheless, the western livestock industry erupted in blind fury and rage—the Forest Service had become too uppity and had to be taught a lesson.

Meanwhile, the Grazing Service, which had been born in chains provided by the livestock industry, had muddled along for several years. The agency was a firm captive of advisory boards of stockmen, and any thought of ministering to a wider public interest in the management of public-domain lands was foreign and unthinkable. Then, despite the careful scrutiny of stockmen and their political allies, a trained range manager, formerly with the Forest Service, slipped in to become Director of the Grazing Service. At that time, ranchers were paying 5 cents (the price of a package of chewing gum) a month to graze a cow and her calf on public-domain lands. In 1944, with World War II drawing to a close and in a time of national camaraderie brought about by the approaching end of that terrible conflict, the new director did the most dastardly thing he could have done—he suggested that public forage on Grazing Service lands ought to be worth 15 cents an AUM (the Forest Service was charging 26 cents). This fellow even hinted an intention to *manage* these lands for the benefit of the resource! That did it—first the Forest Service, now the Grazing Service. It was time for western stockmen to show these swivel-chaired bureaucrats who was running the show.

In former times when ranchers dealt with adversaries, violence was customary—guns, ropes, arson, or other forms of mayhem. But in dealing with federal agencies and employees, such techniques would likely prove to be counterproductive; more devious methods would be required, but, of course, these must carry sufficient force to be convincing. Stockmen prefer power—not talk. But being a minority commodity interest, they have seldom been able to marshal widespread public support for their causes, consequently, most battles have been kept localized and concealed within industry channels so as not to arouse the sleeping masses. Although they are few, stockmen don't often lose—perhaps a battle now and then, but not wars.

In local areas, stockmen have various methods of dealing with errant agency employees. Included are outright defiance of orders and policies, personal harassment and abuse (telephone threats, social snubbing of families, beating of school children, arranging to have electricity turned off, humiliation in local newspapers, etc.) If these measures fail to attain desired results or to bring about voluntary transfer of the federal employee, then ranchers and advisory boards begin writing letters to congressmen, senators, other elected officials, and to administrators of the employee's agency. These complaints state that the employee is arrogant, doesn't sympathize with the industry, doesn't know his job, and that matters have gone so far that the employee can no longer be effective in performing his assigned duties in that community, and should, therefore, be shipped out *for the good of the agency.*

If grazing cuts are an issue, or if fee increases are in the offing, ranchers bring in "experts" from land grant universities. These fellows readily testify that the agency's data are erroneous, that the land is not overgrazed, that cuts are unnecessary, and that higher fees are unfair because the ranchers are already losing money. Invariably, a long-term study of the issues in contention is proposed, but meanwhile cuts will not be made and fees will remain unchanged until the results of the study are available.

Eventually, resolutions seeking the transfer of an employee, threatening agency budgets, or demanding solutions for perceived wrongs are adopted by the local stockgrower's association, then shouted through the convention of the state stockgrower's association, and forwarded to the national organizations. The American National Livestock Association (cattle) and the National Woolgrower's Association (sheep), whose members formerly murdered and maimed each other, ravaged one another's property, killed each other's livestock, and perpetrated every manner of mutual mayhem, have become the closest allies and speak with a common voice in opposition to federal grazing regulations and policies. Professional lobbyists for these organizations mingle among the powerful of the nation's capitol—urging, pressuring, cajoling, and never ceasing to extoll their positions. Ranchers always complain of hard times, but times never get so bad that these slick dudes must be fired!

Finally, the real power of the livestock industry on public lands is clearly vested in the elected politicians from western states—especially those having a livestock background and those holding grazing permits themselves. As early as 1925, when the Forest Service was building up courage to bring livestock numbers within carrying capacity of ranges, Oregon's Senator Robert N. Stanfield, himself a rancher and Forest Service permittee, went to bat for stockmen and feigned utter shock at the notion that public forage ought to be worth as much as private forage.

In bringing the Forest Service and Grazing Service to heel, stockmen used all these methods and more. But the clout of a few was most apparent in a series of "investigations" of federal grazing policies launched by Nevada's Senator Pat McCarran and Wyoming's Representative Frank A. Barrett.

From 1941 until 1945, McCarran held hearings intermittently in cow towns and remote communities throughout the West. Although he heard testimony on Forest Service grazing matters, he took special aim at the Grazing Service charged with administering public grazing districts under the Taylor Grazing Act and at the General

Land Office charged with administering other public-domain lands. Federal employees were dragged before McCarran in a kangaroo court atmosphere, humiliated, badgered, and grilled. Stockmen were invited to relate details of every complaint against federal agencies, no documentation of charges was necessary, and when ranchers failed to volunteer damaging evidence against agencies, McCarran led witnesses in the proper direction. Friendly stockmen were invited to sit with the senator and to interrogate and cross-examine federal employees.

While McCarran was instilling fear into the Grazing Service and making certain that it stayed under the thumb of the livestock industry, he managed to slash the agency's budget, as a form of added insurance. By the end of his investigations, he had thoroughly gutted the Grazing Service, then managed to destroy it and the General Land Office altogether, by merging them into the Bureau of Land Management in 1946. Then, he saw to it that the BLM was set adrift without sufficient budget to do a proper job of managing the public grazing lands and with a staff that was totally demoralized and castigated.

While Senator McCarran was molding the Grazing Service, Representatives Barrett (chairman), D'Ewart (Montana), and Rockwell (Colorado), all stockmen themselves, were castigating the Forest Service with a similar series of hearings. For these hearings, the national associations had lined up so many complaining stockmen that a parade marshall was necessary to arrange order of testimony and call witnesses in proper order. Meeting halls were crammed with boot-stomping ranchers who were encouraged to applaud, jeer, boo, and lend a circus-like atmosphere to the proceedings. With the Chief of the Forest Service at a front table with members of his regional staff, a parade of ranchers complained about lack of stability in the industry, being subjected to experiments, the service's arbitrary and dictatorial policies, failure of the service to keep agreements, big game eating all the forage, and so forth. The Forest Service was not permitted to answer charges at the hearings, but could put them in the written records at a later date. Time and again, members of the committee threatened to cut the Forest Service's budget. Every stockman was given all the time he wished, but Forest Service witnesses and the testimony of conservation organizations were delayed, usually until late afternoon or evening sessions, when time was short and testimony had to be limited to 5 minutes per person. After one hearing, a witness complained that of 15 hours of testimony, only one and a half hours were given to witnesses outside the livestock industry. These hearings were such a travesty of justice and filled with so many boisterous excesses that the *Denver Post* called them "Congressman Barrett's Wild West Show." Testimony ran to 1,500 pages. However, much to Congressman Barrett's chagrin, toward the end of the hearings, irate mayors, civic organizations, engineers, and many other groups began to appear and insist upon being heard as they told how overgrazing was destroying city water supplies. Barrett decided to call it quits.

Now, one might imagine that with the McCarran and Barrett hearings whipping the federal agencies into submission that the stockmen could afford to relax a bit. Not so. They had still another ace up their sleeves—one that would really put the fear of God into land management agencies.

In 1946, the American Livestock Association and the National Woolgrower's Association met in Salt Lake City and formed the Joint National Livestock Committee on Public Lands whose purpose was to prepare legislation for one of the greatest land grabs ever attempted. The stockmen intended to gain title to 157 million acres of public-domain grazing lands, some 80 million acres of national forest grazing lands, plus sizeable acreages of grazing lands in national parks. Senator Pat McCarran attended the meeting and lent support to the plotters.

The scheme called for "returning" public lands to the states (of course, the states never owned them in the first place), after which, the lands would be sold for a few cents (10 cents seemed fair!) an acre to the ranchers who then held permits to graze the lands. A rancher would have 15 years in which to decide to buy, and if so, would have an additional 30 years in which to pay, with the interest on the mortgage being 1.5 percent. Of course, any stockmen choosing not to buy would be allowed to continue grazing under the permit system. Initially, the timber and minerals on the land were to be included in the sale.

Before the Joint National Livestock Committee on Public Lands could get their land-grab scheme perfected, Senator E. V. Robertson (Wyoming), a sheep and cattle rancher who held Forest Service grazing permits, let the cat out of the bag. He introduced in the 79th Congress a bill to transfer all public-domain lands including mineral rights to 13 western states for ultimate sale or disposition as the states saw fit, except that coal, oil, and gas lands had to be leased, not sold. The bill stipulated that ranchers would have first choice to buy the lands they were currently grazing. Forest Service grazing lands were included in the bill, as were certain national park lands. Imagine the effects of such legislation on employees of federal agencies charged with the management of these lands. The cowboys were tightening the screws.

But the stockmen had gone too far. The bluster, threats to dispossess fellow Americans, greed, and abusive behavior began to backfire. Bernard DeVoto, the influential writer and historian, began describing the entire sordid scheme of western stockmen in *Harpers*. Soon, with a lot of help from conservation groups, his indignation spread to an aroused and angry public. Robertson's bill died in committee, and soon the would-be land grabbers were in full retreat—many, including Robertson, made hurried trips home to explain to their electorate that it was all a mistake, they really hadn't intended to steal the public's land. Several of the schemers were turned out of office in the next election.

But did the stockmen really want the public land? Probably not. Why trade a wealthy landlord for a poor one? What they actually wanted was all the rights of ownership, without any of the attendant responsibilities of ownership. By threatening to take the land, they had put a jolting scare into management agencies. Furthermore, McCarran and

Barrett's Wild West Show had done an excellent job of bloodying the agencies and their employees. The Grazing Service didn't even exist anymore, and the BLM was certainly not going to be giving ranchers any trouble for awhile. And even before the Barrett hearings ended, the Forest Service had decided to give up the fight—the service resolved to find a way to get along with the cowboys, and that meant no more cuts. And, of course, there could be but one alternative—range improvements. The cost of getting the stockmen off the agency's back would be transferred to the nation's taxpayers. The vehicle for this new policy was the Anderson-Mansfield Act (1949), which, while recognizing the overgrazed condition of Forest Service lands, authorized $133 million for reforestation and range rehabilitation—and promised more as needed to get the job done.

So the stockmen had won—there would be no more cuts, no matter how badly the land was hurting. From that time on, the Forest Service hardly had to bother counting livestock on and off the lands—just shovel tax money and keep a step ahead of the cows with newly planted grass.

But there was some tidying up to do. What about all those employees who had done a good job of making cuts—as ordered? They had infuriated ranchers, and in this new era of "don't rock the boat" range policy, they represented a discarded philosophy and objected to caving in at the expense of range resources. Although they were the cream of the service's range managers and had served well, they did not fit into the new scheme of spending tax dollars instead of managing range resources. Something had to be done, and that something became the most shameful maneuver ever taken by the U.S. Forest Service—the agency will never live it down.

Region 2, the Forest Service's Rocky Mountain Region, includes Colorado, most of Wyoming, and parcels of Nebraska and South Dakota. Much of the rangeland is in arid lowlands or at high elevations, and the region had been severely devastated by livestock. Furthermore, Region 2 was a hotbed of livestock politics—many of the national livestock association officers and spokesmen lived there. Region 2 was a challenge.

About the time the Forest Service was readying its campaign to gain control of grazing, Earl D. Sandvig was transferred to Region 2 (Denver) as Assistant Regional Forester for Range and Wildlife Management. Sandvig was a professional range manager and seemed destined to advance up the Forest Service ladder. He came to Denver from Montana, where grazing cuts had already been completed, ample rainfall had hastened the range recovery, and stockmen were delighted with the results. Sandvig was obviously the man to bring grazing within the carrying capacity of rangelands in Region 2. The service had set the policy—Sandvig was to carry out service orders. Sandvig had a competent staff of field men, and decisions were based on trend and condition of range, and every effort was made to persuade stockmen to cooperate. Although trouble spots and rancher resistance existed, the job progressed well, and Region 2 was setting a high example with its professional range management program. Even most ranchers recognized the benefits of what was being done in their behalf.

Then the Forest Service buckled—changed its policies from adjusting grazing pressures to the carrying capacity of the land to a policy of range rehabilitation through range improvements. Sandvig and his associates were caught out on a limb. In other words, although Sandvig was doing precisely what he had been ordered to do, and was probably doing it better than anyone in the entire Forest Service, the rug was jerked out from under him. In 1951, Sandvig was shipped out, sent to a desk job in Portland, Oregon—he was carefully steered away from rangelands, and eventually retired as Deputy Regional Forester for Hawaii.

As Voigt says, the stockmen provided the whetstones and knives, but Sandvig's superiors in the Forest Service did the skinning and hung the hide on a corral fence. Stockmen had won again. Furthermore, nearly every range forester associated with Sandvig in Denver was eventually transferred to an innocuous position where he stood properly repudiated for having carried out official policies as directed.

When federal employees are axed and publicly repudiated for political reasons, the word spreads like wildfire throughout management agencies. What had happened to Sandvig and his staff carried a message of immense clarity—get along with stockmen or get out. It would be a long time before anyone in the Forest Service or BLM would muster the courage to put the welfare of the land and vegetation ahead of the welfare of the cowboys. Many dedicated employees took early retirement as the only honest escape from such a repressive system.

After Sandvig and his staff were sacrificed at the booted-feet of stockmen, a period of peace came to the rangelands. The industry was content—they had exorcised the last bit of pluck from management agencies, they had gained almost unlimited access to public funds, and they had successfully converted a public privilege in the use of grazing lands into as solid a right as is possible, short of outright ownership. During those less hectic years, they continued to talk about taking the public lands and "returning" them to the states or private ownership, and various legislation was sought to tighten their grip on the public lands and the agencies administering them. The industry was firmly in charge. Stockmen could sit back and declare their western individualism, which translated meant, "get the federal government off our backs, but keep those federal dollars flowing, but of course, with no strings attached."

Then in the late 1950's, environmentalism began to stir in America. These stirrings soon grew into a force that would sweep the entire nation. Congress tested the wind and jumped into the fray—first with the Multiple Use and Sustained Yield Act of 1960, then the National Environmental Policy Act of 1969, the Federal Land Policy and Management Act of 1976, and others. This was heady stuff— suddenly the rules had changed—grazing was not the only use of public rangelands, citizens had a legal *right* to participate in decision-making processes, the public lands would remain in public ownership, all values of public lands would be taken into account in management, and so forth. But what had changed out on the range? In Nevada, a 1975 BLM report stated, "uncontrolled, unregulated, or unplanned livestock use is occurring in approximately 85 percent of the state, and damage to wildlife habitat can be expressed only as extreme destruction." Such conditions were standard throughout the West.

Thus in 1973, the Natural Resources Defense Council (NRDC) and other environmental groups in the West, filed suit under the provisions of the National Environmental Policy Act to force the BLM to write individual environmental impact statements on specific grazing districts throughout the West. They won in a 1974 court decision. Interestingly, when the NRDC was seeking a professional range management expert to help them in preparing the suit, they searched through range departments of western land grant universities but came up empty-handed—these fellows only worked for cowboys. But guess who came to the rescue and did a bang-up job for NRDC—none other than Earl Sandvig, the old scapegoat from Denver! It must have been sweet to toss a few stones back in the other direction, for any serious study of public lands would reveal desolation and trigger new demands for grazing cuts.

Sure enough, it happened. Suddenly, the cowboys were frantic—their buddy system with federal agencies and their stranglehold on public lands was disintegrating—right before their eyes. Obviously, it was time to drag out the clout again—time to scare the hell out of the bureaucrats once more. This time the great land grab would be called the "Sagebrush Rebellion," although environmentalists called it by such epithets as the "Great Terrain Robbery," the "Cheatgrass Rip-Off," and the "Public Lands Rip-Off."

It began in Nevada in 1979, when the cattleman-dominated legislature seized 49 million acres of BLM land and appropriated a legal fund to contest the issue of ownership "all the way to the Supreme Court." Later that same year, Utah's Senator Orrin Hatch and others introduced a bill that would transfer title to all BLM and Forest Service lands west of the 100th meridian to 13 western states. Sound familiar? Again, the stockmen and a few powerful allies had the entire nation in an uproar. Again, old battle cries of "states' rights" and "returning" the land were dragged out. Ronald Reagan, then a candidate for President, announced that the sagebrush rebels could "count him in"—he was one of them.

Of course, Nevada didn't take the issue to the Supreme Court—they never intended to, for they knew full well that they didn't have a legal foot to stand on. Nor did Hatch's bill or any of the others floating around congress ever come to a vote—the supporters knew the rest of the nation would not stand for such ridiculous nonsense. Eventually, a U.S. District Judge knocked the props out from under the Sagebrush Rebellion by dismissing Nevada's claim that the federal government holds public lands in *temporary* trust and is obliged to dispose of such lands for the benefit of the state and its citizens. That ruling created hardly a stir in western newspapers. The judge pointed out, "No state legislation may interfere with Congress' power over the public land." But, of course, the cowboys didn't really want the public land. They only wanted to put federal employees back in line, to dominate the use of public land, and to keep milking the federal treasury. In fact, because of the furor, congress got busy and passed the Rangeland Improvement Act—promising $365 million of taxpayers' money for the troublemakers over the next 20 years—and the McClure Amendment—requiring a gradual phasing-in of any planned grazing reductions on an allotment.

But as grand as the Sagebrush Rebellion was for the stockmen, it wasn't quite enough. Stronger medicine was required—a few bureaucrats needed to be bloodied. This time it would be in Kingman, Arizona—a town of 22,800 including 18 BLM grazing permittees.

A draft environmental impact statement was being completed. It showed that excessive grazing had left the area in a pitiful state—dominated by snakeweed, rabbitbrush, turpentine bush, and other unpalatable plants. Much of the land would support only 3 cows per square mile.

In 1977, Gary McVicker arrived to become the new BLM area manager, replacing a former employee who had gotten along well with the local stockmen. Ranchers were realistic enough to realize that cuts could be in store. Furthermore, McVicker found 1,000 extra cattle on an allotment—he had them removed, suggesting that he was not playing the good-old-boy routine, but intended to follow the rules. Suddenly, complaints began to surface about McVicker—he was curt, unsympathetic, negative, undiplomatic, etc., etc. The Mohave County Livestock Association requested that the state BLM Director, Robert O. Buffington (remember that name) replace McVicker with someone who would work with Kingman ranchers.

Eventually, the state's congressional delegation became involved and the McVicker case was being discussed in high places in Washington. At one such meeting, an official in the Department of Interior gave Arizona's Congressman, DeConcini, reason to believe that McVicker would be shipped out. Thus, although Buffington and others of McVicker's superiors were convinced that McVicker had acted within the law and for the good of the public, it was also evident that the stockmen were going to persist. If the program at Kingman were to get moving again, McVicker had to go—he was transferred—with a promotion and pay raise. Once again, federal employees learned that the public and public agencies cannot be counted upon to back them when they attempt to carry out assigned duties. Ranchers all over the West were jubilant with the victory and wrote Kingman stockmen for instructions on how to do it.

The real irony is that Buffington was eventually transferred to Idaho as state director of the BLM. In 1981, unhappy ranchers began to complain about him, and various letters were supposedly written to the state's congressional delegation and to the national BLM office. At the urging of Idaho's Senator Steve Symms and Representative Larry Craig, the Director of the BLM, Bob Burford—a cattle rancher—replaced Buffington, who was given a choice between early retirement and a desk job in Washington. Once again, the kangaroo court system of the livestock industry had prevailed, and another dedicated public employee had been sacrificed. Word quickly spread, and federal employees were put on notice—despite all the legislative foofaraw and fancy bills and acts in Washington D.C.—the cowboys were still running the show out on the range!

In 1930, President Herbert Hoover offered to *give* the western states all unappropriated federal lands (minus the mineral rights) within their borders—the governors politely declined his offer. As Bernard DeVoto has pointed out, Montana has no desire to own the Custer Battlefield National Monument and Cemetery, even though it could be rented out for grazing at $30 to $60 a year. Western states don't want public lands, because they already get from these lands whatever values they are producing—without the expenses and tribulations of management. It's interesting that President Reagan is pushing a scheme to sell off "excess" federal properties to help pay the national debt. Stockmen *oppose* this program, because Reagan isn't promising to give them the public lands for a few cents per acre, he has in mind selling them to the highest bidder—and that won't be the stockmen.

Western states have an abysmal record at managing state lands. On being admitted to the Union, most western states were granted two sections (usually 16 and 36) in each township. In addition, many other large grants of land were given to states for various other purposes. Arizona, New Mexico, and Montana have retained most of their land endowments, while Oregon, California, and Nevada have disposed of most of theirs. Nevada, the state most anxious to rip off large chunks of public land during the Sagebrush Rebellion, squandered its endowments of more than 4.5 million acres, selling most at $1.25 per acre, mineral rights included. In 1980, Nevada retained only 134,417 acres of state lands, including the last 2,591 acres of the public school endowment, which were saved by a clerical *error* during the rampant rush toward disposal. Even where lands are retained, they get little management. Arizona has one employee for each 99,000 acres, New Mexico spends 19

cents an acre each year for management, and isolated sections are often grazed without charge. Most states have laws demanding that state lands must earn a maximum return—thus, the law requires that state lands be overgrazed! Furthermore, because the states share revenues from public lands, they have a vested interest in the commercial exploitation of these lands.

Today, only 3 percent of the ranchers control 40 percent of the public forage privileges in the 11 western states. These large operators have managed to convince many westerners, including most small livestock operators, that what is good for the big operators is good for the West. The hotheads and the greedy gain control of the associations—especially at the national level. Sagebrush Rebellions help the big operators, but offer little to the small operators, who, nevertheless, are willing to do the footwork for the big fellows. Many writers have apologized for small livestock operators and contend that they are victims dragged along unwillingly by the big boys. There is surely some truth in this assertion. But when it comes time to testify at public hearings or to drive a federal employee out of town, the mob is always made up of the small ranchers. Furthermore, although they may not agree with actions taken by associations, they have seldom stepped forward to rein in excesses. Also, *all* ranchers have benefited from the spoils of hell-raising battles.

The western livestock industry has kept the region in constant turmoil. It has blackmailed the public by threatening to take the public lands, when in reality it wanted the prerogatives of ownership, while letting the public pay the bills. The industry has held the public land management agencies hostage and has dispensed intolerable abuses upon loyal and dedicated federal employees. Without so much as cringing, the industry has greedily raided public tax funds for personal gain. Yet, today, as always, the western livestock industry is absolutely dependent upon the use of public lands. By no stretch of the imagination can this segment of the livestock industry be considered a form of private enterprise. And perhaps the most remarkable aspect of all this is that the industry is constantly seeking public sympathy—the poor ranchers are going broke. In the West, such whining is more predictable than the seasons. And these pitiful tales of woe are spread by the very same lobbyists who deal out the fury and abuse in Washington during the heat of battle.

So what's the answer? Stockmen return again and again to the same bag of tricks. Whenever they go too far, the public is aroused, hot letters are written, and the fire is extinguished. Usually, by that time the ranchers have already accomplished their goals. Then, the public goes back to sleep, until the next great emergency.

The solution is simple. If the public expects management agencies to manage federal rangelands for the benefit of the general public, they must step in and defend and protect the agencies and their employees from the industry. Ranchers are a tiny minority. But unless the public is willing to be *constantly* alert and lend *continuous* reliable support, the agencies cannot risk stirring the industry to anger. The industry plays hardball and never sleeps. Until the public is willing to do the same, nothing will change. And meanwhile, there will be no cuts.

WASHED IN PUBLIC SUBSIDIES

The history of the livestock industry on public rangelands depicts a generous and indulgent public being exploited by a small but grasping commodity interest. That theme has surfaced repeatedly in preceding chapters. At this point, it's time to examine the economic factors that assure ranchers such a favored position at the public trough.

Stockmen operating on public ranges have long contended that those lands be used to inject *stability* into the western livestock industry. In their view, rangelands should be available to ranchers for long periods of secure and uninterrupted tenure. Also, economic structure should serve to perpetuate the industry and sustain rural areas of the West where the livestock industry is deemed essential to local economies. Congress has accepted these notions and elevated the concept of stability to a dominant principle in the administration of public rangelands.

The results have not been exactly what congress had in mind. In an effort to attain stability, congress has created undeserved wealth, fostered unfair competition at the marketplace, and shielded uneconomical livestock operations—all at extraordinary public expense. Consequently, the current economic policies governing the use of public rangelands are shameful and illogical—amounting to little more than a public swindle.

Under a secure congressional franchise, rich and powerful ranchers are encouraged to extract enormous personal wealth from public rangelands and public coffers. Thus, despite nearly 64 percent of the state being in public owner- ship, Idaho, a farming and ranching state, has a greater percentage of millionaires than any other state in the nation. Today, the most secure and pampered users of public grazing lands are the nation's wealthiest and largest livestock operators, including corporate ranches. An incredible 90 percent of the U.S. cattlemen owning 1,000 or more cows graze them on public rangelands. Furthermore, 63 percent of all western sheep are owned by only 6 percent of the sheepmen. Is this the stability congress intended?

Under congressional mandate, grazing on public land, a privilege bestowed by the public, has been converted into a right—a commodity sold on the open market, thus garnering enormous profits for ranchers fortunate enough to have been granted such a privilege. For example, in 1979 a large cattle operation in southeastern Oregon was advertised (without cattle) as a "vast ranch complex of 558,000 acres," but only 147,750 of those acres were *deeded*. In other words, the selling price of $11.5 million included grazing privileges (rights?) on 410,250 acres of public lands belonging to the people of the United States. Advocates of such cozy arrangements justify them as being in the public's interest—they confer stability to the livestock industry.

In Kingman (Arizona), where Gary McVicker was railroaded out of town, 18 ranchers graze BLM allotments, but 15 of them depend on other income, and the average ranching income for the 18 permittees is only $6,500 per year. In 1978, the BLM collected $94,500 in grazing fees in the Kingman area, while spending about $366,500 on management and operations. What this tells us is that the ridiculously low cost of public forage invites overgrazing and makes profitable the grazing of degraded public lands that could not support grazing in a free-market economy. Thus, the current system subsidizes and perpetuates operators who mine a subsistence living from public rangelands, but who would not survive in a truly competitive market. In short, large numbers of uneconomical ranches are being kept afloat by federal largesse.

Federally subsidized ranchers on public lands enjoy an immense competitive advantage over private, unsubsidized stockmen who use their own lands, pay local property taxes on private grazing lands, and contribute to a free economy. According to the Oregon Cattlemen's Association, more than 300 Oregon ranch families went out of business in 1982, but one can safely bet that few of the failures were ranchers operating on public lands.

The greatest contribution of congress to the economies of the rural West is a wash of public subsidies, which could just as easily be granted as outright gifts, like foreign aid, thus dispensing with the charade of western stockmen pretending to contribute to the national economy. For example, in Mohave County, Arizona, which includes Kingman, ranching and all other agriculture account for only 0.8 percent of the county's total income. The handful of cattlemen in the area are not businessmen—they are on a public dole. In 1981, the federal government collected $24.9 million in grazing revenues, but spent $58.5 million on public rangeland management and payment to local governments in lieu of taxes—thus the U.S. Treasury deficit amounted to $33.6 million. Surely those numbers are clear—the western livestock industry is borne squarely on the backs of the nation's taxpayers.

Now, let's take a closer look at how this enormous program of welfare ranching operates.

Grazing fees charged stockmen for use of public lands have always been absurdly low, but have become more so with passing time. For example, in 1977 near Kingman, ranchers were paying a grazing fee of 7.9 cents per acre per year—that's about $15 per cow per year. But with the passage of the Public Rangeland Improvement Act of 1978, grazing fees were set by a formula taking into account current beef prices and rancher's production costs. If beef prices fall, costs rise, or both, the grazing fee is automatically reduced, as happened between 1980 and 1983 when the fee dropped from $2.36 to $1.40 per AUM. Today, no matter how badly a rancher misjudges the market, how poorly an operation is managed, nor how unsound the economic potential of an operation, the fee system endeavors to keep the rancher in business. Normally, of course, when production costs exceed profits, an enterprise

is discontinued as being no longer worthwhile. However, during the economic depression of the early 1980's, when bankruptcy claimed thousands of small and even many large businesses, including free-enterprise stockmen paying 4 to 9 times as much for forage on private lands, stockmen using the public lands enjoyed a privileged status and were insulated and protected from normal economic vagaries. A profound mystery is why stockmen who do not use public lands, but produce 97 percent of the nation's beef, are willing to accept second-class citizenship by being forced to compete in an open market with lavishly subsidized westerners. Apparently, eastern states do not elect senators and representatives interested in protecting *their* livestock industries.

Stockmen using public lands attempt to conceal their economic pillage of the tax-paying public by contending that federal grazing fees represent a "fair market value" for forage. Such a contention, however, is pure nonsense. A fair market price is one acceptable to buyer and seller alike, provided neither is compelled to buy or sell. Obviously, when the U.S. Treasury spends $33.6 million more than it collects in a year to support private grazing on public land, the sellers are being ripped off. If ranchers are, indeed, paying a "fair market value" for BLM and Forest Service forage, how can they afford to pay 3 to 4 times as much for other public grazing lands (e.g., Department of Defense lands, etc.) sold on competitive bid? By being willing to pay these higher rates, ranchers destroy the credibility of their own contentions.

Meanwhile, the western livestock industry and its apologists in land grant universities issue a continuous barrage of propaganda about "hidden" costs of grazing public land. Included are such assertions as the land is of poorer quality and ranchers must pay more for fence repairs, transportation, horses, horse food, riders, and so on. In 1983, one such press release stated that the *real* cost of grazing public land in eastern Oregon is $9.28 per AUM compared to $10.36 per AUM on private land. Though containing a grain of truth, such statements are absurd in implying that riders, horses, horse food, transportation, and so on are not necessary when livestock are grazed on private land. These cowboy economists even credit private ranchers with costs of building and amortizing their own fences on public land, fences that are generally provided with public funds. For example, in 1977, the total private range improvements constructed on all BLM rangelands in 11 western states included 9 miles of pipeline, 17 springs, 1 water catchment basin, 1 well, 24 cattle guards, and 14 miles of fencing.

In New Mexico, where public land (the McGregor Range) has been offered on competitive bid, Earl Sandvig cites a 10-year comparison of average fees paid for an AUM of forage as follows: BLM land—$1.45, private land—$6.61, and McGregor Range—$4.36. If claimed hidden costs are valid and if BLM fees are actually equivalent to costs on private land, how can ranchers afford to offer 3 times as much for forage sold by competitive bid? Obviously, claims that current federal grazing fees represent fair market value and claims of hidden costs in grazing public lands should be laid to rest. A foolproof way to challenge such claims would be to put the sale of all public forage on a competitive bid basis. Currently, private grazing of public lands is done at public expense, and the public fails to recover costs. Competitive bidding is the basis of a free-market economy, is democratic, and is standard practice in most federal operations—timber sales, oil leases, supply purchases, etc. Why not for public forage? The reason, of course, is that western stockmen know that their perverse use of "fair market value" is simply a euphemism for public subsidy. Currently, the buyer of public forage is delighted—the seller, which is us, is being swindled. All past efforts to alter the fairness of this distorted relationship have triggered vicious tantrums by the western livestock industry, so the public capitulated and nothing changed.

By paying bargain rates for public forage, avoiding local property taxes on rangelands, and enjoying fee reductions during times of economic adversity, stockmen operating on public lands reap maximum profits from current operations.

But that is only part of the scam. Because public grazing fees have consistently been priced far below the true fair market value of the forage, grazing permits save permittees a certain amount of money each year. Because the permit carries with it this assurance of savings, the accrued value of such savings is customarily added to the permit, giving it a cash value. Thus, when a ranch or other base properties are sold, the price includes an added cost of $400 to $1,500 for each cow authorized by the federal grazing permit. Not uncommonly, the cash value of the grazing permit may actually exceed the value of the ranch's deeded property. If grazing fees really were set at fair market value, grazing permits would have no cash value. In purchasing a grazing permit, a rancher is buying future subsidies.

In many instances, when a ranch is sold, no distinction is made between the value of deeded property and the cash value of the grazing permit, and asking prices are quoted in a way that conceals the value placed on the grazing permit. For example, a 300 animal unit ranch (one that supports 300 cows) including the BLM grazing permit might be advertised for $1,800 per animal unit, thus masking the assigned value of the grazing permit in the total selling price of $540,000. Nevertheless, about 75 percent of the selling price is likely to be an asset actually owned by the general public. In any event, ranchers fight adamantly to avoid grazing cuts, for if the BLM were to cut this hypothetical rancher's grazing by 25 percent, the market value of the ranch would be reduced by $135,000 to $405,000! Because of this relationship, the law specifies that the BLM must notify the permittee's bank when grazing reductions are to be made on a rancher's allotment.

The cash value of grazing permits, while often hidden in the selling price, is nevertheless recognized as a reality by federal agencies, stockmen, bankers, and others. In a recent newspaper article, a realtor in Grant County, Oregon, stated, "When I started selling ranches (25 years ago), $200 a cow unit was right in there where you could make a living. It's close to $3,000 a cow unit now. You can't make a living on $3,000 a cow unit unless you write it off on taxes." A 1979 survey of 50 ranch appraisers and loan officers in New Mexico revealed that Forest Service grazing permits were assigned a value of $944 to $1,163 per animal unit, while BLM permits were worth $667 to $888. Ranchers point out that they buy the permit when they purchase a ranch, and, therefore, are entitled to sell the permit as a part of the capitalized value of the ranch. That's true, however, the selling of a public privilege is an unsavory practice and a major impediment to reducing grazing pressure on over-grazed rangelands. Ranchers will not accept cuts. Further-more, the cash value of permits is also an obstacle to offering public forage on competitive bid, because bids would abolish the cash value of permits. But as Earl Sandvig points out, ranchers who have held a grazing permit for 10 years have probably recovered their capital investment. Permits held less than 10 years could be purchased for the value of their remaining years by the federal government from funds collected from the sale of forage on competitive bid. More than anything else, this policy change would go a long way toward getting western stockmen out of the public trough and back into the mainstream of the free-market economy under which other Americans must operate.

Because of the escalating values of grazing permits and of general property values, large numbers of western stockmen have attained the status of "paper" millionaires and would become actual millionaires if they elected to sell their holdings. Although such people obviously relish being subsidized, no one has demonstrated that they actually *need* federal subsidies to remain profitable. Perhaps congress is providing economic stability to operators who do not have a legitimate need. In fact, many ranchers using public rangelands are obviously economically secure and could afford to pay a *true* fair market value for forage, just as their counterparts on private land must do. Ranchers who cannot pay a fair market price for forage should get out of the business.

Besides those mentioned, there are additional subsidies and public costs relating to range management and range improvements. For example, in 1979, after collecting grazing fees, the Forest Service and BLM showed a total deficit of $27.8 million on their grazing programs. Moreover, another 25 percent must be added to that loss to cover costs relating to overhead, fire protection, and so forth. Furthermore, a large but unknown amount must be added to cover costs of personnel, travel, and other administrative expenses not directly budgeted to grazing programs. Next, add special appropriations, such as the $365 million promised ranchers by the Public Rangelands Improvement Act—that's $9,865 for each and every grazing permittee using BLM and Forest Service lands. And remember, when large crested wheatgrass seedings are planted, roads built to them, fences constructed, wells drilled, pipes and watering troughs installed, etc., all at public expense, the rancher will still pay $1.40 per AUM—the same amount as before improvements. Finally, there is a long list of special subsidies to ranchers—disaster relief during droughts and storms, pest control funds for grasshoppers and rodents, weed control, predator control funds, and so forth. Despite all these public handouts, western stockmen have successfully convinced much of the nation to believe their incredible claims of *independence*. Steve Johnson, Southwestern Field Representative for the Defenders of Wildlife, summed it up simply and accurately when he titled one of his articles, "Ranching: High cost of an American myth."

Although dollar costs are appalling, in the long run, they shrink to trivial proportions in comparison to other costs passed to the public by stockmen using public lands. A nation with expectations cannot barter or risk its substance, fundamental assets, or future. Loss of soil, siltation of reservoirs and stream systems, depletion of water supplies, pollution of water sources, degradation of watersheds, destruction of wildlife habitat, loss of biological diversity, conversion of native vegetation to communities of exotics, reduction of animal populations (especially big game, major predators, and endangered species) are just a few of the environmental costs being foisted upon the public by the western livestock industry. Add to these such social costs as diversion of valuable grain supplies into the production of large quantities of inedible and unhealthy fat, exposure of the general population to diverse pharmaceuticals, insecticides, and herbicides used by the industry, extravagant campaigns to encourage Americans to increase their cholesterol intake, generation of enormous amounts of litter by fast-food industries based on beef, and reduction of the quality and quantity of out-of-door experiences available to all other users of public rangelands. Western beef does not come cheap. By being willing to bear the brunt of such insults, the West is committing regional suicide—the nation is ignoring an inevitable day of reckoning.

In contemplating matters discussed in this chapter, the reader might be tempted to grant that stockmen using the public lands have, indeed, become highly parasitic upon their fellow citizens, but conclude that the deed is done, the process has run its course, and, therefore, the situation is stabilized and unlikely to get worse. Such logic is a mistaken delusion. Western stockmen are just beginning—grander things are yet in store. A recent scheme illustrates the point.

In 1982, Americans imported automobiles, television sets, tape recorders and other high-technology items and managed to run up a $17.5 billion trade deficit with Japan. In January 1983, when Japanese Prime Minister Yasuhiro Nakasone visited Washington, the Reagan Administration used our huge trade deficit to pressure the Japanese to open markets to more American export products—especially beef. Simultaneously, an officer in the Oregon Cattlemen's Association, which is dominated by cattlemen using public lands, announced that one of the most important objectives of the beef industry is to work toward increasing beef exports worldwide with particular emphasis on Japan. He said that if various restrictions, such as beef quotas and high tariffs could be reduced or eliminated, American beef shipments to Japan could more than double.

All this may seem perfectly reasonable, but consider the following: 1) The United States is currently and has been for several decades the world's *largest importer of beef*—no other nation comes close to challenging our gluttonous demand for beef; 2) From 1976 to 1982, American beef consumption plummeted from 95 to 77 pounds per capita per year, and in 1982, an expert panel of the National Academy of Sciences issued a study report recommending that for better health, Americans should further reduce their beef consumption; 3) Using the BLM's grazing receipts for 1981, the Oregon Natural Resources Council calculated that American taxpayers paid a subsidy of nearly $14 that year for each animal grazed on BLM land in Oregon and Washington. Other western states would be comparable.

Some questions seem to be in order. If the United States is the world's largest importer of beef, why would we want to export American-raised beef to Japan? With the public rangelands suffering from overgrazing and our own beef consumption dropping, why not seize this opportunity to reduce grazing pressures on public ranges? Furthermore, when nutritionists are warning of the unhealthy aspects of a beef diet, should we be working to force Japan to import more of a commodity that is being increasingly shunned by our own people? If massive public subsidies are required to raise beef on public land, can the nation realize a true profit from selling that beef to others? Finally, beef grazed on public rangelands has been nurtured on the nation's lifeblood—it has been produced at the expense of our common heritage of soil, water, wildlife, and other natural assets. Are we willing to make a business of scalping public land for the sake of export trade?

Exporting beef raised on public land would reduce our nation to the status of a banana republic—the economic rape of national interests for the economic gain of a privileged few. Stockmen are understandably dazzled by the promise of big bucks. Television accounts of Japanese spending more than $10 a pound for beef have triggered a veritable fever among western cattlemen. Moreover, the terms are ideal— our government forces the Japanese to accept more beef as a concession for our continued import of high-technology items. Thus, we export a commodity that is lavishly subsidized by American taxpayers and import expensive high-technology items—the cowboys and Japanese get rich, and the general public gets the bill. Once again, the western livestock industry is preparing to dip deeper into the public coffers. But surely, the nation will not tolerate such a larcenous attempt to swindle. Any cow that has ever set foot on public land should be absolutely banned from foreign commerce!

The western livestock industry is intent upon destroying public land, water, soils, wildlife, and much more. Taxpayers have carried the industry a long ways—much farther than anyone could rightfully expect. Americans are generous and often willing to subsidize industries that generate abundant job opportunities or that perform vital functions for the nation at large. The livestock industry on public lands does neither—it provides a small number of unskilled jobs and its 3 percent contribution to the nation's red meat supply is insignificant and is lost in the normal, year-to-year fluctuations in beef supply.

What can be done? Competitive bidding for public forage offers some attractive advantages. Such a system would undoubtedly recover the *real* costs of public range management. It would free the public of paying subsidies to the industry. Furthermore, if public forage were unsubsidized, grazing pressures would be reduced because ranchers would be unwilling to pay a fair price to graze overgrazed rangelands. Also, forage purchased by competitive bid, by increasing federal income from grazing programs, would markedly increase the income to western communities collecting payments in lieu of taxes. After all, these communities and their economic stability were the intended beneficiaries when congress contrived the current system of boondoggles.

The economic administration of public rangelands is a national scandal. But who is to be blamed? Not management agencies—their hands are bound. They do as congress wills. Not livestock owners, for they are merely opportunists, taking whatever the system will yield. Certainly stockmen cannot be expected to forfeit public subsidies voluntarily. Congress deserves a good share of the blame, for it has consistently betrayed the public in setting guidelines and standards for the administration of public grazing lands. But in the final analysis, the blame belongs to the public—the real landlord and also the employer of both congress and agency personnel.

It's a well-worn maxim, but nevertheless true—the power rests with the people. So far, in the administration of public grazing lands, the people have simply shunned their responsibility. Instead of demanding sound and fair policies of rangeland management, the public has been content to condone and even participate in its own embezzlement.

RED MEAT FOR
A HUNGRY WORLD?

When western stockmen or their sundry collaborators are given an opportunity to speak before a public gathering, especially when conservationists are known to be present, they inevitably launch into a harangue intended to justify the industry's use of public lands. Perhaps this compelling need to justify use of public ranges reflects insecurity or guilt. In any event, the arguments made in these presentations have become highly standardized, and to many western listeners, are now a bit shopworn. Nonetheless, to uninformed audiences, certain of these arguments can be tremendously convincing because they are specifically designed to appeal to patriotism, fairplay, thriftiness, and other such virtues. Many of the assertions are wrapped in just enough truth to pass superficial inspection, but easily unravel on more rigorous examination. Still others seem to be contrived fiction fashioned without recourse to fact. In this chapter, some of the livestock industry's favorite cliches are introduced and analyzed.

We are producing red meat for a hungry world.
This outright falsehood may stem from a combination of deceit, naivete, and a Walter Mitty-like desire to be useful. But what nation of hungry people can afford to purchase and import American beef? Even in this country, the wealthiest on earth, plenty of Americans can't afford beef, and many others are limited to meager amounts of the less expensive cuts and hamburgers. Of course, we do export beef, especially to various Arab nations, Japan, Great Britain, and

a few others, but you may rest assured that it does not fall into the hands of anyone suffering from hunger or malnutrition.

Instead of providing red meat for a hungry world, the United States is the world's largest importer of beef, importing about 9 percent of our total consumption (40 percent of all the beef sold on the world market). Although we tend to think of underdeveloped nations as being most dependent upon food imports, it is the developed nations that place the greatest demand on the world's supply of exportable food. Nearly half of the beef imported by the United States is obtained from the poorest, most protein-deficient sections of Central America—Costa Rica, Nicaragua, Honduras, and Guatemala—a region where per capita consumption of meat by the residents is generally declining. For example, in Costa Rica, while meat production increased 92 percent, per capita meat consumption declined 26 percent. American beef imports of about 7 pounds per person per year exceed the annual per capita consumption of beef in many of the poorer countries. Moreover, many underdeveloped nations are diverting land needed for local food production to the raising of exportable livestock. In other words, citizens of such nations are producing beef to sell to Americans and using the cash to buy beans, rice, and other necessities required for subsistence living.

Although American grain could be used to feed a hungry world, about half of our harvest is fed to livestock. About 80 percent of American cattle are sent to feedlots, where an enormous amount of valuable protein is wasted. For example, when an average steer is fed 16 pounds of grain and soy, one pound is converted to edible meat, while 15 pounds are lost as energy, inedible portions of the carcass, or as waste products (in poultry, less than 3 pounds of grain can be converted to a pound of meat). Just the amount of grain "lost" in livestock feeding is twice the amount we export each year and is enough to provide every person on earth a cup of cooked grain every day of the year. Even though protein is a precious commodity throughout the world, much of the world's protein supply is currently being converted into animal fat. Most of the grain exported from the United States is not destined for needy nations as food, but goes to nations like Japan, Great Britain, and the Soviet Union to be fed to livestock.

The western livestock industry is making no contribution whatsoever to feeding a hungry world. In fact, it is making only a trivial contribution to the red meat demands of our own nation—3 percent to be exact. Each year, we import more than twice the amount of beef grown by ranchers using the public rangelands. Because the nation's beef supply varies as much as 20 to 25 percent in 10 year cycles, the contribution of the westerners is lost in the shuffle. In short, while western stockmen have been busy raising hell and making cattle history, the rest of the nation's stockmen have been quietly raising beef. No one can subsist on a diet of western novels and good intentions.

Eat more beef—it's good for you.

Stockmen and their associations are beef pushers. In the past, their efforts have been incredibly successful—they managed to sell Americans the idea that beef is a status food. Both in fiction and fact, the "beef and potatoes man" represents some sort of implied qualities of being macho and virile. In the late 1960's, beef ranked third behind automobiles and television sets as an item most coveted by Americans. In 1981, red meat accounted for one-fourth of the consumer dollar spent in grocery stores, with red meat, poultry, and seafood accounting for one-third of all expenditures for food and beverages. In restaurants, about 20 cents of every dollar was spent on red meat. Altogether, American consumers spend about 3.5 percent of their disposable income on red meat.

In the early 1970's, ecstatic stockmen were predicting soaring consumer demand for beef through the remainder of the century. But after peaking at 95 pounds per capita in 1976, American beef consumption declined drastically to only about 77 pounds in 1982. Beef pushers had fallen on hard times. Part of the explanation relates to a changing life-style, which will be discussed later. Other causes,

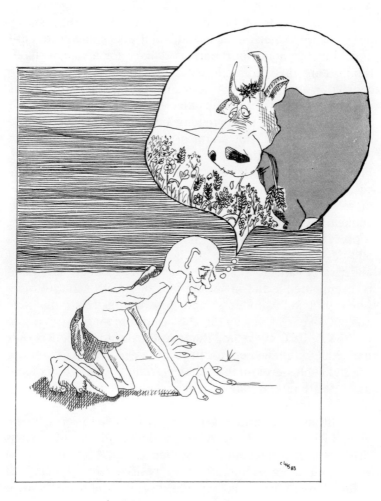

WE FEED COWS FIELDS OF GRAIN,
BUT LEAVE HUMAN STOMACHS
EMPTY.

however, can be attributed to a substantial modification of American perceptions of beef as a food.

A major factor in the decline of beef consumption is price—many Americans can't afford it and many others are unwilling to spend hard-earned dollars for a luxury food. Reinforcing this economic resistance to beef is a growing conviction among many Americans that beef is really not as healthful and nutritious as advertised by the industry. A pervasive concern is a growing national awareness of the hazards of a high cholesterol diet, particularly the adverse effects of such a diet on the heart and circulatory system. Faced with a dramatic reduction in the life expectancy of its citizens, Norway mounted a massive campaign to reduce meat consumption. In the United States, concerns about cholesterol peaked in 1982 when a committee of experts representing the National Academy of Sciences issued a 500-page report dealing with the relationship between diet and risk of cancer. The report confirmed popular fears and recommended a diet including less fat—both saturated fats (meat and milk products) and unsaturated fats (vegetable oils). A 3-year survey by the U.S. Department of Agriculture in the late 1970's revealed that two-thirds of U.S. households had changed their diets for health reasons, chiefly to reduce fat and cholesterol intake. Choice grade beef has 63 percent more fat than standard grade, besides being considerably more expensive.

Additional fears have arisen regarding long-term health risks to humans related to the widespread use of various drugs and pharmaceuticals in animal feeds. According to the Food and Drug Administration, residues of as many as 500-600 toxic chemicals may be present in the nation's meat supply, and residues of 143 chemicals are likely to exceed government tolerance levels. Nearly 40 percent of all antibiotic chemicals produced in the United States go into 75 percent of the feed given livestock. These chemicals are viewed as unacceptable food contaminants as well as contributing causes in the proliferation of drug-resistant strains of microorganisms.

The synthetic estrogen diethylstilbestrol (DES) was widely used as a food additive or tissue implant to increase the growth rate of cattle. Traces of DES remain in the carcasses of slaughtered cattle, especially in the livers. Before 1976, several nations had banned DES when it was found to be a dangerous carcinogen. In the United States, however, DES was not banned until 1979, 7 years after the Food and Drug Administration had declared it to be a proven carcinogen in animals and humans. The livestock industry's willingness to expose consumers to unnecessary health risks for the sake of higher profits seriously eroded confidence in beef as a wholesome food.

Because cattle are long-lived, they are ideal collection depots for chlorinated hydrocarbon pesticides and other chemicals whose residues are consumed and stored in the fat reserves of the living animal. Although fat is trimmed from various types of meat, marbled fat and an ample amount of encasing fat are considered desirable with beef, thus human exposure to toxicants stored in fat tissues is greatly magnified. Also, various episodes of livestock contamination with polychlorinated biphenyl (PCB's) compounds and other dangerous chemicals have received national notice in the press. More recently, a report issued by Ralph Nader's Center for Study of Responsive Law has charged the U.S. Department of Agriculture with extremely serious failures in its meat inspection program. The study contends that millions of Americans are being sold dirty, diseased, and chemically contaminated meat because of too few inspectors, excessive work loads, reduced standards, and political interference with the professional agency and its staff.

All of these revelations have had a substantial impact upon consumers. Today, stockmen pushing beef in the fashion of a circus barker can be certain of finding hecklers in the crowd. In fact, livestock associations, while continuing to push the product, have adopted more subtle sales pitches—instead of urging Americans to beef gluttony, they now tell consumers to eat beef because it is good for them, but to eat smaller servings.

"LET THEM EAT CAKE!"

The sun's energy is captured by range forage and is wasted if not consumed by a cow.

The fallacy of this assertion rests with the common American imperfection in being unable to recognize value unless it is converted into dollars and cents. Obviously, a plant does not have to be eaten by a cow to have value, just as deer do not have to be killed, a river dammed, a tree felled, or an acre tilled to have value. What a rancher perceives as forage for a cow may in fact be duck habitat. Besides filling a cow's belly, plants can hold the soil in place, enrich the organic content of soil, feed and house a bountiful number of naturally occurring animals, guarantee the effectiveness of watersheds, remove pollutants from the atmosphere, replenish oxygen supplies, dress nature in colors and textures that please the beholder, and much more. What nature has so laboriously created and what a rancher so contemptuously labels as forage is vital to the continued existence of humankind upon this planet—cows are not.

Grazing is a useful tool in managing vegetation for wildlife.

After hearing this assertion endlessly repeated by agency personnel, one can almost feel sorry for the millions of large herbivores, the seemingly infinite flocks of waterfowl, and the great droves of upland game birds that had to suffer in pristine America without the miraculous biological services rendered by the cow. Today, we hear that ducks cannot take their newly hatched ducklings to water unless cows first trample a path through the dense vegetation. Big game animals would certainly starve if cows failed to eat old growth vegetation and expose the new. Grasses would become extinct if cattle weren't around to trample the seed into the soil. And if it weren't for the magic stimulating agent in the saliva of cows, plants would probably cease growing altogether. Yes, indeed, American wildlife is certainly blessed to have enjoyed the fabulous benefits of cows as a wildlife management tool.

In truth, cows rival bullets as destroyers of wildlife and have no rivals as destroyers of wildlife habitat. Today, herds of bovine management tools are devouring, stomping, and littering national wildlife refuges, BLM lands are being grazed to dirt, and national forests are being stripped of every edible morsel. This plunder of public lands is nothing more than private enterprise. What possible relationship could exist between filling the bellies of cows and the well-being of wildlife? For the American public to tolerate such a deception does not speak well for our national intellect—we should be embarrassed and ashamed. The historical evidence of the damage to wildlife by cattle is clear and incontrovertible—arguments to the contrary belong in the realm of fairy tales.

Cattle are grazers.

This often-repeated statement is designed to allay fears of hunters and others who might be concerned about cattle competing for food with deer and other browsers. Of course, in an earlier chapter, we saw that hungry cattle will eat tar paper off buildings. The point is, cattle are grazers on good range, but on overgrazed range, they eat whatever is available. For example, on high-quality range, the overlap in diet between deer and cattle is about 7 percent, but on overgrazed land near Kingman, Arizona, cattle have become browsers and the extent of overlap is 20 percent. Nationally, it takes about 18 acres to sustain a cow, but on BLM land 78 acres are required. On such lands, cattle are not exactly knee-deep in grass, and opportunities to "graze" are quite limited.

In the old days, grazing was unrestricted and destructive, but today it is sophisticated, scientific, and carefully controlled.

Certainly grazing in former times was unrestricted and destructive, but the question is, has anything really changed? Today, land grant universities have departments of range management, the cooperative extension service has livestock experiment stations, and agencies are shoveling huge amounts of public funds into range improvement projects. Yet, nowhere is there a clear and indisputable published statement proclaiming public rangelands to be in significantly better condition than in the past. There are more fences, more seedings, more cattle guards, and more sleight-of-hand schemes to rotate cattle from one pasture to another. But there are also more and bigger cattle—the number has doubled since 1950. What is lacking is a concise declaration that public rangelands are more productive, that superior wildlife habitat is more abundant, that soil erosion is diminished, that native vegetation is being restored, that watersheds are healthier, that riparian zones are in better shape, and in general, that public rangelands are on the mend. If such were the case, certainly the news would be shouted throughout the land by everyone associated with the livestock industry. No such claims are being made simply because they would be patently and immediately identified as false. If modern livestock grazing is sophisticated, scientific, and carefully controlled that is interesting, but it is not a substitute for reducing grazing of domestic livestock to the carrying capacity of the public rangelands. Strangely enough, not even the most ardent industry spokesman has made that claim.

Ranchers are the original conservationists.

Some ranchers actually stand up and make this absurd proclamation without batting an eye. Conservation implies planned protection and preservation against unwise use, destruction, exploitation, and neglect of natural resources. As a group, ranchers have demonstrated little propensity for protection and preservation, unless one includes cheatgrass, halogeton, political clout, a place at the public trough, and such. But an assessment of the amount of soil washed to sea, bunchgrass destroyed, riparian zones eradicated, predators pushed to the brink of extinction, and other massive insults to public rangelands and resources severely besmirches the reputation of western stockmen as conservationists. In fact, on the public rangelands of the West, stockmen can claim the undisputed title as the major nemesis of conservation.

The simple act of banishing domestic livestock from the public lands of the West would unshackle conservation throughout the region—protection and preservation of natural resources would quickly and naturally follow. Ranchers were not the original conservationists, they are not significantly represented among current conservationists, and unless the world takes a dramatic turn, they will not be future conservationists. To date, they have demonstrated little interest in the subject.

Stockmen must be kept in business, otherwise they will be forced to sell deeded lands to developers who will subdivide them and build condominiums, housing projects, and other forms of urban sprawl.

This thinly veiled threat has been used very effectively by livestock permittees on public land to gain all types of concessions and to resist unwanted rangeland policies. A number of conservation organizations have bought the idea as being a legitimate threat to rural lands. Of course, some ranches do go out of business and are sold to non-ranching interests. In such cases, if public grazing permits are relinquished and if management agencies seize the opportunity to reduce grazing pressure on public rangelands by that amount, the tradeoff may not be all that bad. But, because the cash value of public grazing permits is so large compared to the value of deeded land, few ranchers are willing to surrender grazing permits and settle for the less substantial value of the deeded property alone. In other words, threats to sell are just that—threats—for if a rancher were to actually sell, the economic loss would be appreciable. Furthermore, this type of verbal sparring can easily be put aside with state laws protecting the sanctity of rural lands. The simple expedient of rigid zoning laws, close supervision of building permits, stringent restrictions of septic tank permits, and such can be used effectively to keep agricultural lands out of the hands of developers. Meanwhile, in most states, ranchers continue threatening the public and making it work.

But ranching is essential to the local economy.

Obviously, ranching does contribute to local economies, but the real question relates to the magnitude of that contribution. From total receipts collected for various programs in 1978 (e.g., oil and gas leasing, mineral leasing, timber sales, grazing, etc.), the BLM disbursed to the 11 western states and appropriate local governments a total of $345.3 million in receipts and in lieu of taxes—but only $2.9 million or 0.84 percent of that amount was derived from livestock grazing. That same year, the BLM spent $68.6 million on its range program and was further obliged to spend an additional $10.4 million from grazing receipts upon range improvements—that's $79 million, which is a very large public expenditure to return only $2.9 million to local governments. An outright gift would have been more sensible.

Currently, ranching communities and ranchers using public lands are principally benefiting from generous public subsidies and from an infusion of funds representing operating costs of agencies at a local level. If these dollars were spent for land improvements unrelated to livestock grazing, local economies would continue to reap enormous benefits. If public forage were sold by competitive bid, income to local governments would double or triple.

Currently, the national economy is in flux. Gas-guzzling automobiles are out. Large industries, such as steel, are fighting for survival in the face of stiff foreign competition. Beef isn't faring so well either. As the economy is increasingly dominated by technology, electronics, service-oriented businesses, and other highly skilled endeavors, American workers will put greater demands upon recreation, hunting, fishing, sightseeing, and other out-of-doors activities—precisely the natural resources currently being sacrificed to the livestock industry. The BLM has been so preoccupied ministering to the demands of the livestock industry that in 1977 it had only 320 recreation sites (12,211 acres) in the 11 western states. Furthermore, one day the tremendous environmental and social costs of the livestock industry on public lands must be borne by that industry rather than passed to others.

Like it or not, small western ranching communities are confronted with change. Change has demanded an end to strip mining in some regions, even though local communities protested the economic loss. When Henry Ford began selling automobiles, the horse economy faded. But, that was progress, and society dictates progress. Sooner or later, progress is destined to strike the livestock industry on public lands. Those lands are simply too valuable to be turned over to a minority commodity interest seeking to grub a quick buck from them. If a local economy lives by the cow alone, then it may well die with the cow.

Ranching is our way of life—we wouldn't overgraze because it would threaten our livelihood.

The history of the livestock industry on public lands and the current conditions of those lands speak for themselves. However, stockmen probably wouldn't be so tempted to overgraze lands if they had to live with the results. But when the federal government accepts responsibility for range rehabilitation, seedings, and other costly improvements, what is the incentive for a rancher to care for public rangelands?

Non-federal lands were the best land, therefore, they were homesteaded or otherwise transferred to private ownership at an early date. Today in 10 western states, 67.9 percent of the non-federal rangelands, despite their initial higher quality, is in fair to poor condition, compared to 82.3 percent of federal rangelands. The severity of range problems on non-federal lands in Oregon, Idaho, Utah, and Arizona is classified as major, but severe in Nevada and California. It would seem that some ranchers are, indeed, threatening their own livelihood by overgrazing!

Ranching should be continued in the West because of its historical importance in the development of the region.

Homesteaders, fur trappers, mountain men, and many others also helped settle the West. They are no longer a part of today's world. Ranchers using public lands are a vestige of that era—one we can ill afford.

Must we continue subjecting public rangelands to abuses of livestock merely to depict the importance of ranching in the settlement of the West? If that's the objective, why not place small, roadside museums at intervals along major western highways, and at each stop display a token cowboy dressed in appropriate western garb, a cow or two, and other suitable ranching paraphernalia? The cowboy could whoop, sing ballads, chase the cows around, and put on a western show for tourists. As usual with other western livestock enterprises, the taxpayers would foot the bill for these historical extravaganzas. And as is currently the case, the nation's red meat supply could be provided by private livestock operators using private lands.

TIME FOR A CHANGE

Our nation and the rest of the world suffer from future shock—fear of uncertainties produced by rapid change. Already, it's too late to go back or even stand still—the tide is flowing. As the nation is confronted with choices, we can only hope that we can muster the needed wisdom to make the proper decisions. One thing seems certain—if we insist upon dragging our past mistakes into the future and if we refuse to profit from experience, we cannot bear these burdens and expect to compete with the swift. The record of the livestock industry on public lands is certainly not a very promising starting point for launching the nation into a secure and bright future.

Public lands belong to *all* Americans. Ownership establishes responsibility for management. For generations, those lands have been trampled by swarms of sacred cows— pawns used by a minority vested-interest group to hold the rest of the nation in economic and political bondage. In modern America, it's high time we discard the notion of sacred cows—they are obsolete relics of a not so glorious past. Cows aren't sacred—they are beef—plain old bloody meat, not religious objects for public veneration. Cows are not American animals—they are exotic imports, like cheatgrass—to a large extent they have supplanted native species. And the people who raise cows are expected to be business people—not publicly subsidized actors performing a fanciful, regional drama.

The record of the livestock industry on public lands is repugnant. Any other interpretation stems from a failure to separate myth from solid substance. Are special privilege, physical force, strong-arm politics, and greed the ingredients of American life that should be perpetuated? Indeed, should these constitute a basis for historical pride? How much longer can the nation afford the outrageous destruction visited upon the public lands by a sacred-cow monoculture? How many more riparian zones must the American people sacrifice to this greedy and insatiable industry? Even if it stopped now, we would continue paying the bill for centuries. What kind of nation would we have if all our businesses existed on a public dole, as does the western livestock industry on public lands? And what hope is there for an industry that stubbornly disregards advice and shuns moderation? In the old days, ranchers were content to gamble on high profits and let thousands of cattle starve and freeze during terrible winters. Today, attitudes have barely changed—warnings about exceeding the carrying capacity of rangelands are rejected out of hand. Modern stockmen simply refuse to consider the notion that today's range problems are anything but a carryover from past times of unrestricted grazing. On the public rangelands today, a distinction between grazing and overgrazing no longer exists —the exploitation of forage amounts to an annual clearcut.

Like pirates, slave traders, and buffalo hunters, ranchers using the public lands have had their time in the sun. The public has been painfully patient. But it's time for a change. After decades of welfare, deceit, and unacceptable behavior, the western livestock industry must grow up—stockmen must become businessmen and good citizens; the myth of western ranching is a luxury the nation can no longer afford.

There are unmistakable signs of a public awakening. For every person grazing livestock on public lands, there are about 195 who read *Outdoor Life*. Add the millions of other hunters, fishermen, sightseers, bird-watchers, members of conservation organizations, and just plain citizens who care about natural resources and you have an imposing constituency. Sooner or later, these Americans are going to tire of getting shortchanged when it comes to the public lands. They haven't organized to defend their common interests in the public lands, but the chances are very good that they will. In fact, they must, for massive neglect of

resources as valuable as the public lands cannot continue forever.

Congress has enacted some excellent legislation governing the use of public rangelands. What is needed now is a favorable political climate in which these laws can produce results. That began to happen during Jimmy Carter's Administration, which triggered the Sagebrush Rebellion, because ranchers knew it was happening. With Ronald Reagan's election, the status quo of the 1890's returned to western rangelands—exploit and let the rich get richer. But the legislation exists, as illustrated by the Natural Resources Defense Council's successful suit forcing the BLM to prepare environmental impact statements for its various grazing districts. To date, the BLM has refused to abide by the law and has made no effort to regulate the livestock industry, but the laws are there and they invite change. Legal avenues are open and the public has gained the right to examine rangeland policy. The stage is set, the time will come.

Agencies have too often been dominated by cowpokes. But younger, better-trained people are moving in, and they are restless. Talk to young college people who have taken summer employment with range management agencies, and you will find them brimming with resentment over the special considerations given commodity interests. Furthermore, the agencies must listen to the public—it's the law. Again, what is needed is a favorable political climate—one in which environment means more than just forage—then the agencies will come around. It's inevitable.

But the most significant changes are those governing the individual life-styles of American citizens. These are personal decisions, but in many instances, seem to reflect a conviction that we must minimize our individual impacts while sharing a very small planet with our fellow human beings. Macho, wild West, exploitation, and the biggest steak in the house are out—small cars, personal health, regard for Mother Earth, and regulated consumption are in.

Nowhere has the change been more evident than in diet. Today, vegetarians number about 15 million in the United

States, and their ranks are growing at a rapid clip. Each vegetarian has a reason for making a dietary change. For some, it's a matter of fitness—like jogging and exercise, a diet of vegetables, high fiber content, and low animal fats is deemed the healthy and wise thing to do. Of course, the medical evidence fully justifies the vegetarian's case.

Others, cognizant of the world's food scarcity and impending famine in many of the poor nations, resent the luxury of meat in contrast to the stark scarcity of protein elsewhere. These vegetarians are sensitive to the lavish waste of valuable food that has become an ingrained custom in our nation. Americans could reduce livestock populations by 25 percent and still have enough to feed every person a half a pound of meat or poultry a day—plenty to meet our total protein requirements. And many foods are as rich or richer than meat in protein content—meat with about 25 percent protein ranks in the middle of the protein scale with nuts, fish, cheeses, and beans, while soybean flour contains 40 percent protein. But in 1973, livestock consumed six times the recommended protein allowance for our national population. Furthermore, an acre used for livestock production will produce 5 times more protein if planted to cereals, 10 times more if planted to legumes, 15 times more if planted to leafy vegetables, and 26 times more if planted to spinach.

Finally, many vegetarians avoid meat because of deeply held convictions relating to a disapproval of killing animals, resentment of livestock on public lands, and similar perceived abuses.

Vegetarians are a diverse lot. Nearly all of them shun beef, most avoid pork, many will not accept poultry, a few do not consume fish, and a small number of truly dedicated individuals will not accept animal products such as milk, eggs, or cheese. Although most vegetarians are young, a significant proportion of all other age groups is represented and many have practiced a vegetarian diet for all of their adult lives.

Regardless of the reason for vegetarianism, this group of Americans is exerting tremendous pressures upon the livestock industry at the marketplace. Unfortunately, the pressure is not just on stockmen on public lands, but on all others as well. Ideally, meat from any animal that has ever set foot on public lands should be so designated with a special label at the marketplace, thus giving consumers a choice if they object to supporting the industry using public lands.

Many other changes in American life-style signal trouble for stockmen using public lands. As pointed out elsewhere, a growing urban population is likely to be less compromising in using the out-of-doors and in demanding genuine multiple uses of public lands. Such people are not likely to be pleased when they drive great distances only to find a national wildlife refuge swarming with cows and littered with cattle droppings. Furthermore, a strong wilderness ethic is growing in the United States, and all the precepts of wilderness run counter to the exploitive principles of commodity interests. Because of satellite communications and other technical innovations in information transmittal, even rural people, who are not actually involved in the exploitation of public lands, are more apt to develop an intolerance for the dogged behavior of their neighbors in the livestock industry. Throughout the nation, a decreased reliance upon smokestack-type industries will tend to focus attention on other environmentally abusive enterprises, and the livestock industry on public lands is destined to attract increasing attention as a villian.

An ecological ethic is growing in the United States. Witness the incorporation of nongame departments into state game and fish management programs. Even land grant universities are anxious to shed the image of being "aggies" and are searching for more acceptable pseudonyms. The word "habitat" is gaining recognition, and an increasing number of citizens are coming to realize that a healthy habitat means more fish, game, water, healthy soil, and all the rest. A cadre of well-informed out-of-door writers is telling the message in a way that is both understandable and convincing. A basic precept of American life is the assumption that our people will do the right thing if armed with the proper information.

Other changes threaten the security of the western livestock industry. For example, as efforts are made to reduce the federal budget and to insure the survival of necessary programs, such as Social Security, increasing attention will be drawn to the gravy train subsidies being enjoyed by ranchers using public lands. Already, writers are pointing out that the fertile lands and high rainfall of the Southeast have made that area a leader in national beef production. More and more, critics of the western livestock industry are questioning the worth of their piddling efforts on public lands. Currently, such notions are only incubating, but they will grow and soon become too conspicuous to be ignored.

There is a gentleness abroad in the land, but these gentle people are bright and persistent. Today, young people are not rioting or burning buildings as they were in the Vietnam days. But they are not totally satisfied with their world either. Today, they tend to be quiet, polite, and dedicated, but they have learned the system and have learned how to accomplish their goals within the system. This trend is destined to have great political significance in the nation's future. National insults to land and resources are not going to be ignored.

Modern conservation organizations are in the charge of extremely bright and savvy people. Moreover, the membership of such organizations is better informed and less likely to be misled by political operators seeking to duck substantive issues or create fuzzy justifications.

Today, environmental groups are voicing protests against predator control, especially at public expense. Others object strenuously to commercial exploitation of public lands by commodity interests. If such reasonable protests are ignored, critics and protestors are invited to take more radical positions. If livestock operators think that reducing grazing to the carrying capacity of the rangeland is unreasonable, let them consider other possible demands. How about a law stating that the number of livestock on a federal grazing allotment cannot exceed the number of big game animals? Or, how about a $2 tax on each cow and a $0.50 tax on each sheep, the funds to be used to restore and reestablish large species of predators extirpated by past predator control programs? Or, consider a provision requiring that every federal grazing allotment turn a profit for the U.S. Treasury. How about repealing all open-range laws and charging ranchers for all damages in automobile-livestock collisions when livestock are trespassing on public highways. Better yet, the nation should resurrect the ancient Greek and Roman rite of the hecatomb (check your dictionary!).

In short, sacred cows are becoming less sacred to most Americans and have never been less welcome on public rangelands than today. While cowboys have been twirling their lariats and strutting around in their pointy-toed boots, Americans have gone to the moon and launched the computer age. A cow is no longer a big deal. Perhaps the cowboys failed to notice, but even cowboy movies have dropped from favor. Today, "western" is an adjective applied more to music than to ranchers, and certainly, those classy dudes want nothing to do with anything as mundane as a cow. Although the nation has a long way to go before it can be free of the great western myth, the evidence that it is moving in the right direction is beyond dispute. The glamour of cows and ranching is rapidly waning.

In this book, we have sought to describe the total impacts of the livestock industry on public lands. These impacts are enormous and decidedly unacceptable. Now there is but one remaining question—what should be done about it?

In the past, federal agencies, conservationists, and others have made what seems to be a most reasonable demand of stockmen using public lands. Specifically, they have asked that grazing be reduced to the carrying capacity of the public rangelands. By any impartial standard, such a demand is reasonable, logical, and in the best interest of all concerned. These efforts, however, have met with stubborn resistance from the livestock industry, and after decades of federal management, the goal seems as unattainable today as in the beginning.

Others have suggested selling public forage on a competitive bid basis, citing a better return to the public, the likelihood of less grazing pressure, an increased opportunity for overgrazed lands to mend, and additional benefits. Again, these efforts have accomplished nothing—stockmen using public lands will have no part of it.

Persuasion, logic, pleading, legislation, and all other forms of public action have failed. The livestock industry stands firm and intends to stay that way. The public could capitulate and let the industry have its way. But we don't think so. The costs—economic, social, political—are simply too unbearable to be tolerated longer. It's clearly time for a change. Public lands are too valuable to the American people to continue subjecting them to the kind of treatment the stockmen have in mind. Until now stockmen have brazenly challenged the rights and wishes of the American public—they have thrown the gauntlet. At this point, the American people have little choice other than to accept the challenge of a recalcitrant, uncompromising, and coddled minority—the public should boot every last one of them off the public lands. The nation no longer needs them.

RECOMMENDED READING

Advisory Committee On Predator Control. 1972. Predator Control—1971. Institute for Environmental Quality, University of Michigan, Ann Arbor, Michigan. 207 p.

Braun, C.E., K.W. Harmon, J.A. Jackson, and C.D. Littlefield. 1978. Management of National Wildlife Refuges in the United States: Its Impacts on Birds. *Wilson Bulletin* 90:309-321.

Cain, S.A. 1978. *Predator and Pest Control*, p. 379-395. *In* H.P. Brokaw (ed.) *Wildlife and America*. Council on Environmental Quality, Washington D.C.

Coggins, G.C. 1983. The Law of Public Rangeland Management III: A Survey of Creeping Regulation at the Periphery, 1934-1982. *Environmental Law* 13:295-365. (Note: This series will include 5 articles.)

Coggins, G.C., and M. Lindberg-Johnson. 1982. The Law of Public Rangeland Management II: The Commons and the Taylor Act. *Environmental Law* 13:1-101.

Coggins, G.C., P.B. Evans, and M. Lindberg-Johnson. 1982. The Law of Public Rangeland Management I: The Extent and Distribution of Federal Power. *Environmental Law* 12:535-621.

Cope, O.B. (ed.) 1979. Proceedings of the Forum—Grazing and Riparian/Stream Ecosystems. *Trout Unlimited,* Denver, Colorado. 94 p.

Dasmann, R.F. 1972. *Environmental Conservation.* John Wiley, New York. 473 p.

Fradkin, P.L. 1979. The Eating of the West. *Audubon* 81:94-121.

Gallizioli, S. 1977. Overgrazing: More Deadly Than Any Hunter. *Outdoor Arizona* 1977:24-31.

Handwerg, K. 1980. Grazing Fees and Fair Market Value. Cascade Holistic Economic Consultants, Eugene, Oregon. 20 p.

Hastings, J.R., and R.M. Turner. 1972. *The Changing Mile.* University of Arizona Press, Tucson, Arizona. 317 p.

Johnson, A.S. 1978. Ranching: High Cost of an American Myth. *Defenders* 1978:324-327.

Lappe, F.M. 1975. *Diet For a Small Planet.* Ballentine Books, New York, 410 p.

Oliphant, J.O. 1968. *On The Cattle Ranges of the Oregon Country*. University of Washington Press, Seattle, Washington. 372 p.

Oppenheimer, H.L. 1971. *Cowboy Arithmetic*. Interstate Printers and Publishers, Danville, Illinois. 246 p.

Sheridan, D. 1981. *Desertification of the United States*. Council on Environmental Quality, Washington, D.C. 142 p.

Voigt, W. 1976. *Public Grazing Lands*. Rutgers University Press, New Brunswick, New Jersey. 359 p.

Wagner, F.H. 1978. Livestock Grazing and the Livestock Industry, p. 121-145. *In* H.P. Brokaw (ed.) *Wildlife and America*. Council on Environmental Quality, Washington, D.C.

Yensen, D. 1980. A Grazing History of Southwestern Idaho with Emphasis on the Birds of Prey Study Area. Bureau of Land Management, Boise, Idaho. 82 p.

OTHER REFERENCES

Alderfer, R.B., and R.R. Robinson. 1947. Runoff from Pastures in Relation to Grazing Intensity and Soil Compaction. *Journal of the American Society of Agronomy* 29:948-958.

Baker, M.F., and N.C. Frischnecht. 1973. Small Mammals Increase on Recently Cleared and Seeded Juniper Rangeland. *Journal of Range Management* 26:101-103.

Behnke, R.J., and R.F. Raleigh. 1978. Grazing and the Riparian Zone: Impact and Management Perspectives, p. 263-267. *In* Symposium on strategies for protection and management of floodplain wetlands and other riparian ecosystems, Calloway Gardens, Georgia.

Berry, K.H. 1978. Livestock Grazing and the Desert Tortoise. *Transactions of the 43rd North American Wildlife Conference,* p. 505-519.

Blackburn, W.H., and P.T. Tueller. 1970. Pinyon and Juniper Invasion in Black Sagebrush Communities in East-Central Nevada. *Ecology* 51:841-848.

Blydenstein, J., C.R. Hungerford, G.I. Day, and R.R. Humphrey. 1957. Effect of Domestic Livestock Exclusion on Vegetation in the Sonoran Desert. *Ecology* 38:522-526.

Branscomb, B.L. 1958. Shrub Invasion of a Southern New Mexico Desert Grassland Range. *Journal of Range Management* 11:129-132.

Braun, C.E., M.F. Baker, R.L. Eng, J.S. Gashwiler, and M.H. Schroeder, 1976. Conservation committee report on effects of alteration of sagebrush communities on the associated avifauna. *Wilson Bulletin* 88:165-171.

Brown, A.L. 1950. Shrub Invasion of Southern Arizona Desert Grassland. *Journal of Range Management* 3:172-177.

Brown, D.E. 1978. Grazing, Grassland Cover and Gamebirds. *Transactions of the 43rd North American Wildlife Conference,* p. 477-485.

Bryan, K. 1925. Data on Channel Trenching (arroyo cutting) in the Arid Southwest. *Science* 62:338-344.

Buffington, L.C., and C.H. Herbel. 1965. Vegetational Changes on a Semi-desert Grassland Range From 1858-1963. *Ecological Monographs* 35:139-164.

Busack, S.D., and R.B. Bury, 1974. Some Effects of Off-Road Vehicles and Sheep Grazing on Lizard Populations in the Mojave Desert. *Biological Conservation* 6:179-183.

Buttery, R.F., and P.W. Shields. 1975. Range Management Practices and Bird Habitat Values, p. 183-189. *In* Symposium on management of forest and range habitats for nongame birds, Tucson, Arizona.

Charley, J.L., and S.W. Cowling. 1968. Changes in Soil Nutrient Status Resulting from Overgrazing and Their Consequences in Plant Communities of Semi-arid Areas. Proceedings of the *Ecological Society of Australia* 3:28-38.

Cook, C.W., and L.A. Stoddart. 1963. The Effect of Intensity and Season of Use on the Vigor of Desert Range Plants. *Journal of Range Management* 16:315-317.

Costello, D.F., and G.T. Turner. 1941. Vegetation Changes Following Exclusion of Livestock From Grazed Ranges. *Journal of Forestry* 39:310-315.

Cottam, W.P., and R.F. Evans. 1965. A Comparative Study of the Vegetation of Grazed and Ungrazed Canyons of the Wasatch Range, Utah. *Ecology* 26:171-181.

Cottam, W.P., and G. Stewart. 1940. Plant Succession as a Result of Grazing and Meadow Desiccation Since Settlement in 1862. *Journal of Forestry* 38:613-626.

Council for Agricultural Science and Technology. 1974. Livestock Grazing on Federal Lands in the 11 Western States. *Journal of Range Management* 27:174-181.

Daubenmire, R.F. 1940. Plant Succession Due to Overgrazing in the *Agropyron* Bunchgrass Prairie of Southeastern Washington. *Ecology* 21:55-64.

Daubenmire, R.F., and W.E. Colwell. 1942. Some Edaphic Changes Due to Overgrazing in the *Agropyron-Poa* Prairie of Southeastern Washington. *Ecology 23:32-40.*

DeVoto, B. 1955. *The Easy Chair.* Houghton Mifflin, Boston, Massachusetts. 356 p.

Duce, J.T. 1918. The Effect of Cattle on the Erosion of Canyon Bottoms. *Science* 47:450-452.

Duebbert, H.F., and J.T. Lokemoen. 1977. Upland Nesting of American Bitterns, Marsh Hawks, and Short-Eared Owls. *Prairie Naturalist* 9:33-40.

Dunford, E.G. 1954. Surface Runoff and Erosion From Pine Grasslands of the Colorado Front Range. *Journal of Forestry* 52:923-927.

Dyksterhuis, E.J. 1958. Ecological Principles in Range Evaluation. *Botanical Reviews* 24:253-272.

Ferry, G., D. Luman, R. Ross, W. Sandau, and V. Schulze. 1981. Review of the Bureau's Oregon and Washington Range Seeding Program. Bureau of Land Management, Portland, Oregon 53 p.

Gallizioli, S. 1977. Overgrazing on Desert Bighorn Ranges. *Transactions of the Desert Bighorn Council,* p. 21-22.

Gardner, J.L. 1950. Effects of Thirty Years of Protection from Grazing in Desert Grassland. *Ecology* 31:44-50.

Gifford, G.L., and R. H. Hawkings. 1978. Hydrologic Impact of Grazing on Infiltration: A Critical Review. *Water Resources Research* 14:305-313.

Gjersing, F.M. 1975. Waterfowl Production in Relation to Rest-Rotation Grazing. *Journal of Range Management* 28:37-42.

Grelen, H.E. 1978. Forest Grazing in the South. *Journal of Range Management* 31:244-249.

Grelen, H.E., and G.W. Thomas. 1957. Livestock and Deer Activities on the Edwards Plateau of Texas. *Journal of Range Management* 10:34-37.

Gunderson, D.R. 1968. Floodplain Use Related to Stream Morphology and Fish Populations. *Journal of Wildlife Management* 32:507-514.

Hanson, W.R., and L.A. Stoddart, 1940. Effects of Grazing Upon Bunch Wheat Grass. *Journal of the American Society of Agronomy* 32:278-289.

Herbel, C.H. 1955. Range Conservation and Season-Long Grazing. *Journal of Range Management* 8:204-205.

Howard, R.P., and M.L. Wolfe. 1976. Range Improvement Practices and Ferruginous Hawks. *Journal of Range Management* 29:33-37.

Hull, A.C., and M.K. Hull. 1974. Presettlement Vegetation of Cache Valley, Utah and Idaho. *Journal of Range Management* 27:27-29.

Humphrey, R.R. 1968. *The Desert Grassland: A History of Vegetational Change and An Analysis of Causes.* University of Arizona Press, 74 p.

Johnson, A.S. 1978. Pronghorns, Fences, and Ranch Mortgages. *Defenders* 1978:8-11.

Jones, K.B. 1981. Effects of Grazing on Lizard Abundance and Diversity in Western Arizona. *The Southwestern Naturalist* 26:107-115.

Julander, O. 1962. Range Management in Relation to Mule Deer Habitat and Herd Productivity in Utah. *Journal of Range Management* 15:278-281.

Julander, O., and D.W. Jeffrey. 1964. Deer, Elk, and Cattle Range Relations on Summer Range in Utah. *Transactions of the 29th North American Wildlife Conference,* p. 404-414.

Julander, O., W.L. Robinette, and D.A. Jones. 1961. Relation of Summer Range Conditions to Mule Deer Herd Productivity. *Journal of Wildlife Management* 25:54-60.

Kindschy, R.P. 1979. Rangeland Management Practices and Bird Habitat Values, p. 66-69. *In* Workshop on non-game bird habitat management in coniferous forest of the Western United States, Portland, Oregon.

Kirsch, L.M. 1969. Waterfowl Production in Relation to Grazing. *Journal of Wildlife Management* 33:821-828.

Kirsch, L.M., and K.F. Higgins. 1976. Upland Sandpiper Nesting and Management in North Dakota. *Wildlife Society Bulletin* 4:16-21.

Klebenow, D. 1969. Sage Grouse Nesting and Brood Habitat in Idaho. *Journal of Wildlife Management* 33:649-662.

Klemnedson, J.D. 1956. Interrelations of Vegetation, Soils, and Range Conditions Induced by Grazing. *Journal of Range Management* 9:134-138.

Knoll, G., and H.H. Hopkins. 1959. The Effects of Grazing and Trampling upon Certain Soil Properties. *Transactions of the Kansas Academy of Sciences* 62:221-231.

Larson, F., and W. Whitman. 1942. A Comparison of Used and Unused Grassland and Mesas in the Badlands of South Dakota. *Ecology* 23:438-445.

Laycock, W.A. 1967. How Heavy Grazing and Protection Affect Sagebrush-Grass Ranges. *Journal of Range Management* 20:206-213.

Leopold, A.S. 1977. *The California Quail.* University of California Press, Berkeley. 281 p.

Longhurst, W.M. 1957. A History of Squirrel Burrow Gully Formation in Relation to Grazing. *Journal of Range Management* 10:182-184.

Lull, H.K. 1959. *Soil Compaction on Forest and Range Lands.* U.S. Forest Service Misc. Publication 768. 33 p.

Marquiss, R., and R. Lang. 1959. Vegetational Composition and Ground Cover of Two Natural Relict Areas and Their Associated Grazed Areas in the Red Desert of Wyoming. *Journal of Range Management* 12:104-109.

McGinty, W.A., F.S. Smeins, and L.B. Merrill. 1979. Influence of Soil, Vegetation, and Grazing Management on Infiltration Rate and Sediment Production of Edwards Plateau Rangeland. *Journal of Range Management* 32:33-37.

McLean, A., and E.W. Tisdale. 1972. Recovery Rate of Depleted Range Sites under Protection From Grazing. *Journal of Range Management* 25:178-184.

Meehan, W.R., and W.S. Platts, 1978. Livestock Grazing and the Aquatic Environment. *Journal of Soil and Water Conservation* 33:274-278.

Morris, M.G. 1971. Differences Between the Invertebrate Faunas of Grazed and Ungrazed Chalk Grassland. *Journal of Applied Ecology* 8:37-52.

Odum, E.P. 1971. *Fundamentals of Ecology.* W.B. Saunders, Philadelphia, Pennsylvania. 546 p.

Pieper, R.D. 1968. Comparison of Vegetation on Grazed and Ungrazed Pinyon-Juniper Grassland Sites in Southcentral New Mexico. *Journal of Range Management* 21:51-53.

Rauzi, F., and F.M. Smith. 1973. Infiltration Rates: Three Soils with Three Grazing Levels in Northeastern Colorado. *Journal of Range Management* 26:126-129.

Reynolds, H.G. 1958. The Ecology of the Merriam Kangaroo Rat *(Dipodomys merriami rom.)* on the Grazing Lands of Southern Arizona, *Ecological Monographs* 28:111-127.

Reynolds, T.D. 1979. Response of Reptile Populations to Different Land Management Practices on the Idaho Engineering Laboratory Site. *Great Basin Naturalist* 39:255-262.

Reynolds, T.D., and C.H. Trost, 1979. The Effect of Crested Wheatgrass Plantings on Wildlife on the Idaho National

Engineering Laboratory Site, p. 665-666. *In* The mitigation symposium: A national workshop on mitigated losses on fish and wildlife habitats, Fort Collins, Colorado.

Reynolds, T.D., and C.H. Trost. 1980. The Response of Native Vertebrate Populations to Crested Wheatgrass Planting and Grazing by Sheep. *Journal of Range Management* 33:122-125.

Rich, L.R., and H.G. Reynolds. 1963. Grazing in Relation to Runoff and Erosion on Some Chaparral Watersheds in Central Arizona. *Journal of Range Management* 6:322-326.

Robertson, J.H., and P.B. Kennedy. 1954. Half-Century Changes on Northern Nevada Ranges. *Journal of Range Management* 7:117-121.

Rummel, R.S. 1951. Some Effects of Livestock Grazing on Ponderosa Pine Forest and Range in Central Washington. *Ecology* 32:594-607.

Schroeder, M.H., and D.L. Sturges. 1975. The Effect on the Brewer's Sparrow of Sprayed Big Sagebrush. *Journal of Range Management* 28:294-297.

Sharp, A.L., J.J. Bond, J.W. Neuberger, A.R. Kuhlman, and J.K. Lewis. 1964. Runoff as Affected by Intensity of Grazing Rangeland. *Journal of Soil and Water Conservation* 19:103-106.

Shreve, F., and A.L. Hinckley. 1937. Thirty Years of Change in Desert Vegetation. *Ecology* 18:463-478.

Skovlin, J.M., P.J. Edgerton, and R.W. Harris. 1968. The Influence of Cattle Management on Deer and Elk. *Transactions of the 33rd North American Wildlife Conference,* p. 169-181.

Smith, A.D. 1949. Effects of Mule Deer and Livestock upon a Foothill Range in Northern Utah. *Journal of Wildlife Management* 13:421-423.

Smith, D.A., and E.M. Schmutz. 1975. Vegetative Changes on Protected Versus Grazed Desert Grassland Ranges in Arizona. *Journal of Range Management* 28:453-458.

Smith, J.G., and O. Julander. 1953. Deer and Sheep Competition in Utah. *Journal of Wildlife Management* 17:101-112.

Tanner, C.B., and C.P. Mamaril. 1959. Pasture Soil Compaction by Animal Traffic. *Agronomy Journal* 51:329-331.

Taylor, W.P., C.T. Vorhies, and P.B. Lister. 1935. The Relation of Jack Rabbits to Grazing in Southern Arizona. *Journal of Forestry* 33:490-498.

Trueblood, T. 1980. They're Fixing To Steal Your Land. *Field and Stream* 1980:40-41, 166-167.

Turner, G.T. 1971. Soil and Grazing Influences on a Salt-Desert Shrub Range in Western Colorado. *Journal of Range Management* 24:31-37.

U.S. Department of Interior. 1972. National Survey of Fishing and Hunting—1970. U.S. Fish and Wildlife Service, Resource Publication 95.

Vale, T.R. 1975. Presettlement Vegetation in the Sagebrush-Grass Area of the Intermountain West. *Journal of Range Management* 28:32-36.

van Voorthuizen, E.G. 1978. Global Desertification and Range Management: An Appraisal. *Journal of Range Management* 31:378-380.

Vorhies, C.T., and W.P. Taylor. 1933. The life histories and ecology of jack rabbits, *Lepus Alleni* and *Lepus californicus* ssp. in relation to grazing in Arizona. *University of Arizona Agricultural Experiment Station Technical Bulletin* 49:471-587.

Weaver, J.E., and F.W. Albertson. 1940. Deterioration of Midwestern Ranges. *Ecology* 21:216-236.

Weller, M.W., B.H. Wingfield, and J.P. Low. 1958. Effects of Habitat Deterioration on Bird Populations of a Small Utah Marsh. *Condor* 60:220-226.

Welsh, G.W. 1971. What's Happening to Our Sheep? *Wildlife Digest,* Arizona Game and Fish Department. 8 p.

Winegar, H.H. 1977. Camp Creek Channel Fencing—Plant, Wildlife, Soil, and Water Responses. *Rangeman's Journal* 4:10-12.

Yoakum, J.D. 1975. Antelope and Livestock on Rangelands. *Journal of Animal Science* 40:985-992.

Zumbo, J. 1979. Hunting—An American Tradition. *The American Hunter* 1979:20-21.

INDEX